"In *Faith Simplified*, Aaron A[rmstrong...] offering readers an accessible [...] With pastoral warmth, he add[s...] of Scripture, and God's redemptive plan through the gospel of Jesus Christ. Armstrong's engaging style invites readers—whether new to the faith or long-time believers—to live with greater devotion, confidence, and joy in the gospel."

Justin S. Holcomb, PhD
Episcopal bishop, seminary professor, and author

"Aaron Armstrong's *Faith Simplified* is a conversation meant to reach those who are curious, questioning, and committed. Armstrong fulfills his purpose with a *profound* simplicity. His rich theological insight and attention to Scripture provides ballast as he considers some of life's deepest questions and many of today's most wily topics. The questions at the end of every chapter engage the reader and provide conversation points for small groups."

Cas Monaco, PhD
Vice President of Missiology and Gospel Engagement at FamilyLife®

"Aaron writes with good-natured humor and a strong grasp on biblical scholarship and theology. This book is accessible without compromising depth. A great resource for anyone looking to understand the Christian faith."

Kristel Acevedo
Author and Discipleship Director at Transformation Church

"Aaron Armstrong's *Faith Simplified* is a masterful invitation into the richness of Christian doctrine. This Christ-saturated book combines theological depth with accessible language, making it an invaluable resource for new believers seeking clarity and mature readers desiring fresh insights. Armstrong stands firmly on the historical convictions of the Christian faith, presenting them in a memorable and transformative way. Readers will walk away from this book not only understanding their faith but inspired to live it out with conviction and joy."

Jamaal Williams
Lead pastor, Sojourn Church Midtown; president, Harbor Network; coauthor, *In Church as It Is in Heaven*

FAITH SIMPLIFIED

AARON ARMSTRONG

HARVEST HOUSE PUBLISHERS
EUGENE, OREGON

Unless otherwise indicated, all Scripture verses are from the NET Bible® copyright ©1996, 2019 by Biblical Studies Press, L.L.C. http://netbible.com. Scripture quoted with permission. All rights reserved.

Scripture verses marked CSB have been taken from the Christian Standard Bible®, Copyright © 2017 by Holman Bible Publishers. Used with permission. Christian Standard Bible® and CSB® are federally registered trademarks of Holman Bible Publishers.

Verses marked NKJV are taken from the New King James Version®. Copyright © 1982 by Thomas Nelson. Used with permission. All rights reserved.

Verses marked NIV are taken from the Holy Bible, New International Version®, NIV®. Copyright © 1973, 1978, 1984, 2011 by Biblica, Inc.® Used with permission of Zondervan. All rights reserved worldwide. www.zondervan.com. The "NIV" and "New International Version" are trademarks registered in the United States Patent and Trademark Office by Biblica, Inc.®

Verses marked ESV are taken from the ESV® Bible (The Holy Bible, English Standard Version®), copyright © 2001 by Crossway, a publishing ministry of Good News Publishers. Used with permission. All rights reserved. The ESV text may not be quoted in any publication made available to the public by a Creative Commons license. The ESV may not be translated in whole or in part into any other language.

Verses marked NASB are taken from the (NASB®) New American Standard Bible®, Copyright © 1960, 1971, 1977, 1995, 2020 by The Lockman Foundation. Used with permission. All rights reserved. www.lockman.org.

Published in association with the literary agency WTA Media LLC, Franklin, TN

Cover design by Faceout Studio, Jeff Miller

Cover images © INORTON, v_kulieva, Marish, Plasteed, tutti_frutti, Oksana Nazarova, Max0070 / Shutterstock

Interior design by KUHN Design Group

For bulk, special sales, or ministry purchases, please call 1-800-547-8979. Email: CustomerService@hhpbooks.com

This logo is a federally registered trademark of the Hawkins Children's LLC. Harvest House Publishers, Inc., is the exclusive licensee of this trademark.

Faith Simplified
Copyright © 2025 by Aaron Armstrong
Published by Harvest House Publishers
Eugene, Oregon 97408
www.harvesthousepublishers.com
ISBN 978-0-7369-9107-0 (pbk)
ISBN 978-0-7369-9108-7 (eBook)
Library of Congress Control Number: 2024945996

All rights reserved. No part of this publication may be reproduced, stored in a retrieval system, or transmitted in any form or by any means—electronic, mechanical, digital, photocopy, recording, or any other—except for brief quotations in printed reviews, without the prior permission of the publisher.

Printed in the United States of America

25 26 27 28 29 30 31 32 33 / BP / 10 9 8 7 6 5 4 3 2 1

For Emily, Whit, and Rachel, who wrestle with God.

ACKNOWLEDGMENTS

To **God our Father, the Lord Jesus Christ, and the Holy Spirit**, thank you for desiring that we know you even as we are already known by you (1 Corinthians 13:12).

Emily, when our powers combine, we make one functional adult. I'm grateful for you, every day.

Abigail, Hannah, and Hudson, thank you for encouraging me in your own unique ways as I wrote. I pray you all read this book and see the beauty of Jesus through your dad's imperfect words.

My friends and my church, thank you for praying along with me through this process.

Dave Schroeder, thank you for advocating for this book and being a great friend. Let's get back to being middle-aged dads doing a podcast.

Tim, Mark, and Fran, thank you for reading drafts as I wrote and helping to make this book better.

Jenaye Merida, thank you for being a better agent than I deserve.

Bob Hawkins, Steve Miller, and the team at Harvest House, thank you for seeing the value of this project for the church and helping bring it to the world.

And, of course, my thanks to **you, dear reader**. I am grateful to be allowed to play a small role in what God is doing in your life through this book.

> *"Grace be with all who have undying love for our Lord Jesus Christ."*
> Ephesians 6:24 csb

CONTENTS

Foreword 11

Try the Untried. 15
An Invitation to the Curious, the Questioning, and the Committed

PART 1: GOD IS

1. One, and Also Three (Who Are One) 23
   Who (and What) Is God?

2. Similar, but Different 37
   The Infinite, All-Knowing, All-Powerful God Is Always with Us. And Separate from Us. All at the Same Time.

3. Perfectly Perfect in Every Way 45
   A Merciful and Loving God Who Is Always Right and Pure and Trustworthy

PART 2: GOD SPEAKS

4. Always, Everywhere, and in Everything 55
   God Doesn't Hide that He Exists

5. In the Words He Gave Us 63
   Why Christians Make Such a Big Deal About the Bible

PART 3: GOD MAKES

6. A Good World That He Rules 77
   The Point We Miss in the Creation Story

7. A World for Beings Like Him 85
   What Are Human Beings?

8. A World Where We Are Not Alone 95
   Angels, Demons, and Maybe Aliens Too

9. A World Where God Is Always Working 105
   The Seen and Unseen Works of God

PART 4: GOD JUDGES

10. The Difference Between Good and Evil 115
    Mysteries, Problems, and the Limits of Our Comprehension

11. The Evil That *We* Do 123
    Why Everything That's Wrong with the World Is Wrong with the World

12. People Who Love What They Should Hate 135
    We Are Not as Free as We Were Meant to Be (But We Can Be)

PART 5: GOD RESCUES

13. According to a Plan for the Whole Universe 145
    The Gospel Is Good News for You, Me, and Even Those Who Don't Believe It

14. By Becoming a Human Being 155
    The Strangest Thing Christians Believe

15. As a Mediator Who Will Never Fail 165
    How Jesus Is Better Than the Best

16. Through the Strange Beauty of Death 175
    A Sacrifice That Satisfied

17. Through an Empty Tomb 185
    Our Only Hope in Life, Death, and Everything That Comes After

18. By Making the Dead Live 197
    What It Means to Be Born Again

19. With a Goal in Mind 205
    How the Holy Spirit Makes Us More Like Jesus

PART 6: GOD RESTORES

20. A United People 213
    Many Metaphors and One Reality

21. Our Relationships with One Another 221
    How the Gospel Makes Us Safe

22. Our Greater Purpose 229
    *Worshiping in Songs, Sacraments, and Every Part of
    Our Lives*

23. Our Great Commission 239
    Good News Worth Sharing in Word and Works

PART 7: GOD REIGNS

24. Over Life *After* Death 247
    *The Question Everyone's Asking (Even When They Don't
    Realize It)*

25. Over a New Creation 257
    And a World We Can't Imagine

What Will You Do with What You Know? 265

Notes 269

FOREWORD

Trevin Wax

Whenever I see a book that promises to lay out the basics of Christianity or present the big story of the Bible, I become immediately curious. There are countless ways to tell the "old, old story." So I begin to wonder: *How is this author going to sum up the Bible? What themes will they choose to emphasize? How will they handle the wide range of Christian interpretation that has taken place over the course of nearly 2,000 years? How will they present the truths of Scripture in a way that speaks to our current cultural moment?*

But the big question that truly makes me lean in is, *How did the author make Christian theology accessible to someone who is just starting out in their exploration?*

How do you simplify the vast, deep waters of Christian teaching without reducing them to something shallow? How do you achieve simplicity without succumbing to reductionism? How do you provide simple speech that isn't simplistic? That is no small task, especially considering the greatest theologians in history have plumbed the depths of Christian teaching and have never run empty of awe-inducing truths.

When I picked up *Faith Simplified*, I was eager to see how my friend Aaron Armstrong would tackle such an ambitious task. I was pleased with what I found. He's done something special in these pages.

Aaron presents the heart of the Christian faith in a way that's clear, engaging, and—*most importantly*—faithful. He's not interested in watering down concepts or lecturing through a surface-level overview. No, this book digs down to the essential truths of Christianity. But in a way that makes them accessible without being superficial. Aaron doesn't shy away from the complexity of our faith, but he also doesn't let it become a barrier to those just beginning on their journey.

Aaron's approach in *Faith Simplified* is to sit down with you and walk you through the big questions about faith, like *Who is God?*, *Why is there suffering?*, *Why did Jesus come?*, and *What does it mean to be born again?* And he does this in a way that's thoughtful and practical. Aaron seeks to help you through the basics without getting lost in a maze of theological jargon. He is the kind of guide who knows the terrain well but doesn't show off his knowledge. He desires for you to love what he loves. And he wants the Christian faith to make sense for you.

If you are new to the faith, this book is a road map to guide you on your journey. If you've been walking with Jesus for years, this book is a chance to see the surrounding landscape with fresh eyes. And if you're reading as someone who is curious but not quite sure what to make of it all, this book is your invitation to try the untried.

Faith Simplified reminds us that theology isn't only for scholars. It's for everyone. Aaron wants you to engage with these truths, to wrestle with them, and to own them. If theology is the study of God, then Christian theology is about knowing God as he's revealed himself in Christ. The heart of our faith isn't simply a set of theological bullet points or a list of ethical dos and don'ts. It's about a Person. All Christian theology is a response to that pivotal question Jesus asked his disciples: "Who do you say that I am?" (Matthew 16:15).

Christian theology is not some tedious exercise in sorting out irrelevant details. It's an invitation to know more about this Jesus who saved us. He said it himself: Eternal life is knowing God and the One he sent (John 17:3). We want to speak in a way that matches his majesty and to proclaim his excellencies to the world.

So whether you're just now dipping your toes into the Christian faith, or you've been swimming in its waters for years, *Faith Simplified* is a book worth diving into. Aaron has given us a gift—one that will help you to know and love God more deeply. Enjoy the swim.

TRY THE UNTRIED

An Invitation to the Curious, the Questioning, and the Committed

It was a sweltering summer day in 2005. I'd been a Christian for about two months and was still trying to figure out what that meant. Not because I wasn't already learning anything from my pastors' messages or reading my Bible. But because I didn't have any significant preexisting knowledge of Christianity before becoming one, I frequently asked, "Okay, so what does that mean?"[1]

That is the mixed blessing of being a blank slate. When everything is new, everything is *new*. Language, concepts, and entire books of the Bible that might be familiar to a more established Christian are fresh to someone experiencing them all for the first time. Depending on your temperament, that freshness can quickly feel overwhelming. You can start to believe you must gain a lifetime's worth of knowledge right away—to know the answers to questions people have spent their entire lives exploring: Who and what is God? How can Jesus be both God and a human being simultaneously? Why do baptism and communion matter? What is heaven supposed to be like—and who will be there?

All of this was brand new to me. So I went to a bookstore. Specifically, a *Christian* bookstore. Now, bookstores are my happy place. I am what a professor I know sometimes refers to as a *promiscuous reader*, meaning I read a lot and I read widely. But in 2005, Christian bookstores were different animals than the indie bookshops and general market big box stores I frequented. The authors, publishers, and topics were all unfamiliar. That sense of not knowing where to start continued to grow.

After looking at different titles, I grabbed a copy of a book by a former pastor from Michigan, one whose messages I heard on occasion. In hindsight, it was a spiritual mid-life crisis in book form. This author spent much time spitballing faux-deep "what if" questions and writing in disjointed

single-

word

paragraphs,

while offering questionable analogies, comparing our beliefs to brick walls and trampolines, and calling important beliefs negotiable.

There were probably better choices.

I tried a few other books, but none of them resonated. Some were too focused on different attitudes—most encouraging men to capture or recapture a wild manly-man spirit. Others seemed more like the authors bragging about how humble they were. But after a few false starts, I found what I was looking for, even though it didn't directly answer my questions. It was called *Orthodoxy* by G.K. Chesterton.

GOD WANTS US TO USE OUR MINDS

First published in 1908, *Orthodoxy* was the first great Christian book I read as a new believer. In it, Chesterton describes his spiritual journey, which began with a desire to find a philosophy that would comprehensively make sense of *everything* in the world. If he had to develop it himself, he likely would have. As he began, Chesterton realized that this philosophy, or worldview, he was searching for already existed.

It was called *Christianity*.

Throughout the book, Chesterton expressed his understanding of Christianity as it truly is: an intellectually, emotionally, and practically rigorous worldview that has been left untried by far too many (including many who profess to believe it—but we'll come back to that).[2] One that speaks to the deepest needs of the human heart in a way that competing philosophies cannot. With cleverness and care, he developed a compelling argument that Christianity is so powerful and life-changing that "even when watered down [it] is hot enough to boil all modern society to rags."[3]

I devoured this book, leaving nary a page unmarked. My mind was on fire as I read each sentence, even if I didn't understand everything I read on the first go around.[4] And whatever else you could say about Chesterton's writing, his passion was evident. He *believed* what he wrote. But more than merely believing what he wrote, Chesterton understood something significant: for Christians to grow, they had to know something of their faith. But satisfying intellectual curiosity wasn't the point of that knowledge. Our knowledge of our faith must lead to something more profound.

Chesterton wasn't the only one who understood this, as I learned when I was introduced to C.S. Lewis. Or rather when I was *reintroduced* to him.

CURIOSITY AND COMMITMENT BELONG TOGETHER

For most of my life, I only knew Lewis as the author of *The Lion, the Witch and the Wardrobe*, a book I adored from the first time I read it when I was around age eight. His writing about reflections on the Christian faith and his delight in working his way "through a tough bit of theology" was entirely unknown to me.[5] I was completely unaware that he was a Christian at all!

Then, I found *Mere Christianity*. As I began reading it, I discovered a kindred spirit: a man who was simultaneously deeply curious and committed to upholding the core truths of the faith—truths that have defined Christianity from the beginning. A man who, like Chesterton, was captivated by big questions, even bigger ideas, and a God simply too glorious for him to comprehend fully. He saw the value of a deep and rich intellectual life because he knew that "God is no fonder of intellectual slackers than of any other slackers."[6] But he, like Chesterton, was not content to see Christianity as a merely intellectual faith, as though the accumulation of knowledge was the pinnacle of godliness. He understood that our faith must affect how we live every day.

> Christianity asserts that every individual human being is going to live for ever, and this must be either true or false. Now there are a good many things which would not be worth bothering about if I were going to live only seventy years, but which I had better bother about very seriously if I am going to live for ever. Perhaps my bad temper or my jealousy are gradually getting worse—so gradually that the increase in seventy years will not be very noticeable. But it might be absolute hell in a million years: in fact, if Christianity is true, Hell is the precisely correct technical term for what it would be.[7]

Together, Chesterton and Lewis encouraged me to seek the answers to my big questions about the Christian faith and to live differently because of those answers. But there was another individual still who not only agreed with their encouragement, but amplified it.

KNOWING *ABOUT* GOD AND KNOWING GOD

I was curious about this book when I saw it on my friend's coffee table. I hadn't heard of the author, J.I. Packer, but that was nothing new at the time. It was the title that intrigued me: *Knowing God*.

"Is it any good?" I asked.

"You should read it," he said. "It will change your life."

That was a bold statement, but let me tell you, dear reader, my friend was not exaggerating. I bought a copy later that week and slowly began working my way through it over the next several weeks. It was a book that demanded that sort of care. In it, I found many chapters devoted to some of the bigger questions I had about essential Christian beliefs—the nature of God, the humanity and deity of Jesus, and so much more. But I also found something more as I read. These were the words of a man who knew much *about* God—but more than that, he was a man who seemed to know *God* intimately. He described knowing God as, in one sense, "dealing with him as he opens up to you, and being dealt with by him as he takes knowledge of you."[8] It is also "a matter of personal involvement—mind, will and feeling," recognizing that we are invited into a relationship with God that involves the totality of our being.[9] And it is a matter of grace, a gift from God to us. "*We* do not make friends with *God*; *God* makes friends with *us*, bringing us to know him by making his love known to us" (emphasis Packer's).[10]

Chesterton, Lewis, and Packer. These three men helped me develop the skills I needed to know the essential truths of my new faith—to pursue knowledge, to be curious, and to do so out of a heart of devotion to God. To live as a person who delights in and is devoted to the truths that define Christianity.

I want the same for you. So, where do we start? With something called *theology*.

STRAINING OUT CAMELS

At its most basic, theology is what you understand and believe about God. Theology comprises the capital *T* truths of who God is, what he is like, and what he has done and continues to do. That includes how he made the world, everything in it, and intended for it to operate. (Including us too.) But for many people, especially Western Protestant Christians within more experientially oriented traditions, *theology* evokes images of giant tomes and academic ivory towers. Of academics discussing issues that don't seem to matter much to our day-to-day lives, who seem content to strain out gnats while swallowing camels (Matthew 23:24). If that's what theology is, it is best to leave it to the theologians. The rest of us have work to do and people to serve.

I understand that impulse. I've sat in enough rooms with professionally very smart people to know this stereotype has some truth. But the presence of some truth doesn't make something wholly true. Theology is not a purely academic pursuit. It is not something we can set aside, downplay, or ignore. It is not something that hinders our lives as Christians or gets in the way of ministry; it is what undergirds everything.

In the Western world, this is more important to understand than ever. According to ongoing studies from Lifeway Research and Ligonier Ministries, American Protestant Evangelical Christians don't affirm what Christians have historically believed about some fundamental matters.[11] Jesus' divinity and eternal nature. The personhood of the Holy Spirit. The scope of sin's effects on the world. The exclusivity of the Christian faith as the path to eternal life.[12] And this problem is not unique to the United States, either. A 2018 study of the state of theology in the UK revealed that many Protestant Christians there may be even *less* Christian in their beliefs than American Protestants.[13]

These matters are not gnats. These are camels.

Which brings us back to Chesterton's problem. For many, it's not that Christianity has been tried and found wanting. It's that they have never tried it. And they haven't tried it because they don't know what is central to that faith.

Christian beliefs shape the Christian heart and the Christian life. That is why we need to know these truths. Our minds, hearts, and actions are all informed and transformed by what we know about God, the universe, and everything else. It is why theology is good news for you and me. It is *practical*, leaving no area of our lives untouched as we all draw on the Bible's teaching to live faithfully day by day.[14]

AN INVITATION TO TRY THE UNTRIED

As you engage with this book, dear reader, I don't know from what background you are approaching it. Perhaps you are where I was in my first years as a Christian. You believe, but there's a lot that you don't know that will help shape your faith. Perhaps you're a long-time believer who wants to learn more about the faith that is yours because of Jesus. Or maybe you're reading this book from a more questioning perspective; you're not a Christian at all, or you're a professing Christian who is as confused about our faith as the world is. Or you may be a deeply committed Christian who knows the truths we cling to but seeks a way to help others understand what is unique and special about the faith.

And while some of the material in the following pages may stretch you, you won't find heady academic explanations filled with highly technical jargon. While there is a place and time for technical material, exploring and explaining the deep truths of the faith should not sound like the technobabble on *Star Trek* sounds to most everyone watching—or the way a mechanic sounds to me when trying to explain the maintenance being done on my car. It shouldn't be this way because theology—our beliefs about God, his words, his works, and his promises—is for everyone. Theology is for *you*.

And wherever you're coming from, whatever brought you to the place of reading it, this book is for you too.

Because I'm one of you.

This book isn't the distillation of an advanced seminary degree. It is the fruit of 20 years' of ongoing Bible study, reading, and conversations. These are tasks all of us can do, no matter our backgrounds, educations, and interests. They are habits I hope you will practice as you read this book. That is the reason there are so many Bible references throughout these pages, questions at the end of every chapter, and a lot of extra information for you to investigate in the endnotes. I don't want you to read these pages and simply take my word for it. Explore on your own, consider these truths and where they are represented in the Bible, and ideally, talk with others as you do. But most importantly, I hope this book will aid you in discovering, delighting, and ultimately devoting yourself to the truths you find in its pages. These truths that make Christians *Christian*.

GOD IS

1

ONE, AND ALSO THREE (WHO ARE ONE)

Who (and What) Is God?

Once upon a time, on a frigid February morning in a townhouse complex in southwestern Ontario, a man and a woman knocked on my door. They were Jehovah's Witnesses and were on a mission to share literature and what they believed to be a message of hope for anyone who didn't pretend they weren't home or slam the door in their faces. (Yes, Canadians are indeed that rude regarding door-to-door proselytizing.)

I was delighted to speak to these missionaries from another religion. Early in my faith, I decided to engage in conversations like this whenever God brought the opportunity. I wasn't looking to be convinced to convert. I just wanted to have a respectful discussion about the differences in what we believe. So, despite the icy temperatures, I kept the door open as they diligently worked through their script:[1]

1. The Bible is full of wisdom and has an important message for the world.

2. The world is falling apart because of immorality, famine, and war, they said, carefully tying in a relevant recent event from the news.

3. The answers to these problems are found in obedience to God's commands in the Bible and a renewed relationship with humanity's Creator through Jesus Christ.

On the surface, these are true statements that few, if any, Christians would disagree with. But surface-level agreement is one thing. Genuine agreement requires something else: a shared foundation.[2] And to get to this, I asked one question, "Who is Jesus?"

Without missing a beat, the male missionary said, "We believe Jesus is, as he said, 'the way, the truth, and the life,' and no one comes to the Father except through him."

"He gave his perfect human life as a ransom sacrifice, and his death and resurrection make it possible for those exercising faith in him to gain everlasting life," said his teammate.

"Sure, but that doesn't answer my question," I replied.

They paused and looked at each other as if having a telepathic conversation:

> Female Missionary: *Where is this guy going with this?*
>
> Male Missionary: *Not sure; let's see how it plays out.*

I continued. "Well, you've said Jesus had a perfect human life, right? So, you believe Jesus was a created being, right?"

"Yes…?"

"Okay, cool. But how can any human being be perfect? Doesn't the Bible say that's impossible?"

The female missionary's eyes widened. She knew where I was going with my questions—and she would have none of it. "The Trinity isn't taught in the Bible," she exclaimed. They quickly left.

Rats, I thought. *We hadn't even gotten to John 1:1 yet.*

STARTING AT THE STARTING POINT

So why begin this chapter with a story about Jehovah's Witnesses? I mean, that would probably make more sense if we were talking about evangelism or looking at Jesus' nature, right? While it might seem like this is just a cute story, it reveals something important. Even though we have some superficial agreement on the problems of the world, and we use similar language to define the problem, Christians and Jehovah's Witnesses have a profound disagreement about God. The same is true between Christians and Muslims, as well as Jews, Mormons, Buddhists, Hindus, and every other religion and worldview. We disagree on the starting point of our theology.

All theology ultimately centers on God, the One at the center of everything—on who he is, what he has done, and how he requires us to live. So to begin with God means to begin exploring his nature and being—to answer the question of *who* (or what) is God.

If you had asked me this question when I was in my early twenties, I wouldn't have been able to give you a particularly compelling answer, largely because I didn't know. But when I became a Christian, I learned that answering this question was *really* important. It is the most important question to be able to answer because what we believe about God himself shapes everything else we believe.

WHO DO CHRISTIANS TALK ABOUT WHEN WE TALK ABOUT GOD?

Up until about the 1960s, there was at least some semblance of a shared cultural answer in the West. It was an answer that somewhat resembled the God Christians worship. However, those days have long since passed. You may have atheist friends who might say God is a myth our ancestors devised to help make sense of the world or, more cynically, an idea to maintain control over a population and legislate morality. Perhaps a Muslim coworker would tell you that God is an otherworldly, supreme being who cannot be known or comprehended by human beings. Or maybe a spiritual-but-not-religious classmate would suggest that we all carry the divine in us—in effect, we are all God.

Then, there is what Christians believe.

The Christian understanding of God is unlike any other religion or worldview. Our beliefs about God have led to some of the most beautiful and inspiring teachings in the church's history. But they have also resulted in some of its greatest controversies and errors. This is because what the Bible teaches about God is mysterious and strange, but also the only way God makes sense.

If you had to condense what we believe about God's nature—meaning *what* God is—into three key points, it might look something like this:

1. There is one God, who has eternally existed.

2. This one God is entirely self-sufficient, lacking nothing.

3. This one God eternally exists as three persons who are fully and equally divine, one in essence, or substance, yet distinct from one another.[3]

While there's much to be said about all three, these points make up the heart of Christians' understanding of God. There is one God, and only one God, who needs for nothing—including relationships—because God is three distinct persons who are all equally and fully that one God.

Yeah, I know; it can all seem overwhelming. It's a lot to take in, especially that last point. So before we go any further, remember this: God wants you to know who he is. He has made it possible for you to understand something of what he is like. But before we can dig into that last point, this very simple explanation of what we call the *Trinity*, we must explore the first two. So, let's answer this question together: Why do Christians believe there is only one God?

THERE IS ONLY ONE GOD

Among those who believe God exists at all today, the idea of there being only one God does not seem particularly mind-blowing. There are no less than three religions that hold to the view there is only one God, a view known as *monotheism*—Christianity, Judaism, and Islam. This doesn't mean, however, that Christians and Muslims believe in the same God (nor modern Jews, for that matter). We have fundamental disagreements about his nature, so it is wrong to say that we do. But we do agree that there is only one God.

In the days of Abraham, Isaac, and Jacob, and in the times of Moses, Joshua, and David, though, this was a *radical* concept. People were largely polytheistic in their beliefs, meaning that they believed in the existence of, and worshiped, many gods. It was not uncommon for people to have a tribal or household deity that they would primarily worship, while offering sacrifices to another god in the hopes of having a child, and another for a prosperous harvest, and so on.

But humans were not meant to be polytheists. Our worship has always been intended to belong to only one God—the only God who *actually* exists. The biblical authors went to great lengths to depict other gods for what they were: lifeless, useless, and powerless. These handcrafted gods were not worthy of worship but mockery.[4]

Nowhere does the Bible teach that there are many gods, of whom the Lord is but one option to choose from.[5] Instead, the Bible emphasizes this truth from beginning to end—there is one God, and only one. For example:

- "The Lord is our God, the Lord is one" (Deuteronomy 6:4; Mark 12:29 NASB).

- "O Lord, there is none like you; there is no God besides you" (1 Chronicles 17:20).

- "I am the Lord, and there is no other; there is no God besides Me" (Isaiah 45:5; and variations: 45:18, 21, 22; 46:9 NKJV).

- "I am the Lord your God and there is no other" (Joel 2:27 NKJV).

- "There is no God but one" (1 Corinthians 8:4).

This one God is not merely any god, though. He is not a stand-in for one of the deities of the Greek and Roman pantheons. He is not born of violence and lust as they were. He has no beginning, and he has no end (Isaiah 44:6; Revelation 1:8; 22:13). The God of Israel, the God of the Bible, is the Maker of heaven and earth, uncreated, and eternally existing as the One who was there *before* the beginning (Genesis 1:1; Psalm 121:2; 146:6).

A COMPLETELY SELF-SUFFICIENT GOD

There is one God, and there is no other. He has always been and always will be. He lacks nothing; he is self-sufficient. He is not "served by human hands, as if he needed anything, because he himself gives life and breath and everything to everyone" (Acts 17:25). He doesn't *need* sacrifices from humanity because everything comes from him; it is already his (Psalm 50:9-12; 1 Chronicles 29:14-16). He doesn't need our worship, even as all humanity is called to worship him

(1 Kings 8:41-43). He doesn't need anything at all from us—not our love, adoration, affection—he needs none of it. And as we'll explore in chapter 2, even though he is extremely relational—revealing his existence, nature, power, and will to the entire universe (Romans 1:20)—he doesn't even need *external* relationships. He doesn't need us, the people he made (Job 22:2). He has all he needs in himself.

A GOD WHO IS THREE PERSONS

But how can that be? How can this one God, who has always existed and will always exist, and is actively relational, be self-sufficient the way the Bible describes? As we read the Old Testament, God drops hints that his nature as One is more complex, or maybe mysterious, than we might think because, even as the Bible speaks of one God, it seems to depict a multiplicity to God. That there is one God, but more than one *person* is God.

Some of this is revealed in language, such as when God speaks singularly and refers to himself plurally. For example, in Genesis 1:26 we read, "God said, 'Let us make humankind in our image, after our likeness.'" Other times it's situational, such as when Joshua "bowed with his face to the ground in homage" before the commander of the Lord's army (Joshua 5:14 CSB). While these examples alone aren't definitive proof, when we consider other events such as God being among the three visitors who were with Abraham before the destruction of Sodom and Gomorrah (Genesis 18), the appearance of the Lord to Gideon (Judges 6:22-23), and God's apparent appearance in bodily form to Samuel (1 Samuel 3:10), it sparks curiosity enough to make you take notice.[6]

And in the New Testament, what seems curious becomes clear.

The Lord, God the Father

God's deity and personhood are never truly in question at any point in the New Testament writings. In fact, by and large, the New

Testament authors speak of him in precisely the same way as the Old Testament, with one exception: a deepening of relationship.

The New Testament authors, taking their cues from Jesus, began to refer to God not simply as "Lord" and "God," but also as "Father." This moniker is used interchangeably with God throughout the Gospels (see Matthew 6:26-33; Mark 11:22-25; Luke 23:46-47). However, "Father" is not the only name used in relationship with God in the New Testament, but those others do not apply to the Father.

The Word, God the Son

Then John's Gospel opens with a dramatic prologue, set before the beginning of time: "In the beginning was the Word, and the Word was with God, and the Word was God. He was with God in the beginning" (John 1:1-2 CSB). That same Word, John wrote, came to earth and dwelt among his people, revealing the glory of God as his one and only Son (John 1:14).

Who is that "Word"? *Jesus.*

While he is shown to be a human being by the Gospel writers, those same writers take care to demonstrate that Jesus is not simply human. He did (and does) things only God could do—because he was and is God (Philippians 2:5-11). For example:

- Jesus demonstrates the authority to forgive sin (Mark 2:1-12).
- Jesus issues authoritative commands on par with Scripture (Matthew 5:21-48).
- Jesus has power over life and death (John 11).
- Jesus has authority over creation (Matthew 8:23-27).
- Jesus commands angels and demons (Matthew 8:28-34; 13:41).
- Jesus describes himself as equal to God and receives worship *as* God (John 5:39; 20:28).

When Jesus did and said these things, those around him—including those who opposed him—understood. Jesus was "making himself equal to God" (John 5:18 csb); in other words, Jesus was saying that he *is* God. Equal to the Father, but distinct from him. The Word, God the Son, "is the radiance of God's glory and the exact expression of his nature" (Hebrews 1:3 csb).

That is who Jesus is.

But the Bible does not stop with only these two persons; there is not simply God the Father and the Word, Jesus, who is God the Son. There is one other—God the Holy Spirit.

God the Holy Spirit

The Holy Spirit is, in some ways, the most difficult person of the three to comprehend. If we aren't reading Scripture carefully, we can incorrectly conclude that the Spirit is a manifestation of God's power or an impersonal force. A *what* rather than a *who*, if you will. But the Scriptures themselves reject this idea. The Holy Spirit is described as eternal (Hebrews 9:14), having been present at the beginning of creation as the Father spoke the world into existence through the Son (Genesis 1:2). The Spirit is omnipresent (Psalm 139:7-8), all-knowing (1 Corinthians 2:10), and all-powerful (Zechariah 4:6). He is holy, faithful, just, truthful, gracious, and merciful.

The Holy Spirit has personal characteristics. He speaks, teaches, and leads (Luke 12:12; Acts 13:2; Romans 8:14; 1 Corinthians 2:10-11). He counsels and comforts (John 14:26; 15:26). He seals and sanctifies (Ephesians 1:13; 4:30; 1 Peter 1:2). He can be grieved, resisted, and insulted (Isaiah 63:10; Acts 7:51; Ephesians 4:30; Hebrews 10:29). And if that weren't enough, the Holy Spirit is explicitly called "God" in Acts 5:3-4 and 1 Corinthians 3:16-17 (see also 6:19-20). The Scriptures themselves are emphatic: The Holy Spirit is God—fully divine, just as the Father and Son are divine (Matthew 28:19; 2 Corinthians 13:14), and their equal in every way. (And, I should add, there's a *lot* more to say about who the Holy Spirit is and what he does in our lives, which we'll get to in chapter 19.)

GOD AS SCRIPTURE DESCRIBES HIM

This is God as the Bible describes him: God is one in essence and three in person—Father, Son, and Holy Spirit (Matthew 28:18-20). Each is fully and equally God. The Father is God, the Son is God, and the Spirit is God, perfectly and eternally united in their essence and will, free from subordination or hierarchy.[7] But even as they are eternally united in essence and will, they are also distinct from one another. While the Father, Son, and Spirit are God, the Father is not the Son nor the Spirit, the Son is not the Father nor the Spirit, and the Spirit is not the Father nor the Son (Matthew 11:27; John 10:30; 14:16).

And yes, that is the simplest way to explain it.

This is what Christians refer to as the doctrine of the Trinity. While the word *Trinity* doesn't appear in Scripture, the concept does. But that doesn't mean that it is easy to understand.

THE STUFF (ACCIDENTAL) HERETICS ARE MADE OF

Remember how I said that what the Bible teaches about God's nature is the source of some of our greatest controversies and errors? Well, that's because our attempts to explain the mystery of God's three-and-oneness always fall short, as a laundry list of heresies—teachings that contradict or deny an essential truth of the Christian faith—attests.[8]

One teacher attempted to explain the Persons of the Trinity as *forms* or *modes* of existence, that at certain times God acted in the mode of the Father and at others in the mode of the Son or the Spirit.

This heresy, called *modalism*, is alive and well in our day, as it is part of some churches' doctrinal statements (such as the Oneness Pentecostals), and finds its way into popular songs and books.[9]

Another teacher, Arius, believed Jesus and the Holy Spirit are not coeternal and equal with God the Father. Instead, he taught that both are created beings and subordinate to God the Father. His heresy, *Arianism*, is alive and well in religions such as the Jehovah's Witnesses, which, despite using Christian language, does not align with historic Christian teaching, believing Jesus is a created being and the Holy Spirit is an impersonal force.[10] Some teachings about the relationship between the Father, Son, and Spirit within otherwise faithful Christian circles also risk being a reframing of this heresy.[11]

A third common heresy, *tritheism*, teaches that the Father, Son, and Spirit are not one but fully separate divine beings. A form of this is taught by the Church of Jesus Christ of Latter-day Saints (commonly known as the Mormons), another religion that, despite using similar language, does not align with historic Christianity.[12]

This is why we shouldn't try to use analogies to describe the Trinity. They all wind up making us accidental heretics. For example:

- The Trinity is not like water, which exists at different times as gas, liquid, or solid. That's *modalism*.

- The Trinity isn't like a star from which light and heat emanate. That's *Arianism*.

- The Trinity isn't like a family with a mother, father, and child. That's *tritheism*.

While analogies might make for entertaining YouTube videos, they make for terrible theology.[13] The Trinity is a grand mystery. God's revelation of his nature is incomparable—there is *literally* nothing else like him in all the universe.

A BEAUTIFUL MYSTERY TO BEHOLD

This is probably the most theologically intense piece you're going to read in this entire book. And let's be honest; it's tempting to skip over some of this kind of stuff—to put questions about God's nature in the "I'll-find-out-when-I-get-there" folder, alongside the problem of evil and why American reality TV shows continue to draw audiences. But the Trinity matters because there is no Christianity without it. For that matter, there are no Christians without the Trinity. Everything about how we "do" Christianity depends on it:

We read the Bible through a trinitarian lens and with trinitarian power. The Bible is the revelation of the Father through the Son by the power of the Spirit. The Spirit helps us understand and rejoice in this revelation to the glory of the Son and the Father.

We pray with a "trinitarian grain," as one author put it. Our prayers run "from the Spirit through the Son to the Father."[14] We're not on our own with our prayers bouncing off our ceilings. The Spirit carries our prayers to Jesus the Son, who intercedes on our behalf with the Father.

We are rescued by and share a gospel that involves every Person of the Trinity. The Father planned for the salvation of sinners incapable of rescuing themselves, loving those who did not first love him (1 John 4:10). The Son accomplished that salvation through his sinless life, death, and resurrection. And the Spirit applies it to "everyone who believes" (John 3:16), anyone who calls upon the name of Jesus to be saved, by breathing new life into dead hearts. And we are commissioned to share this good news in the name and power of the Trinity—the Father, the Son, and the Holy Spirit (Matthew 28:19-20).

This is only scratching the surface, of course. But when you begin to look at the world through a trinitarian lens, it changes everything. Is it a mystery? Absolutely. But it is a beautiful mystery to behold.

REFLECT, EXPLORE, AND DISCUSS

1. What idea or concept stood out to you as you read this chapter? Why?

2. Read some of the Bible passages that describe the deity of the Father, the Son, and the Holy Spirit referenced in this chapter. How do they help you grasp the truth of God's nature?

3. What new questions do these passages raise?

4. What does looking at the world through a trinitarian lens mean for your life?

2

SIMILAR, BUT DIFFERENT

The Infinite, All-Knowing, All-Powerful God Is Always with Us. And Separate from Us. All at the Same Time.

I'm a reader of books of all sorts and kinds. Give me a good mystery, apocalyptic sci-fi, epic fantasy, or a moment of "ordinary" from a small town in Sweden…all of it is amazing. But there's something that's always fascinated me about mythology. The Norse gods—Odin, Thor, Loki, and the rest—are so often seen scheming against one another. They are petty, vindictive beings. Then, there are the Greek and Roman pantheons who come to the aid of human heroes (who, often, also happen to be their children) in one moment, and then focus all their vindictiveness on these same heroes the next.

Sometimes the gods of mythology have admirable qualities. Most of the time, they're terrible. Actually, that's not quite right. It's not that they're terrible. It's that they're a little bit too much like *us*. They lust, lie, steal, manipulate, and murder at least as much as they care for those who worship them. They have virtues and vices. They act in exactly the ways we would if we were gods. For all their bluster, the fear they inspire, and all the evils they perpetrate in their stories, these gods are safe. They are unchallenging to us in any meaningful way.

They are exactly the kind of gods people would make up. Which is why the God Christians believe in seems so different.

A GOD INFINITELY UNLIKE ANY OTHER

Christianity's God isn't like any of the gods of mythology. He is entirely different. He is entirely bigger and better—and not just in the ways that we already looked at in the last chapter. This one God is entirely self-sufficient, lacks absolutely nothing, and exists as three persons—Father, Son, and Holy Spirit—who are all one in essence, equally divine but distinct from one another. (You didn't skip over chapter 1, did you? If you did, go back and read it before you go further. I'll wait.) As mind-blowing, awe-inspiring, and head-scratching as the reality of his nature is, there is so much more to God than even that. So much that can, and should, leave us slack-jawed in wonder. Infinitely so.

Infinite is exactly the right word to use here. It sums up everything about God. It is a catchall word that begins to describe the absolute lack of boundaries or constraints on God's qualities and his existence (Job 11:7-9; Psalm 147:5).

Now, here's the problem: To go no farther than to say God is infinite fails to do justice to God's nature. It is too *conceptual*, perhaps even too theoretical, to help us truly begin to grasp the greatness of God's being. Fortunately, the Bible illustrates this in a few different ways for us:

- **God is everywhere:** Time and space place no constraints on him because he is outside of both (1 Kings 8:27; Acts 17:24). And because he is not bound by the limitations of time and space, God is everywhere simultaneously, or *omnipresent.* He is with us all the time, even when we don't realize it or act as though he weren't (Psalm 33:14; Jeremiah 23:23-24; Matthew 18:20).

- **God knows everything:** When it comes to knowledge, he is *omniscient,* having all knowledge, perfect and complete, extending to the past, present, and future (Job 37:16). This also means that there isn't anything he *can't* know. Nothing is hidden from him. No one gives him counsel or teaches him (Job 21:22; Isaiah 40:13-14). He knows the mysteries that no one else does (Deuteronomy 29:29). He knows our hearts in a way that even we do not (John 2:24). He even knows exactly how many hairs are on your head, because he numbered each one (Matthew 10:30). And if you are among the follicly challenged, he knows how many remain or have been lost.

- **God can do anything:** God is all-powerful, that is, *omnipotent,* capable of doing anything and everything that conforms to his nature, character, and decrees (Genesis 18:14; Job 42:1-2; Isaiah 14:27; Daniel 4:35; Ephesians 1:19). This also means that he is incapable of doing anything and everything that conflicts with his nature, character, and decrees. So in case you're curious, no, God cannot create a boulder so big that he cannot lift it, because he cannot create something that negates his God-ness.[1]

INFINITELY DISTINCT FROM US

The whole notion of an all-knowing, all-powerful, ever-present God is difficult to grasp. That God can be all these things reminds us that he is so completely unlike us. And we're right to recognize that. God is different from us. He is *distinct* from everyone and everything in the universe—including the universe! He is unique, entirely *other* from us. The technical word that is used to describe this is *transcendence*. This is a fancy way of saying that God is infinitely above and beyond his creation. He is not a part of the world in the way that we are, and it is not a part of him.

This is part of the reason that the Bible emphasizes his eternal nature to the degree that it does. While I touched on this ever so briefly in the last chapter, it's worth repeating: God has no beginning; he simply *is*. He has no starting point because there is none. Instead, when the Bible begins, it begins with God already present. Before the foundations of the world were laid, before anything else was, God was already there, perfectly fulfilled in all his three-in-oneness (Genesis 1:1). There has never been a time when God was not, nor will there ever be a time when he will not be. He is the God "who was and who is, and who is still to come…the Alpha and the Omega, the beginning and the end" (Revelation 4:8; 21:6). And because God has no beginning and no end, because he *is* the beginning and the end, he exists outside of our finite, linear existence. He *transcends* it.

INFINITELY INTIMATELY INVOLVED WITH US

Now this whole concept of transcendence, God's otherness, can be misunderstood. Because God is distinct and separate from the universe, we can make the mistake of believing that he is not involved in the universe.[2] But what we see in the Bible presents a very different perspective. We see that God is both distinct and separate from the world, but also, he is deeply and personally involved in the events of the world.

And truly, he is.

Despite not needing humanity for relationship (that whole "self-sufficiency" thing), God delights in being involved with us, down to the most minute detail of our lives (Zephaniah 3:17). So he reveals his existence, nature, character, and actions to us in many different ways: through the natural world, through the events of history, and through the Bible itself (we'll discuss all this in coming chapters). And God's self-revelation—his self-disclosure—brings him near to us. It makes him personal.

This is what we mean by the word *immanence*. God is intimately involved in his creation, particularly in making human beings in his image. We bear the image of God, which makes us unique from the rest of creation (again, we'll come back to this in a bit, so just hang tight). We see God's intention in this regard through the creation account, when he was not content to speak the first man and woman into being, something he did for everything else. Instead, God formed the first humans with his hands (Genesis 2:7, 22). And there is a sense in which this direct formation continues, for the psalmist declares that God "made my mind and heart; you wove me together in my mother's womb" (Psalm 139:13). It is only fitting that a sovereign, loving God would play a "hands-on" role in the formation of every person because every person is made in his image.

But God's moment-by-moment involvement with us does not end at our birth. It continues throughout our lives. Jesus goes so far as to tell us that God "knows the things you need before you ask him" (Matthew 6:8 CSB). He provides for our daily needs, such as what we will eat and drink (Matthew 6:25-34). He equips and empowers us (Acts 1:8). He is actively working in our lives to make us more like Jesus (Romans 8:29; 2 Corinthians 3:18). Indeed, Jesus himself is the epitome of the immanence of God, humbling himself to take on flesh, becoming like us so that he might redeem us. This is not the description of a far-off, unknowable, uninterested divine being. Instead, it is a glimpse of a close, deeply personal, and involved God. God is immanent; he is near and knowable.

OUR INFINITELY EXISTENTIAL ANGST

But let's be honest: Even trying to wrap your head around the idea of an infinite being can seem like a lost cause. It's so far outside our experience. We can't even imagine what that could be like. And if you are prone to a particular sort of existential angst, you may fear that even attempting to understand God is not only a lost cause, but also wrong. After all, to be infinite is, by definition, to be without limits. But definitions, by their nature, create limits. Wouldn't our definitions put God in a box? Wouldn't they limit him and limit our thinking about him, reducing our wonder?

And so we spiral.

All kidding aside—and with apologies to the first-year philosophy students reading this—while we can look at definitions as limiting, I think there's a healthier way to approach them, especially when it comes to God. When trying to understand an infinite being, definitions can be illuminating. Rather than creating hard boundaries that negatively limit us, definitions help us to begin to grasp the shape of God. To understand *something* of God's majesty—his awe-inspiring wonder. These facets, these attributes, of God help us to begin to see his infiniteness, increasing our awe of him.

That God's knowledge is infinite—that there is *nothing* he does not or cannot know—should give us confidence that there is nothing that can be unknown to him. Nothing can surprise him or catch him off guard. God's infinite power reminds us that nothing is too great for him to overcome. God's infinite presence means that he is always with us, even in the darkest places.

This is who God is. This is how God delights in making himself known to us. And even if we can only know him in part (the fullness of God's nature is far beyond our perception or ability to comprehend), what *can* be known is truly majestic.

THE ONLY GOD WORTH BELIEVING IN

That's why all these concepts matter so much, all these characteristics that are tied to God's infinite nature. They reveal that the God Christians worship is completely unlike anything else—no other religion's deity comes close in comparison. No other philosophy has at its center, a being who evokes such a powerful sense of wonder. The majestic, infinite, and transcendent God, who exists apart from the world he created, cares deeply about his creation. He cares deeply about you and me and every other person who has ever lived or will ever live—to the degree that he stepped into creation to rescue us from our sins! No other god did this. No other god *could*. No other god is worthy of our praise.

REFLECT, EXPLORE, AND DISCUSS

1. What idea or concept stood out to you as you read this chapter? Why?

2. Read some of the Bible passages describing God's nature and attributes referenced in this chapter. How do they encourage or challenge you?

3. What new questions do these passages raise?

4. Even though it is meant to be reassuring, God's omnipresence makes some people uncomfortable. Why might that be?

3

PERFECTLY PERFECT IN EVERY WAY

A Merciful and Loving God Who Is Always Right and Pure and Trustworthy

Everyone has an opinion about God. Even people who say they don't believe God exists, who have never given a first thought to the existence of anything supernatural, have an opinion. And for many people, their beliefs about God are distilled in two contradictory points:

1. God is not real.

2. If he exists, I hate him.

These points might seem extreme, or at least overly simplistic. Few people would express their beliefs about God in these exact ways, in part, because they are so direct.[1] But even if we might not be this forward about what we believe, practically, it's how many of us live.

The reasons behind this are complicated. For some people, their opinion may be the result of a distorted understanding of who God is or what it means for God to be good. Perhaps a beloved family member died, or some other tragedy occurred, resulting in their rejection of God (because their understanding of God's goodness means nothing bad is supposed to happen to *them*, and therefore, he cannot be trusted when they do experience these events). For others, it may be because of the failures of those who profess to be Christians to represent God adequately—for example, church leaders and members who abuse power and harm people. As the thinking goes, if those are the kind of people who worship God, he must be terrible.

But there's something else at work, something that we all struggle with—even those of us who profess to be Christians. And it's that even the *idea* that God *might* exist challenges our self-image. God's existence tells us that we aren't as great as we think we are.

THE BAD NEWS FOR OUR SELF-IMAGE

The late R.C. Sproul, a well-known author and founder of Ligonier Ministries, shared the story of a pro golfer who once played in a tournament alongside several well-known figures, including the late evangelist, Billy Graham. During the experience, another golfer asked what it was like to play alongside Graham.

> The pro unleashed a torrent of cursing, and in a disgusted manner said, "I don't need Billy Graham stuffing religion down my throat." With that he turned on his heel and stormed off, heading for the practice tee.
>
> His friend followed the angry pro to the practice tee. The pro took out his driver and started to beat out balls in fury. His neck was crimson, and it looked as if steam was coming from his ears. His friend said nothing. He sat on a bench and watched. After a few minutes the anger of the

pro was spent. He settled down. His friend said quietly, "Was Billy a little rough on you out there?"

The pro heaved an embarrassed sigh and said, "No, he didn't even mention religion. I just had a bad round."[2]

So what was it about Graham's presence that caused this outsized reaction? He was a representative of Jesus—and for the golf pro to be in the presence of someone who followed Jesus caused him to respond with hostility. The holiness of God was seen clearly enough in Graham that it made the pro recognize his lack of holiness; he was personally convicted and condemned by it, even if only on a subconscious level.

So what does this have to do with who God is? In a word: everything. In the last two chapters, we looked at God's nature, seeking to understand him to the degree that we are able. We surveyed what we might call his attributes as they relate to his being, qualities that are inherent to him. Those sorts of attributes primarily focus on *who* and *what* God is. But there are others still that help us grasp what God is *like* and how he *acts*. And a key aspect that helps us understand God's other attributes is holiness.

THE HOLY—PERFECT—GOD

We use the word *holy* quite regularly in our culture, even if in many cases it's only as one-half of an exclamation. But we've all heard of specific people being referred to as "holy" in a positive sense based on the merits of their actions on behalf of others (many refer to Mahatma Gandhi and Mother Teresa in this way, for example). It is used as an honorific for others, such as the Pope in the Roman Catholic Church. And virtually all of us have, at one time or another, been to a specific place and were left with a feeling that this location is somehow special—set apart and distinct from the rest of the world. That is, in one sense, what holiness means; to be holy is to be separate or set apart from others. (This is what the biblical Hebrew word we translate as "holy" means.) And that certainly is true of God. He is distinct; he is unique, unlike any other.

If that sounds a lot like a concept we talked about in the last chapter, that is, God's transcendent nature—his existence outside of and apart from the world he made—you're right. God is set apart, separate. But when referencing God, holiness isn't referring to his set apart-ness in terms of his nature, but in the sense of his moral character. To say God is holy is to say that God is perfect, ethically and morally. Everything he does, everything he says, and everything he *is*, is good and right. There is not even a hint of wrong motive, selfishness, conceit, or any other sinister intent.

This is important for us to try to wrap our heads around because holiness is the central attribute of God's character. This complete moral perfection is his default mode, and it never changes. Every other attribute of God that can be identified in Scripture—love, faithfulness, trustworthiness, justice, graciousness, and mercy to name but a few—is best understood in light of it.

Holy Love

Because God is holy, it is not enough to simply say that he is loving. Instead, we can and should say, along with the Bible, that "God is love" (1 John 4:8). Every word, thought, and deed is grounded in, motivated by, and a display of his love: his love for his people, for his creation, and for his glory.

God's love is perfect, pure, and good. It is not given out of compulsion. It is not self-seeking. It is not boastful. It cannot be earned or coerced. It is freely given and shown to all—even those who reject him. It is a reflection of his very essence, the perfect love that resides and resonates within the Trinity—Father, Son, and Spirit (John 5:20; 2 Corinthians 13:13).

Holy Faithfulness

Because God is holy, he is faithful. He always keeps his word. He always keeps his promises. And from the beginning, the Bible shows us that God is a promise-making and promise-keeping God. These promises are what we sometimes call *covenants*, holy vows about which God defines the terms and promises to fulfill them. And everything God does in the Bible is best understood through the lens of these covenants.

God first made a covenant with humanity, whom he made to rule over the rest of creation as his representatives within it (Genesis 1:26-28). He promised eternal life with him if they obeyed his commands—which at the time was only one command: Do not eat the fruit of one very specific tree (Genesis 2:15-17). If obeyed, they would live forever in peace and joy and harmony with him. If disobeyed, they would die. And when humanity disobeyed, deceived by a serpent (we'll come back to this), God kept his promise and sent them out of his presence, but not without hope—though their lives would be difficult, and they would eventually die, one of their descendants would someday destroy the one who deceived them (Genesis 3:14-19).

When the descendants of humanity filled the earth and their only desire was to do evil continually, God wiped them out in a flood. But before he did so, he made a covenant with Noah, who found favor with God and was a righteous man, sparing him and his family to begin humanity anew. After the waters subsided, he promised to never again flood the world in its entirety (Genesis 6–9).

God made a covenant with Abram, later Abraham, promising him as many offspring as there are stars in the sky (Genesis 15). He promised Moses and the Israelites (Abraham's descendants) that they would be a nation under his rule, a nation that served as a symbol of a greater kingdom yet to come (Exodus 6:4; 19:5; 34:10). He promised David, who was the archetypal faithful king of Israel, that his throne would be established for eternity and that one of his sons would rule forever (2 Samuel 7:11-16). And then, on the night of his arrest, Jesus made another promise—a final one: that the forgiveness of sins would be paid for through his death and resurrection. His body being broken and his blood shed, during his arrest and crucifixion, and then his rising from the dead on the third day, were the signs (Luke 22:14-20).

If that weren't enough, these promises—these covenants—were made in the context of another, one that Jesus' new covenant is the completion of. A covenant made before creation existed; before any finite being had taken a breath. The Father, Son, and Spirit agreed together on a plan to redeem his people, a covenant of redemption that all other covenants point toward in its fulfillment (Ephesians 1:4).

But God's faithfulness isn't limited only to the past, or to the big picture of these promises. He is faithful in the small and seemingly insignificant moments of our lives as well. He promises to provide for our needs, and he does it (Philippians 4:19). He promises to finish the work he began in our lives when he saved us, and he is doing it (Philippians 1:6). He promises to forgive our sins and cleanse us of all unrighteousness when we confess them, and he does it (1 John 1:9). He promises to never leave nor forsake us (Deuteronomy 31:6; Hebrews 13:5), and he will remain with us for eternity. Why? Because his "steadfast" (ESV), "loyal" (NET), or "faithful" (CSB) "love endures forever" (Psalm 136:1 NIV).

Holy Trustworthiness

Because God is holy, he is trustworthy. Just as we can trust him to keep his promises, we can trust what he says. He always and only speaks the truth. He never lies like a human being might (Titus 1:2;

Hebrews 6:18). (Which, again, brings us to that whole being-unable-to-do-something-that-would-conflict-with-his-nature-, character-, and-decrees thing we touched on last chapter.)

As you can imagine, this is especially difficult to believe for many people in our society. After all, we're told "truth is subjective." We are encouraged to live our truths—to be who we are and follow our hearts. A universal or objective truth is contrary to this whole notion. Yet this is what Christians believe. We believe God is trustworthy—always. And it's not simply that he always tells the truth. It is that truth exists because *God* exists. God is the embodiment of truth—he is the *source* of all truth (John 14:6). And we can believe him, even if we don't understand what he has said—or, more often, even when we don't like what he has said.[3]

Holy Justice

Because God is holy, he is just. His judgments are always right and uncompromised. They are always in line with his righteous standards (Psalm 119:137). And his judgments are never a mystery. He does not leave us wondering about what the consequences might be for sin. We know, and have known from the beginning, that the consequence of sin is death (Genesis 2:17)—and that everyone who experiences it does so, not because God is cruel, but because he is just. In the same way, God forgiving our sins does not make him unjust—God is justified in forgiving us because Jesus willingly took the punishment for our sins for us (John 10:15-17).

Holy Grace and Mercy

Because God is holy, he is gracious and merciful. It delights God to show unmerited favor—to show grace—to undeserving people like you and me. People who reject him at every turn, and yet, are bestowed the gift of grace through faith in Jesus (Ephesians 2:4-9). (And if you want your head to explode, Ephesians 2:8 also says even that faith is a gift!) But God doesn't just show grace to those who trust in Jesus. He shows grace to everyone in this world, the righteous and unrighteous alike, providing for their needs out of his sheer kindness (Matthew 5:45).

And in God's mercy, he shows compassion to undeserving people—to every person who has ever lived and will ever live. He withholds his just punishment for sin, rather than immediate death being the consequence of our first transgression (Genesis 3:20-22). He provides forgiveness for our sins through the death and resurrection of Jesus. And he invites all who live to trust in Jesus to enjoy that forgiveness and eternal life with him forever (John 3:16).

HOLY (AND WHOLLY) UNCHANGING

Can you see why holiness troubles people? That God could be so different from us isn't merely difficult for us to grasp (although it is). His holiness—his purity—brings our failures, impurities, and sins into the light. It forces us to realize that our self-image is entirely different than our reality. We are people of "unclean lips"—prone to speak, think, and act in profoundly unholy ways (Isaiah 6:5 NIV).

If God were not holy, if he were not perfect the way that he is, what would it mean for us? We couldn't have any confidence in who he is, what he does, and his ability to rescue us from sin. God would be too much like *us*. And if God were like us, we could only live in uncertainty, if not outright fear.

But that's not who God is. That is why God wants us to know everything Scripture says about him. Everything we have already looked at in this book so far: He wants us to know that he is unique, being one God existing as three persons. God is entirely self-sufficient, lacking nothing, and having no need for anything—including external relationships. He is infinite, without constraint or boundaries on his qualities and existence. He is eternal, with no beginning or end.

He is all-knowing, all-powerful, and ever-present. God exists outside of space and time, and yet, is intimately involved with all he made. He is holy—morally perfect in every way. He is love—not simply loving, but the epitome of love itself. He is merciful, gracious, faithful, just, trustworthy, and so much more.

God wants us to know that he has all these characteristics and attributes. He perfectly embodies them all because he *is* all of them. Completely. Totally. Perfectly. And just as he has been all of them from the beginning, he is all of them forever (Hebrews 13:8). He does not, will not, *cannot* change.[4] So we can count on God being God no matter what; and we have good news to believe and share as a result.

The God who forgives us isn't going to change his mind. The God who gives rest to those who are weary and heavy-laden won't suddenly throw their burdens back upon them. He isn't going to give up on his plan to rescue the world until every single point of it is completed. And to that end, even now, he is calling people out of darkness and into his marvelous light. This is the good news that lets us sleep in peace at night. This is the good news that secures our future. This is the good news worth believing—and sharing with the whole world.

REFLECT, EXPLORE, AND DISCUSS

1. What idea or concept stood out to you as you read this chapter? Why?

2. Read some of the Bible passages describing God's attributes referenced in this chapter. How do they encourage or challenge you?

3. What new questions do these passages raise?

4. Sometimes, people who don't know Jesus react to Christians with hostility. How can we tell the difference between hostility that is due to a Christian faithfully reflecting Jesus and hostility that is due to a Christian's un-Christlike behavior?

GOD SPEAKS

4

ALWAYS, EVERYWHERE, AND IN EVERYTHING

God Doesn't Hide that He Exists

How do you know God exists? Whether you're a Christian or not, this is an important question to consider. When I wasn't yet a Christian, I didn't get that having an answer to this question mattered. It wasn't that I simply didn't understand. I didn't have a response because I didn't care. And because I didn't care, I never gave it any serious consideration. I might have given some half-hearted affirmation that there might be something supernatural in the world, but there was no conviction on the matter. But then something shocking happened: I started to care. I didn't realize it at first, of course. But when I started to believe that God might possibly be real—something that occurred around the time I started to read the Bible—I was consumed with a need to know.

THE GOD-SIZED WALL WE RUN INTO

Back then, when I read the Bible, I didn't know if God was real. I was only reading the Scriptures because I was looking for material to make fun of a friend of mine who was a Christian. But as I got into it, I hit a wall. A God-sized one.

The Bible is written with God's existence—his *pre-existence*—as a given: "In the beginning, God…" (Genesis 1:1 ESV). His existence is assumed, even obvious. And for the more skeptical among us, this assumption might seem like a cop-out on the part of the author of Genesis. Yet it is anything but. This assumption is the first clue to knowing *how* we know God exists at all.

So far, we've looked at some significant truths about God—specifically, who and what he is, and what he is like. Among those key truths are these:

- There is one God who exists as three persons—Father, Son, and Holy Spirit.

- He is eternal, always existing without beginning or end; he just *is*.

- He is holy, perfect in every way, in his character and actions.

- He knows everything, is all-powerful, and is everywhere.

- He is transcendent, exists apart from the universe, outside of space and time, and therefore he is unconstrained by them.

- He is immanent, meaning that despite existing apart from the universe he made, he is actively involved with it.

But how can we know all these things? After all, it is one thing to say (or write) them. But simply making a statement doesn't make it true. It is a whole other matter to provide the truth behind the statement.

For generations, this has been a "gotcha" argument that has been leveled by atheists and agnostics against the belief in any kind of supernatural being. And while on the surface this might be enough to satisfy those who want to be affirmed in their skepticism, the question itself does have an answer.

So what is the answer? For us to know anything about a being so unlike us, we need to be told about him *by* him. And that is exactly what God does.

God tells us about himself.

This is what Christians mean when they use the term *revelation*. It is the act of God communicating the reality of his existence, his nature, and his will to the creatures he made. So how does God reveal what he wants us to know about himself? The short answer is: Through literally everything. But that's not all that helpful. Over the centuries, theologians—people who have dedicated their lives to studying the things of God—have divided God's revelation, his self-disclosure, into two very broad categories: general revelation and special revelation.

WHEN EVERYTHING THAT CAN BE KNOWN ABOUT GOD IS PLAIN TO US

These two types of revelation can be thought of as a distinction between showing and telling. It's kind of like an activity we used to do in kindergarten (if you weren't homeschooled). For show-and-tell, you would bring a special or interesting object from home to school. During show-and-tell time, you shared it with the class and told everyone about it: what it is, how you got it, and why it was special.

General revelation is kind of like the "show" part of show and tell. It is the term we use to describe God making himself known by showing something of himself through all that he has made. (I'm getting ahead of myself here, but hang tight.) He reveals his "invisible attributes"—his "eternal power and divine nature"—as Romans 1:20 (CSB) puts it. And those invisible attributes, that divine power and nature, are seen in everything. We can see them in the world around us. We can see them as we reflect on history. And we can even see hints of them as we look at ourselves—at humanity. Through all of these, God shows us something of who he is and what he is like.

THE NATURAL WORLD DECLARES HIS EXISTENCE

"The heavens declare the glory of God; the sky displays his handiwork," sang David (Psalm 19:1). The vastness of the universe, with all its variety and splendor, and the intricate and observable orderliness with which it operates reveal to us the existence of God (Romans 1:19-20).

For example, in North America, Niagara Falls (the Canadian side, at least), Thor's Well in Oregon, and Spotted Lake in British Columbia all inspire wonder. In Europe, England's Micheldever Wood, Scotland's Isle of Skye, and Iceland's Vatnajökull amaze us. In Asia and Oceania, the Tianzi mountains of China, Lake Hillier in Australia, and Mount Fuji in Japan fill us with awe. And moving beyond our planet and even our solar system, images of the Crab Nebula, the Orion Nebula, and the Eagle Nebula astound us.

All these places and vast spaces reveal God's power; the ability to make them all is astonishing. But they also reveal what he is *like*. He is orderly. He is creative. He is attentive to detail. He loves beauty. All of that is communicated to us by merely looking at the world God made—a world that screams of his existence.

HISTORY REVEALS HIS HAND AT WORK

It's not only the world God made that reveals his existence. The events of history reveal his hand at work as well (Daniel 2:21). He appoints leaders and rulers according to his plans and purposes, acting as his instruments to bring about justice and judgment—*even* when they are antagonistic toward God and his people (Romans

13:1-5). Nebuchadnezzar, a ruler of the Babylonian Empire during the sixth century BC, is merely one of the many examples the Bible provides of this type of leader. King Nebuchadnezzar was an idolator who set himself up as a god, yet he was the instrument God used to judge the people of Judah for their idolatry (2 Chronicles 36:15-21).

Another example is Cyrus the Great, whose empire succeeded Nebuchadnezzar's decades after the Jews were exiled from their land. Cyrus issued the command that allowed the Jewish people to return to their homeland, fulfilling God's promise that they would not be exiled forever (2 Chronicles 36:22-23; Ezra 1:1-4). And if that wasn't enough, God refers to Cyrus *by name* as his instrument for this task, centuries before Cyrus's birth (Isaiah 44:28)!

But it's not only biblical examples that reveal God's hand at work. Observing history helps us to see that God has a plan and purpose for the world, despite appearances to the contrary. Nothing happens flippantly. Nothing catches God unaware. Ultimately, mankind's march through time declares God's glory as much as the natural world does.

HUMANITY REFLECTS HIS CHARACTER

Even you and I are markers of our Creator. Despite sometimes being walking train wrecks who say, do, and think things we'd never want to be known (notwithstanding, readily posting those things on social media for all the world to see). Humans were made to reflect God's character and nature into the world as moral, rational, relational, and creative beings. (We will explore this in greater detail in chapter 7.) We make and appreciate beautiful and interesting things, just as the creator God does. We are relentlessly relational, incapable of existing entirely in isolation, which reflects the God who lives in eternal, self-sustaining relationship as Father, Son, and Spirit. We are hopelessly moral beings who know that right and wrong exist, even when we don't agree on what is *right* or *wrong*. Everything we do, everything we *are*, points to the reality of God's existence.

MOVING TOWARD THE SPECIFICS

Everything around us in this simultaneously beautiful and horrifying world proclaims the glory of God. In form and function, everything reveals his power and divine nature. This world and the creatures who inhabit it are no happy accident. The universe is not the coincidental confluence of time and chance. (Hang tight; we'll cover that in chapter 6.) It is a glorious sight to behold. It is an intentional work of its Creator, whose fingerprints can be seen throughout.

But as much as this world is a testament to the existence of its Creator, it doesn't tell us *everything* about God. Or, more accurately, it doesn't tell us everything *he* wants us to know about him.

God's general revelation shows us enough to know that he is real, that he is here, and that he is good. It unveils that he is far above us, yet still involved in this world. It leaves us without excuse for failing to honor and worship him (Romans 1:19-20)—because truly, who or what else could be so worthy? And it reveals enough to condemn us as fools if we say there is no God (Psalm 14:1; Romans 2).

But for humans to know everything God wants us to know about him—and for us to truly know him—he doesn't leave us to figure it out on our own. God doesn't leave us guessing. Like you may have done during kindergarten show-and-tell time, he shares. He tells us about himself. He tells us *specifically* in a revelation of a different sort. A special revelation that helps us to know God in a personal sense. This special revelation takes two forms—one a person, the other a collection of writings—both sharing the same name or title: the Word of God.

JESUS, THE WORD OF GOD

John's Gospel introduces us to the Word, one who was "in the beginning" *with* God and who *was* God (John 1:1 NIV). Everything was made through the Word, and not one thing was created apart from him. This Word came into the world and dwelt among us; he took on human form and became known to us as the man Jesus Christ (John 1:2-4; 14). Jesus was and is "the radiance of God's glory and the exact expression of his nature" (Hebrews 1:3 CSB). He is God's special revelation to us. To know Jesus is to know God the Father; to see him is to see God the Father (John 14:8-9).

THE BIBLE, THE WORD OF GOD

God's special revelation is the Word—Jesus Christ. But God's special revelation is also the Word that was spoken through and written down by prophets and apostles (2 Peter 3:2). This is the Word we can read today: the Bible. The Bible reveals God's nature and character. It tells us of God's will for us and his purpose for the world. It demonstrates his extravagant love for us as he came into the world to rescue and redeem humanity and all of creation. The Bible is God's special revelation to us.

Jesus, the eternal Son of God, the Word of God—a divine Person upon whom our faith rests. The Bible, the living and active Word of God (Hebrews 4:12)—a book in which we can discover what God is saying to us right now, if we have eyes to see and ears to hear. Both revealing all we need to know about God in order to love, honor, and obey him every day.

REFLECT, EXPLORE, AND DISCUSS

1. What idea or concept stood out to you as you read this chapter? Why?

2. Read some of the Bible passages describing God's revelation referenced in this chapter. How do they encourage or challenge you?

3. What new questions do these passages raise?

4. Look up one of the natural wonders that was highlighted in this chapter. How does what you've read in this chapter affect what you see?

GOD SPEAKS

5

IN THE WORDS HE GAVE US

Why Christians Make Such a Big Deal About the Bible

The night before I got married, a friend—my best man—and I were talking about my then-recent conversion to Christianity. He was respectful, but skeptical. Not of my sincerity but of something essential to my faith. Something that had played an important role in my becoming a Christian. His problem was with *the Bible*.

Was his problem something to do with its message? No, at least not directly. Did he have a concern with how people sometimes use (and misuse) it? Again, kind of, but not so much. His issue was that he couldn't get on board with what Christians believe about the Bible—what we understand it to be.

WHAT CHRISTIANS DON'T BELIEVE ABOUT THE BIBLE

I understand my best man's concern. What Christians believe the Bible to be is both simple and complex. After all, the writings that make up the Bible are rooted in space and time, primarily within a specific people group's relationship with God as it has played out over thousands of years. And because of that, it's tempting to see the Bible as merely a record of that people group's evolving understanding of God.[1] But if the Bible were simply that, I don't know that my friend would have had a problem with it. Likewise, the Bible contains many proverbs and parables—stories and sayings that teach practical moral and spiritual wisdom. Because of that, it would be easy to put the Bible in the same category as something like Aesop's Fables.[2] But again, if that were the case, my friend probably would have been fine with it.

The Bible is treated, particularly by Christians, with great respect. To us, it is *sacred*. We revere it (but don't worship it). Many other religions have their sacred texts too. For example, Muslims have the Qur'an; Buddhists, the Tripitaka; and Bahá'ís, the Kitáb-i-Aqdas. If we view the Bible as one of many sacred writings that all carry the same weight, my friend likely would have had no issues at all.[3] I don't know that he, or anyone else for that matter, *could*.

Why is that? Simple: If the Bible were any of those other texts, it could be respected and appreciated, but it could also be *ignored*. It would be a book that might offer guidance and encouragement, but it would lack the power to give you commands. It couldn't make any lasting claim on you. And that's where the issue arises. Christians do not believe that about the Bible because we cannot; and we cannot because the Bible does not allow for that. That might sound like a nifty bit of circular logic, but bear with me. It will make sense shortly, I promise.

REVELATION REVEALS OUR DILEMMA

To understand what Christians believe about the Bible, we have to go back to the idea we explored in the previous chapter: God chooses to make himself known in two ways that we call general and special revelation. God reveals his existence, his power, and his divine attributes through everything he made—through nature, history, and even people (Romans 1:19-20). And he does this to such a degree that to deny his existence is a failure to be honest with ourselves.

But God doesn't stop at simply showing us that he exists. He also tells us what he is like, what he desires, what he has done, what he is doing, and what he will do in this world. And he accomplishes this in two forms that are both called the Word of God. A person: Jesus Christ, God the Son, the Word who came into the world as a human being to dwell among his people, perfectly revealing to us what God is like (John 1:1-4; Hebrews 1:3). And also, the living and active Word, spoken through and written down by prophets and apostles, teaching us God's character, his attributes, his activities, and his will for us (Hebrews 4:12; 2 Peter 3:2). These are the writings we call the Bible.

And *that* is exactly what tripped up my friend. How could human beings call the Bible the Word of God? Calling it that has…implications. Like being true—and not just "kind of" true, but *entirely* true. Being free from errors, being reliable, useful, and meaningful for our lives no matter when and where we live. Basically, the Bible is *perfect* in all the ways God means it to be.

But how can the Bible, which was written by human beings thousands of years ago, be *perfect*? To my friend, this authorship seemed to directly contradict what Christians believe about mankind's condition and what we all know to be true about human beings, that humans are imperfect. If humans are imperfect, then anything we are involved with will also be imperfect. And if anything we are involved with is imperfect, then the Bible can't be perfect. That this book could be God's Word to humanity—that it correctly and faithfully records events that really happened and that it could be entirely accurate and trustworthy—didn't seem logical. Something *must* be wrong with it.

On the surface, the logic holds. Human beings *are* imperfect.

(Which is putting it lightly.) And whatever we are involved with is necessarily imperfect because we can't make anything perfect on our own. It is the "on our own" part that is key. If the Bible were something entirely invented by human beings, my friend would be correct. It could not be the kind of book that Christians hold in such high regard. But Christians do not believe that humans were left to their own devices to write the collected works we now call the Bible. We believe God himself was intimately involved in its writing—and God's involvement changes everything.

GOD'S GOD-BREATHED WORD

While God's participation in the writing of Scripture is seen throughout its pages, one of the most important passages that helps us to understand how he was involved is 2 Timothy 3:16-17: "All Scripture is inspired by God and is profitable for teaching, for rebuking, for correcting, for training in righteousness, so that the man of God may be complete, equipped for every good work" (CSB).

In this passage, Paul (the author) uses a Greek word that appears in the New Testament only once—*theopneustos*—to describe God's relationship to Scripture. He calls it "inspired by God," or more precisely (if not potentially confusing), "God-breathed" (NIV). The big idea behind this phrase is: Although written by humans, the words of Scripture—every word of Scripture, in both the Old and New Testament writings—are not merely human. They aren't something that human beings made up (2 Peter 1:20). They are of divine origin. God is their ultimate source; the Bible's words are *God's* words.

In one sense, they are God's words because they are words that he spoke to a human author. Throughout Scripture, we find examples of God giving a command for a message to be recorded and repeated. Sometimes he gave a specific order to write, as he did with Moses

(Exodus 34:27), Isaiah (Isaiah 30:8), Jeremiah (Jeremiah 36:2, 28), Habakkuk (Habakkuk 2:2), and even John (Revelation 1:19; 21:5). Other times, God commanded a prophet to speak directly in his name; his message was delivered using phrases like "the Lord says" (1 Kings 21:21; Isaiah 3:16; 38:1) or "this is the Lord's declaration" (1 Samuel 2:30; Jeremiah 7:30 csb). And these commands are not limited to only the Old Testament. In the New Testament, we see at least one instance of a prophet directly saying, "This is what the Holy Spirit says" (Acts 21:11 csb).

These instances are hardly infrequent—these sorts of explicit statements appear more than 200 times in the Old Testament alone—but we need to make sure we don't make more of them than we ought to. The majority appear within the Bible's historical narratives and prophetic writings.[4] And in their context, they have a purpose. They are part of an event being retold or they serve to validate a message, as to say, "This is a message from God: listen to what he is saying."

Also, historical narratives and prophetic writings are only two of the many forms of writing found within Scripture. There's also moral and religious law, poetry, proverbial wisdom, biography, and formal doctrinal teaching. So it begs the question: How are these other forms of writing—ones in which the phrase "the Lord says" doesn't appear, or have a human author's name that is attributed to them—also God's Word?

This is where things get overtly supernatural in a different way. Second Peter 1:21 describes how a prophecy—a message from the Lord—comes about by the messenger being "carried along by the Holy Spirit" (csb). Now, that doesn't mean that God took over people's bodies and used them as a mechanism to deliver a message. He didn't override their will to make them unaware of what they were writing.[5] Instead, the message was inspired through the Holy Spirit's supernatural influence over Scripture's human authors. He worked through everyone's unique personality, grammar, and perspective in such a way that what was written down was what they desired to write, and what God desired his people to know.

This means, for example, the message Jude wrote (the book of Jude) was both what he felt necessary to write (Jude 3), and what God wanted Jude's audience—*and* us today—to know about the need to contend for the faith once delivered to all the saints. Likewise, Paul's letter calling for holiness and purity in the church at Corinth (the book of 1 Corinthians) was the message he was compelled to deliver, and the one God wanted to make known (even the parts that some might be tempted to explain away).[6]

Inspiration means that the human authors' words are *their* words, but they aren't *only* theirs. With the writers' perspectives and stylistic peculiarities fully intact, their words were (and are) also God's words. All of them—whether the verses that we read in are in Deuteronomy, Obadiah, Luke's Gospel, 2 Timothy, or any other writing that's found in the Bible—are inspired (2 Timothy 3:16). All of them are God's Word (2 Peter 1:19-21). And all of them are true.

GOD'S PROTECTED AND PRESERVED WORD

And for many people, it's that "true" part that is hard to take, including for my friend. (And I will add, also me, back before I ever read the Bible.) But what makes believing the Bible to be true so difficult? It goes back to the seemingly circular logic I referred to at the beginning of this chapter: It appears like we're just taking the Bible's word for it. Christians say the Bible is true because the *Bible* says that it is true. But how do we know that it *is* true? Because the Bible was written thousands of years ago, how do we know that what we are reading today is what the authors originally wrote down? And couldn't the human authors have made a mistake or gotten something wrong?

These are good and important questions. They are the questions that are at the heart of all the varied questions people have about the Bible. And, thankfully, they're questions with answers.

How Do We Know That What We Read in the Bible Is What the Authors Wrote?

We know that the Bible is a collection of ancient writings dating back more than 2,000 years. But original copies of the writings no longer exist. So how do we know that what we read in the Bible is what was originally written if we don't have the originals?

For many who view the Bible with skepticism, this is a deal breaker. They posit that without the originals, we should cast doubt because we can't compare what we have *now* to what was first written down. Several times over the years, I've heard this reasoning from people who question Christianity, both as a "gotcha" argument, but also with sincerity. Let's focus on addressing the concerns of the sincere.

The sincere are genuinely curious; they see the logic of the argument as sound. But what they don't see is that positioning the argument in this way holds the Bible to a different standard than any other historic writing. If we apply the same logic to other ancient works, we wouldn't trust that the editions of *The Iliad* and *The Odyssey* we read today contain the same epic sagas that Homer wrote.[7] The same is true of significantly more recent works, like those of William Shakespeare (written between roughly 1590 and 1613), as none of his original manuscripts exist either. But there is very little debate that the lines recited by multitudes of actors from that time to today are any different from the words that the Bard originally wrote down. What remains of these examples, and most other ancient documents, are copies.

The same is true of the Bible. From the moment they were first penned, scribes and scholars diligently made hundreds and thousands of copies of the Bible's writings. (This was the primary way *any* writing and mass correspondence was distributed.) The Bible we have today is based on the copies available to us. Focusing on the New Testament writings alone, nearly 6,000 Greek manuscripts exist (most of which are fragments of recognizable texts), the oldest of which dates to within 30 to 50 years of the original's writing.[8]

There is an entire discipline built around studying ancient documents. It is called textual criticism. Scholars in this field work comparing available and accessible ancient manuscripts against one another and to more recent copies in order to reconstruct the original message. And those who focus on the Bible have found a remarkable degree of consistency between all the available manuscripts. Where disagreements between copies exist, most often they are typos, such as transposed letters (think, "their" and "thier"). But in the few places where more substantial disagreements exist, they are most often in the form of a passage or verse that appears in a later manuscript, but not in manuscripts dated earlier. Passages such as John 7:53–8:11, the extended ending of Mark (16:9-20), Matthew 18:11, and a handful of other verses fall into this category, and are most often included in modern English Bibles by surrounding them by boxes or with a notation in a footnote. But even in these instances—only about 1 percent of all inconsistencies that cannot otherwise be accounted for between manuscripts—no major doctrine of the faith is affected.

That consistency isn't found solely in the copies of the various biblical manuscripts available to us. It also applies to the canon, the received writings we recognize as Scripture, as well. The earliest lists of the New Testament books include virtually every writing we have in our Bible. Only seven New Testament writings were ever questioned between the second and fourth centuries, but all of them were ultimately recognized for what they are: God's Word for his people.[9] From the earliest days of the church to today, the canon of Scripture—the 66 books that comprise the Old and New Testaments—has remained largely unchanged, despite periodic debates that have risen up from the sixteenth century onward.[10]

On its own, this level of consistency is remarkable and should give us great confidence that the Bible we read today is what its authors wrote. But more than that, it should encourage Christians to see God's care for his Word. Throughout history, he has preserved these writings for our benefit. Through these manuscripts, church councils, and even controversies, God has kept his Word from being lost or distorted so that *every* generation can know him and his will.

How Do We Know What We Read in the Bible Is Really True—Couldn't It Be Wrong?

Okay, even if we can agree that we don't have to worry about the message of the Bible being corrupted and what we read today is what its authors originally wrote (albeit in a different language), how do we know that what the Bible says is true? Couldn't it be wrong about certain people or events—or even have errors in what it teaches?

Throughout history, Christians have always affirmed the truthfulness of the Bible, that there are no genuine errors, internal conflicts, or contradictions in its pages. That what it says inside is true. Today, we use a couple of shorthand terms to describe this attribute of God's Word. One of those, largely popularized by American evangelical Christians in the mid- to late twentieth century, is *inerrant*, meaning that the Bible is "free from all falsehood, fraud, or deceit."[11] The other, which has a much longer and broader historical and contemporary use, *infallible*, does not simply mean that the Bible contains no errors, but also that it *cannot err*. Ultimately, Scripture cannot be wrong in what it teaches, even if a Bible teacher is wrong in how he or she interprets and applies it.[12]

These concepts tie in closely to what Christians believe about inspiration—that as God worked through human authors and their unique vocabularies and perspectives, he supernaturally protected the message from being distorted by human error. And, again, this is not a new or novel idea. Christians have believed this for as long as there have been Christians. Clement of Rome, a church leader in the first century, encouraged Christians to "Look carefully into the Scriptures, which are the true utterances of the Holy Spirit."[13] And he wasn't alone. Polycarp (69–155), Irenaeus (130–202), Tertullian (c. 166–220), Origen (185–253), Augustine of Hippo (354–430), and John Chrysostom (347–407) are among the many teachers of the early church who unashamedly taught that the Bible was of divine origin, true, and trustworthy, and encouraged their hearers (and later, readers) to believe it.

But when it comes to the Bible's reliability regarding certain events, the existence of specific locations, and its key figures, that has been a subject of debate for decades. A segment of scholars who are critical of the Bible have treated a lack of extrabiblical (outside of the Bible) evidence for a place or person to mean that they likely did not exist. Meanwhile, there is an ever-increasing body of archaeological evidence that supports the Bible's reliability in these areas.[14]

When it comes to the Bible's utility, lived experience shows that its wisdom is reliable for all the aspects of life that it addresses. But ultimately, all the evidence in the world won't convince a person of the trustworthiness of its message. Nor will explorations of the perceived conflicts between the Bible and scientific discoveries, societal values, or personal experiences, which covers everything from the age of the earth to sexual expression and everything in between. (Although these are all worthy of discussion—and we'll get to them.) Evidence might win an argument, but it doesn't always win a person.

Instead, the main reason we can trust the Bible comes back to the God who inspired it. Christians believe it is true because of what it says about *God*. God never lies. He doesn't change his mind the way that human beings do. He is always reliable. God is trustworthy. And because he is trustworthy, we can trust the Word he inspired.

GOD'S KNOWABLE WORD

If God wants us to know him through his Word, he also wants us to understand it. The Bible's central message and teachings can be understood by using the same basic principles we use when we read any other book.[15] By paying attention to context clues, verb tenses, and the literary forms used—everything we are doing when we read anything else—we can discover several significant truths. For example, we can know who God is and what he is like. We can discover why it seems like the world is a giant mess. And we can learn what the God of the universe is doing about it.

But this doesn't mean that all portions of Scripture are equally clear. Some parts *are* hard to understand (2 Peter 3:16). We are, after all, trying to comprehend the infinite God with finite minds. There are aspects that we are incapable of grasping on our own (1 Corinthians 2:14-16). And so, God himself helps us to understand it. For example, after his resurrection, Jesus explained the Scriptures to his disciples (Luke 24:27), and he opened their minds to understand (verses 44-45). In the same way, the Holy Spirit illuminates the Scriptures in our hearts and minds (John 14:15-18; 16:7-15). God helps us understand what we could not otherwise and gives us the desire to be transformed by the truth of His Word.

GOD'S AUTHORITATIVE WORD

And if what we've explored about the Bible in this chapter is true, then the Bible has a special kind of authority in our lives as Christians.

Pastors and teachers in our local churches carry an amount of authority (Hebrews 13:17). The historic creeds and confessions of the Christian faith do as well. Beyond the church, parents, civil government, and even experts within specialized fields have differing degrees of authority.[16] But in every one of these cases, *none stand on equal footing with the Bible*. The Bible sets the standard for all of life and faith in all the areas that it addresses and is sufficient to equip us for every good work (2 Timothy 3:17). It is the authority that is meant to keep all other authorities in check because it is God's Word, written for us.[17]

THE TRUE STORY WE NEED

I think this is why people get so uncomfortable with the Bible. Its message is entirely contrary to the story we tell ourselves about how the world works. Humans, particularly in the West, have built our lives on the belief that we are in authority over our own lives. We are the masters of our fate, free to pursue our truth, and define and redefine every aspect of our being. And no one can tell us differently.

But telling people differently from what they think is exactly what Scripture does. It tells us a story that presents humans in a very different light than any other book. It doesn't present us as being on a journey of progress or as heroic figures, as any human author naturally would. Instead, the Bible confronts us with an ugly truth: We are responsible for the problems of this world (Genesis 3). And we aren't good enough, smart enough, or strong enough to pull ourselves up by our bootstraps, realize our potential, and clean up the mess we made. But the Bible isn't bad news about us. It is good news *for* us. It is the true story of a Hero who comes from a far-off land to rescue people who live in this darkness of our own making. A Teacher who doesn't tell us how to be better people, but who makes us new people. A King who is building a kingdom where all who believe in him will live in peace, freedom, and joy forever—not only as his subjects but also as his friends (John 15:15; Revelation 21:4).

My friend couldn't see that. Before the Holy Spirit opened my eyes, I couldn't see it either. But when my eyes were opened, I understood. The Bible is not one sacred book among many others. It is not a collection of moral wisdom and practical guidance. And it is not a record of one people group's evolving understanding of God. The Bible is the Word of God. It is God's revelation of his nature and character, of his plans and purposes. The Bible tells us the truth about ourselves and offers us good news to share with the entire world. It is a book like no other, the most humbling, frustrating, and awe-inspiring book you'll ever read. And it is the only one that answers the questions we don't even know to ask.

REFLECT, EXPLORE, AND DISCUSS

1. What idea or concept stood out to you as you read this chapter? Why?

2. Read some of the Bible passages about Scripture referenced in this chapter. How do these passages encourage or challenge you?

3. What new questions do these passages raise?

4. Think about the accusation of circular logic that is leveled against Christians' views of the Bible. Do you think this accusation is fair? Why or why not?

5. Why is it important that understanding the Bible to be infallible does *not* mean that Bible teachers are always without error?

GOD MAKES

6

A GOOD WORLD THAT HE RULES

The Point We Miss in the Creation Story

What makes a great story? This is a question my avid reader friends and I discuss regularly. Typically, the responses settle down to three factors: the characters, the plot, and the setting. No matter the genre—fiction or nonfiction, mystery or biography, sci-fi adventure or grounded exploration of the human heart—and no matter which of the three is emphasized most, all three are present in every great and lasting story.

This is what makes the tales of J.R.R. Tolkien endure. It's why we continue to read the works of Jane Austen and the Brontë sisters centuries after they were first written. And it's what makes the stories of the best modern authors such as Leif Enger, William Kent Krueger, and Michael Chabon stand out among their peers. There is an authenticity to all their work—relatable and recognizable characters, believable and compelling journeys, and worlds with rich histories.[1]

There's a sense in which the Bible is no different. Because whatever else we might say about the Bible (like everything that I talked about in the previous chapter), we cannot forget that it is a story. A *true* story written by human authors and inspired by God the Holy Spirit, but a story, nonetheless. Its cast of characters is all too relatable. Its plot is compelling. And as for its world? It's this one.

THE BEAUTIFUL WORLD GOD MADE

Starting with how it all began, the Bible tells the story of how everything came to be, how the world we live in became the mess it is now, and what God has done (and will do) to restore it all. A story that begins with the most incredible—and controversial—opening line ever penned: "In the beginning God created the heavens and the earth" (Genesis 1:1).

With language that resembles a poem or song, Genesis describes God creating everything in the universe, *including the universe itself*, out of nothing. Rather than reshape eternally existent matter, God simply spoke, and where there was nothing, suddenly there was everything.[2]

Over six days, God said, "Let there be…" and whatever he said came to be. Light and darkness. Earth, sea, and sky. Grass, trees, and plants of all kinds (oh my). The sun and moon. (And the stars too.) Land animals, birds, fish, and insects. And finally, God made the first human beings, male and female. He made them not with his words but fashioned with his hands, all before God rested from his work.

As God spoke and saw what he made, he said that it was good. It was good because it had a purpose, to put his beauty and wonder and power on display (Romans 1:20). It was good because it pleased him, good because *he* is good, and whatever he does is good (Exodus 33:19; Psalm 25:8). And it still is, even if that is difficult to see at times. God made a world filled with beauty and wonder that leaves us marveling. An endlessly interesting world, with resources meant to be creatively and carefully harnessed, consumed, and renewed. A world perfectly designed for all life to flourish.

The world, as it was intended to be, is beautiful. And when understood, the story of how the world came to be is equally so.

OF ARGUMENTS ABOUT ORIGINS

Yet few portions of the Bible have been as hotly debated as the creation story, which is a shame, because as we've seen, its message is beautiful. But this beauty gets lost in how we approach the creation narrative. At least, it gets lost in the way many Western evangelical Christians do.

When we read this passage, we tend to try to settle specific debates, and therefore focus on certain questions: Are the first chapters of Genesis recording historic events or are they akin to other ancient creation tales such as the *Enuma Elish* of the ancient Babylonians, or the *Atrahasis Epic* of the ancient Mesopotamians?[3] Does "day" mean *day* as we understand it (24 hours), is it figurative language, or something else altogether? How old is the earth? And for some reason we ask, Did the first people have belly buttons?[4]

We approach the creation account from a specific kind of apologetics standpoint.[5] We make arguments against competing perspectives and ideologies, particularly those that reject the idea of a creator God altogether and view all life as the result of a process of ongoing, incremental changes and mutations successfully occurring over millennia, and all governed, essentially, by chance.[6] We focus on fossil records and offer alternative explanations of current scientific perspectives. We talk about dinosaurs, make replica arks, and fund institutes that explore the evidence that this world was purposefully made. But too often, we approach these topics defensively. We attempt to counter a narrative born from the Enlightenment Movement of the eighteenth century, a narrative that attempts to pit faith against reason, or science against Scripture. It's a narrative that claims that *reasonable* people don't believe in fanciful creation stories like what we see in the Bible. A narrative that creates a conflict out of nothing, because it's a conflict that doesn't exist.

REJECT RED HERRINGS AROUND THE CREATION STORY

There are reasonable discussions to be had about the relationship between science and Scripture. For those of us who grew up assuming the Enlightenment's "faith versus reason" narrative is true, we need to have those conversations.

But the debate, as it is commonly framed, is also a red herring. After all, there is no genuine conflict between the two. Untold hundreds of scientists throughout the centuries were (and are) committed Christians. Isaac Newton, Blaise Pascal, and George Washington Carver are just a few worth mentioning. They recognized what we need to as well: Rather than faith being a barrier to scientific inquiry, faith is fuel for it—a desire to understand the world God made.

That is why I don't buy the common framing. The faith versus reason, or science versus Scripture, dichotomy is a distraction from a much more significant issue. Or rather, a more significant conflict that revolves around the Bible's central plot, and its central character.

THE CREATOR AND HIS CREATION

Go back and read Genesis 1:1. Who is the first character introduced in this story? It is God, the Lord of all things.[7] Already present; already existing. Outside of all that is. By introducing God as the preexistent Creator of everything, the Bible reveals a profound truth: *All creation belongs to him*. It is *his*. Because he made everything, God has the right to determine how everything works. To say what is right and what is wrong. To say what is good, beautiful, and true—and what is *not*— in every area of existence. The flow of time. The speed at which every planet in our solar system orbits around the sun. What humans are, and what we are not. No area of creation is outside of his authority.

And that authority isn't limited to one person of the Trinity either. The Father, Son, and Holy Spirit are equally in total authority over everything because all were present and involved at the beginning. The Father and the Spirit are the most apparent, with God the Father the declared creator of all things, and the Spirit of God moving, preparing for the work of creation to begin (Genesis 1:1-2). But what about the Son? Where was he in the beginning? John's Gospel provides the answer as its first verse calls back to the opening line of the Bible: "In the beginning was the Word" (John 1:1 NIV). The Word who was with God and was God, and came into the world as the man Jesus Christ. (We looked at this back in the first chapter of this book, remember?) Jesus, God the Son, "was in the beginning with God" (verse 2 NKJV), and all things were created by him, for him, and through him (verses 3, 14, 17). He sustains everything, holding all things together, with the same authority that the Father and Spirit have over creation (Colossians 1:17; Hebrews 1:3).

THE SCANDAL OF THE CREATION STORY

That is the real scandal of the creation story. And that is exactly why people are desperate to debunk it. Or, at least, try to put those who do believe it on the defensive.

People don't object to the creation narrative because it's ludicrous or intellectually dishonest. In truth, it is no more or less intellectually credible than the belief that the universe as we know it exists, effectively, by accident.[8] They object because, if there is a Creator who made everything, we are not autonomous beings. If we came into the world as the result of the equation of time plus matter plus chance successfully adding up again and again and again, we are beholden to no one. We don't have to worship, and more pointedly, obey God, because that God isn't real.

But if the creation narrative is true, and so is the rest of the Bible's narrative for that matter, it's a different story. It means the God who made everything is in authority over everything—including us. He is not a distant deity content to let us run amok, doing whatever pleases us. God has a plan for his creation, a design for how it works, and a purpose he is working toward. He is so personally invested in his creation that when we tried to deviate from his plan—to do our own thing—he revealed himself to the world by entering into it as the man Jesus of Nazareth.

Jesus put his authority over all creation on display with signs and wonders, forgiving sins, refuting human tradition, and even overcoming death itself. And to him, as Lord over all creation, every knee will bow and every tongue will confess his authority, to the glory of God the Father (Philippians 2:10-11).

BEHOLD THE BEAUTY OF THE STORY

That is the point of the creation story. That is the point of the entire Bible: All authority belongs to Jesus. It is beautiful *and* scandalous. And this is what we need to remember whenever we find ourselves drawn into discussions and debates about faith and reason, or science and Scripture. There are honest discussions to be had, and we should *want* to have them. But they aren't really about faith and reason. They're about how the world works and how we were meant to live.

The story we're told by the culture around us (and what it wants us to believe) is that we are entirely self-autonomous. That we are masters of our fates, free to define ourselves and to do as we please. It promises a kind of freedom it cannot deliver; and instead of freeing us, it stifles us.

But the story of Scripture invites us to embrace a view of the world that is bigger and brighter and more wondrous than anything mankind can imagine. One that welcomes questions and exploration, because by exploring the world we come to know better the One who made it all, the One who is in authority over all things (Psalm 8:1; Romans 1:19-20). We are meant to live under God's authority, not our own. Under his rule, we find the freedom we seek. And our hearts will remain unfulfilled until we finally yield to him.

REFLECT, EXPLORE, AND DISCUSS

1. What idea or concept stood out to you as you read this chapter? Why?

2. Read some of the Bible passages about God's creative work referenced in this chapter. How do these passages encourage or challenge you?

3. What new questions do these passages raise?

4. How does this chapter affect your perspective on "faith versus science" discussions and debates?

GOD MAKES

7

A WORLD FOR BEINGS LIKE HIM

What Are Human Beings?

My wife and I adore a short-lived, action-comedy TV series called *Chuck*. The basic premise was simple: A computer geek working at a big-box electronic store downloads a government supercomputer into his head; becomes an asset, and later, a special agent of the CIA; falls in love with his handler; and saves the world every week. Admittedly, the show required a fair amount of suspension of disbelief. But the writing was fun, the acting was strong, and the leads had great chemistry. (Also, it has a terrific soundtrack.)

I've watched this series multiple times over since it was canceled in 2012. With every rewatch, I appreciate to a greater degree the profound questions at the show's heart. Questions that its creators, and its cast along with them, may not have realized they were even asking.

Throughout the series, what it means to be human is explored through varying conflicts as a human brain meshes with computer programming. As its hero, Chuck, grows from a goofy nerd to a capable (but still goofy) spy, it considers whether the supercomputer changed

Chuck into someone new, or merely unlocked his potential. When the computer was blocked and later removed altogether, the show shifted focus to one's value: Does our value come from what we do, or who we are? And when a corrupted version of that program began to wipe out users' memories, it left viewers hanging on another question: What does it mean for us to forget who we are—are we still *us*, or are we someone different? (Am I overanalyzing the plot of a TV action-comedy drama? Maybe. But that doesn't mean I'm wrong.)

WRONG ANSWERS TO RIGHT QUESTIONS

These questions probably sound familiar. They boil down to: Who are we and what is our value? They're the same questions we've been asking for as long as we've been introspective. And they are the questions at the heart of every major debate in Western society—abortion, sexuality and marriage, gender and transgenderism, genetic manipulation, cloning, euthanasia, animal-human hybrids, artificial intelligence, and the list goes on. The nature of humanity is at the root of every one of these issues. We've spent centuries asking if there is anything that intrinsically makes humans *human* and if a human can be *less* than human. We want to know if our lives have value, where that value comes from, and if it can be lost. These are good questions; more than that, they are the right questions for us to be asking. But too often we try to find solace in the wrong answers.

Most often, we gravitate to answers that focus on utility, which means our value—and in some cases, our very humanity—is based on what we might become, or what we do. When someone asks us what we do for a living, for example, we say "I am a (fill in the blank)." When we talk about protecting the most vulnerable, it's usually with an eye toward what they could be, whether a doctor, dentist, or delivery person. But this kind of utilitarian approach to defining humanity doesn't work. It doesn't make *sense*. Because if we are human because we do X, Y, or Z, then if we cannot do those things anymore (or before we can do them), we are not *really* human, right? This line of thinking is problematic.

If thinking about ourselves in utilitarian terms is one wrong way to answer the question of what defines humanity, another wrong way is to look to ourselves for the answer. To take the perspective that, individually, we are the only ones who can define who and what we are. But with no objective standard to measure against, what standard do we use? Our feelings. What we *feel* about ourselves is what is *true*. And those feelings lead us to define and identify ourselves—often focusing on sexual orientation and gender—based on what we think will make us happy, no matter how fleeting that happiness might be.[1] This also is in error.

If our identity and value are based on our utility or what we feel is true, we're thinking in ways we were never meant to. We aren't our job, education, intelligence, sexuality, or anything else we're tempted to define ourselves by. None of those makes us who and what we are. To think like that is to think too small. It's the kind of thinking that stems from the story we tell ourselves of our world—a story that strives to find meaning in meaninglessness. If our existence can be boiled down to a semi-happy accident, then there isn't anything about us that makes us particularly special or distinct.[2] Such a story effectively demands us to define our humanity on our terms.

MADE LIKE GOD

But we don't live in a world that stems from a story of meaninglessness. We live in a world rooted in a much better story, one where there is a Creator who made us and imbued us with value and purpose. So if we want to understand what it means to be human, we have to go to the source, to what our Creator says about us. And what does God say?

> Then God said, "Let us make humankind in our image, after our likeness, so they may rule over the fish of the sea and the birds of the air, over the cattle, and over all the earth, and over all the creatures that move on the earth." God created humankind in his own image, in the image of God he created them, male and female he created them. God blessed them and said to them, "Be fruitful and multiply! Fill the earth and subdue it! Rule over the fish of the sea and the birds of the air and every creature that moves on the ground" (Genesis 1:26-28).

Genesis 2 adds the following additional details:

> The LORD God formed the man from the soil of the ground and breathed into his nostrils the breath of life, and the man became a living being...So the LORD God caused the man to fall into a deep sleep, and while he was asleep, he took part of the man's side and closed up the place with flesh. Then the LORD God made a woman from the part he had taken out of the man, and he brought her to the man (Genesis 2:7, 21-22).

Central to the description of humanity we see in Genesis is that we are made in God's image. Everything else that is said about us flows from this. But what does this mean? Christian teachers have spent centuries exploring the pieces of the answer the Bible offers about this distinction between us and all other created beings. If you had to boil down what they've learned so far, it looks something like this: As God's image bearers, we reflect and represent something of what God is like to the world.

This whole idea of reflecting and representing is bound up in who we are—the truth that we share certain characteristics with God.

Of course, we do not share *all* his characteristics. Some aspects of his nature belong to him alone: we are created, whereas he has no beginning; we are rooted within space and time, whereas he exists everywhere all at once; we are limited, whereas he is limitless; and so forth. But the characteristics we do share reflect God's goodness *in* the world through our minds and morals, our relationships, and our purpose in the world.

Our Minds and Morals

Except for in particularly esoteric philosophical circles, few people question the existence of rational thought and morality (even if they don't know *why* they exist).[3] Anthropologists and sociologists have long noted how societies with no connection to one another share similar moral standards. The same is true with the development of language, technology (tools), art, and even scientific inquiry (even if that term wasn't used).

The Bible answers why this is possible: Both morality and rational thought are expressions of our being made in God's image. Because God is rational and logical, we have the capacity for logical and rational thought. Because God is creative, we are creative. Because God communicates, we also communicate. Because God is moral, just, and compassionate, we are also made to be moral, just, and compassionate.

Our Relationships

We all have different relational needs. Some of us need to be surrounded by people all the time. Others, like me, thrive with significant amounts of personal time. But regardless of our individual needs, one thing is true for us all: We all need relationships with other people. We cannot exist apart from other people. And this, too, is an expression of our being made in God's image.

Because God is three-in-one—Father, Son, and Spirit—he exists in a perfect, eternal relationship. He is the only being who is entirely fulfilled in himself. So it should be telling that, out of everything God created, the only thing he deemed "not good" was the man being alone (Genesis 2:18). By "alone" the Bible is referring to the man's singular nature, without a partner—one equal *to* him and distinct *from* him to share life *with* him. And when God made his equal—the woman—and presented her to the man, what else could the man do but rejoice (Genesis 2:21-23)?

While this passage specifically shows the first marriage, it isn't only about marriage (something we'll explore in chapter 21). Marriage is just one way our relational wiring is expressed. Platonic relationships allow us to express our relational wiring as well. Friendship exists because it is not good for us to be alone. Communities exist because it is not good for us to be alone. Without other people in our lives, we are, in a sense, incomplete. We can only truly flourish and fulfill our purpose in the world in relationship with other people.

Our Purpose

The creation story tells us that human beings were made with a purpose: to have authority and responsibility over the rest of creation (Genesis 1:26). In Genesis 1:26, 28, this is what is meant by the terms "rule" and "subdue" (NET, CSB), or "have dominion" (ESV). The first man expressed that purpose as he named all the animals God made (Genesis 2:19). People continued to express that purpose as they cultivated the land, made art and music, and developed the skills to create wondrous structures (even if those structures were meant to draw attention to their builders, not the Creator—see Genesis 11).

This purpose is still ours today. We are called to "subdue" the earth, to harness its resources for human flourishing. This naturally encourages wise, responsible, and sustainable technological and scientific development. In our dominion or ruling over creation, we not only resemble God using our shared characteristics, but we reflect God in responsibly managing the resources he has provided.

MADE MALE AND FEMALE

These characteristics, abilities, and responsibilities are expressions of our being God's image bearers. But they are not the only expressions of it. Our biology, being either male or female, also expresses being made in God's image. This doesn't mean that God is male or female, of course. God is not a man, woman, or human being (Numbers 23:19). "God is spirit," and does not have a body (John 4:24). (That said, God the Son, Jesus, *is* a man and has a glorified physical body.) But human beings are either male or female, with physical, biological, psychological, and neurological characteristics that both complement and differentiate one from the other.

Our bodies have basic similarities in terms of general form and function.[4] Men and women are simultaneously physical and spiritual beings who experience the world that way; we are holistic beings who cannot be divided into body and soul.[5] We share the same basic needs and desires. We carry within us the same sort of rational and moral capacity, the same relational drive and desire, and the same responsibility to cultivate and care for the world around us. And yet, how we express and experience those is distinct from one another. And this is no accident, for "every cell has a sex," meaning that our being male or female shapes how our bodies develop, how our brains work, and even how we respond to illnesses.[6] Our biology is essential to our experience of the world and the way we reflect and represent God in it, which includes the special honor women have of carrying the innate potential to bring new life into the world.[7] God did not make us with a distinction between biological sex and gender, in the sense of conformity to a set of approved societal behaviors for men and women.[8] The Bible doesn't idealize men being dominant over women; nor does it suggest that women should rule over men. It also doesn't show us as fully representing and reflecting God in isolation from one another. Instead, the Bible presents the ideal of men and women as *partners*, walking and working side by side as they represent God in the world in ways that honor their distinctiveness.

THE KEY TO HUMAN FLOURISHING

Fundamentally, being made in God's image is not something we *do*—it is what we *are*. To be a human being is to be God's image bearer.[9] Regardless of our mental, physical, and relational capacity, regardless of our realized or innate potential, that is who and what we are. And with everything we are, from our biology to our actions, we are always reflecting something about what God is like. And when we begin to grasp that, it changes everything.

If all people are God's image bearers, we need to be compassionate, especially toward those with whom we might disagree (even those who might perceive us as an ideological "enemy"). It means that we must meaningfully and practically protect and care for the vulnerable, including the unborn, people living in poverty, the elderly, and the infirm. It means we must uphold and defend the dignity of *all* people, seeking to put every last semblance of racism, classism, sexism, and every other-*ism* to death in our hearts and our societies. It means upholding the goodness of God's design for humanity as distinctly male *and* female, honoring both as partners in representing God in this world. And for those of us who are Christians, it means sharing the gospel with our fellow image-bearers who do not know Jesus, introducing them to the One who has the power to redeem and restore them so they might reflect their Creator in the world in the way they were meant to.

God gives humanity a greater identity than we can create for ourselves. An identity that *gives life*. One that is the key to pursuing human dignity and flourishing. One all the people of the world need to know.

REFLECT, EXPLORE, AND DISCUSS

1. What idea or concept stood out to you as you read this chapter? Why?

2. Read some of the Bible passages about humanity referenced in this chapter. How do these passages encourage or challenge you?

3. What new questions do these passages raise?

4. What are you most tempted to use as the basis of your identity? How does what you've learned in this chapter affect that?

GOD MAKES

8

A WORLD WHERE WE ARE NOT ALONE

Angels, Demons, and Maybe Aliens Too

I probably think about pop culture a lot more than I should. I'm typically quick with references, quotes, and random facts. If I'm not careful, I can wind up talking about things that no one cares about for way too long. Which is fine. For me. For other people, I'm sure I am insufferable, especially when I'm being a bit *too* obscure.

But part of why I think about pop culture so much is that I notice how effective music, movies, TV shows, books, and comic books are for exploring big questions and ideas. (Like, for example, a spy dramedy exploring what it means to be human.) And the reason it is so effective is because it's a safe place to be curious. To consider alternative perspectives that we couldn't otherwise. To develop empathy for those whose life experience differs significantly from our own. And, most importantly, to ask, *What if?*

Think about speculative fiction—stories exploring science fiction, horror, fantasy, or supernatural elements. Books and films about vampires, werewolves, mummies, and demons. Stories of strange visitors from other planets, or other dimensions within this one. These kinds of stories have been a pop culture staple since at least the eighteenth century. While many modern stories range between the banal and the creepy, all are asking the same question: What if there is more to this world than we can see—what if we are *not* alone?

THE QUESTION WE'RE AFRAID TO ASK

"What if we are not alone?" should not be a controversial question. Yet, if asked outside of designated "safe spaces" like speculative fiction, it often puts the person asking under undue scrutiny. This is, again, the fruit of the Enlightenment and its false dichotomy between faith and reason, and overreliance on the scientific method as the tool to determine what is true. Now, here's the thing: We cannot prove *or* disprove the supernatural using the scientific method. The supernatural doesn't work that way. But being unable to apply the scientific method doesn't prevent us from making a value judgment. And judge we do.

It's one thing to say you're open to the possibility of the existence of supernatural or other unexplained phenomena. For the most part, such an admission would warrant a raised eyebrow or an eye roll, but that's about it. But to admit to having an *encounter* with any kind of supernatural or otherworldly being, people will react to you very differently. And by differently, I mean they will most likely look at you as if you've suddenly grown a second head, or possibly even say, "But you seem so normal…"

I know this because I've experienced it multiple times over. That's what happens when you tell people that a part of the story of how you became a Christian involved being attacked by demons. (See, now you're doing it too.)

Christians should not be afraid of talking about the supernatural. Our faith is a supernatural one. After all, Christians believe that God created everything in the universe out of nothing. We believe that this same God, who exists outside of time and space, entered into it as the man Jesus Christ who was born without a human father. We believe that Jesus performed miracles. He healed the sick and infirm and gave sight to the blind. We even believe that he died and rose from the grave to forgive our sins. But when it comes to supernatural beings—specifically, angels and demons—we are far more skeptical and undereducated as a result.

What we know about angels and demons has more in common with what is portrayed in pop culture. We treat them as being generally approachable, if not likable. As funny, flawed, learned, and growing. As controllable. Exactly the kind of supernatural beings humans would be inclined to make up. And nothing at all like the real thing.

In case that wasn't clear enough, we need to realize that supernatural beings, angels and demons, are real. They not only exist, but they are active in this world right now. We might have even encountered one without realizing it (Hebrews 13:2). So what are they like, and what would we do if we encountered one?

ANGELS: WONDROUS AND TERRIFYING

Pop culture's depiction of angels gives us a very skewed picture. Pop culture inclines us to think of angels as gentle beings that are eager to lend a hand, offer a hug, and possibly give us a pat on the head. They are beings who do good in the world to earn their status in heaven. In Western societies, especially in North America, angels are also popularly treated as an elevated state for humanity. Death becomes a promotion to this state.[1] We have guardian angels watching over us, often casting our deceased loved ones in those roles, but we leave little or no room for who sent them.[2] In other words, our popular understanding of angels has nothing to do with what Christianity has taught for centuries. And what we see in the Bible is equal parts more wondrous and terrifying.

What Are Angels?

The Bible does not describe angels as an elevated form of humanity. They are something other, another form of created being, with their exact number unknown to us (Nehemiah 9:6). These beings are entirely distinct from human beings but can also appear to be indistinguishable from us (Matthew 28:3; Judges 13:3).[3] There are different types of angels, including cherubim (Genesis 3:24), seraphim (Isaiah 6:2), and the more mysterious archangels (Jude 9). And unlike us, they can move between heaven and earth (Genesis 28:12).

What Purpose Do Angels Serve?

Angelic beings exist to bring God glory and to carry out his plans and purposes. The primary way they do this is by functioning as messengers of God.[4] Angels were charged with guarding the gates of the garden after the first humans were expelled (Genesis 3:24). Angels acted as agents of God's wrath against the cities of Sodom and Gomorrah (Genesis 19:1-15). Angels gave visions to prophets, such as Ezekiel (Ezekiel 10:1-22) and Daniel (Daniel 10–12). An angel, Gabriel, appeared to Zechariah and told him he would have a son, and his son would be the forerunner to the Messiah, the rescuer and redeemer of God's people (Luke 1:5-25). Gabriel also announced to Mary that she would be the mother of Jesus, the promised Messiah (Luke 1:26-38). Angels announced Jesus' birth to a group of shepherds (Luke 2:1-14). An angel warned Joseph to take Mary and Jesus to Egypt to escape Herod (Matthew 2:13-15). Angels declared Jesus' resurrection from the dead (Luke 24:1-8). When Jesus had ascended to be with the Father, angels assured the apostles that Jesus would return (Acts 1:10-11). An angel even served as John's companion as he experienced a vision of the end of all things and the glorious return of Christ (Revelation 22:8-9).

What About "the Angel of the Lord"?

And then there is the one called "the angel of the Lord" (Genesis 16:7; Exodus 3:2). This angel appears throughout the Old Testament, but especially during Israel's wandering in the wilderness and in the conquest of the promised land. This angel is distinct from all others and does things no other angel appears to do. He speaks for God in a way that suggests he is God. He acts in a way that suggests he is God. He even accepts worship from humans, something he can only do if he is God.[5] This has led several Christian teachers throughout the centuries to conclude that the angel of the Lord may have been a preincarnate form of Christ himself.[6]

What Would You Do If You Met an Angel?

While they often remain hidden, angels do operate in our world today. This is why Hebrews 13:2 describes the possibility of unknowingly encountering one. But what if you were to encounter one in a way that made it evident that you were not dealing with a human being? And I don't just mean being suddenly confronted by whatever it was that Ezekiel saw, with its many wings, eyes, and wheels. The chances are solid that you would fall over in terror, and then you might start trying to worship it. And if you did, you'd be in good company, because that's what so many did when they encountered an angel in the Bible (Luke 1:13, 30; 2:9-10; Revelation 19:9-10). Thankfully, the angel would stop you from doing the latter reaction.

DEMONS: DANGEROUS, DEADLY, AND DEFEATED

Angels are not the only sort of supernatural beings in this world, nor the only ones that Western pop culture has warped our understanding of. Like angels, demons have been remade in our image, as likable, empathetic, and misunderstood. (Although, to be fair, misunderstanding them is the one thing pop culture gets right.)

What Are Demons?

Demons appear frequently in both the Old and New Testaments. While their precise origins are unknown, it is traditionally believed that they were once angels themselves who rebelled against God (Revelation 12:4-9). Throughout the Bible, they are called "demons" explicitly (Leviticus 17:7; Matthew 7:22), but also "evil spirits" (Luke 8:2), "spiritual forces of evil" (Ephesians 6:12), and more enigmatically, "prince" on at least one occasion (Daniel 10:13). Like angels, they can appear human, as well as in the form of an angel from heaven (Galatians 1:8). These beings are not to be trifled with as they are capable of oppressing, tempting, and even possessing people (Matthew 4:1; 8:28-34; Acts 10:38).

Is Satan God's Equal?

Chief among the demons is one referred to most frequently as Satan, though he is also referred to as "the devil" (Matthew 4:5), a "liar and the father of lies" (John 8:44), the "serpent" (Revelation 12:9), the "dragon" (Revelation 20:2), and "the tempter" (Matthew 4:3). He is most often associated with the serpent who tempted the first humans to question God's commands in the garden and was cursed as a consequence (Genesis 3:1-15). The devil is a "roaring lion" (1 Peter 5:8), who desires to "steal and kill and destroy" as he works in opposition to God's plans and purposes in this world (John 10:10). And were he able, he would surely do it.

But despite how he is popularly portrayed, and how he seems to imagine himself, Satan is not God's equal. He is a created being. An extraordinarily powerful one, without question, but a created being nonetheless. He cannot be everywhere all at once. His knowledge, and even his power, is limited. Although he is called the "ruler of this world" (John 12:31), Satan rules as a usurper, and his power is not absolute; he can only operate within the limits that God gives him (Job 1:6-12).

Do We Need to Be Afraid of Demons?

Although it's tempting to bore you with a thousand caveats, there *is* a sense in which we should be afraid of demons. I mean, we're talking about very real and very powerful supernatural beings here. Beings that are unlike us and do not have wonderful plans for our lives. Demons are dangerous and deadly, capable of wreaking great havoc through their influence over, or even possession of, people (Mark 5:15; Luke 22:3). Although, it should be noted that a demon cannot possess a Christian, because the Holy Spirit lives within us (Ephesians 1:13-14).

So yes, we should have a biblically healthy fear of demons. To behave as though they are not a threat of any kind and to allow ourselves to be conditioned into believing they are not a danger is foolishness. But our caution has a limit: While they wield tremendous power and influence in the world, their power and influence will come to an end. The devil might be a roaring lion, but he is also a cornered and, ultimately, defeated one. His fate, and the fate of all like him, has already been determined, and it is not a future in which they rule over God's creation for their purposes. The only future that awaits them is "the eternal fire," a place of punishment created for them (Matthew 25:41 CSB).

WHAT DO WE DO WITH EVERYTHING ELSE WE CAN'T EXPLAIN?

Angels and demons are one thing (okay, two things). But what about all the other unexplained phenomena that people experience, or at least claim to? What do we do with stories of spirits, ghosts, fairies,

Bigfoot, and other creatures that go bump in the night? What about claims of unidentified anomalous phenomena (UAP) and (often disturbing) encounters with nonhuman intelligence?[7] Are people just making these things up? Are they having waking nightmares? Or is the answer something much more straightforward—that they've had an encounter with something they cannot explain or understand?

There is no simple answer to any of these questions. And a reason for that is because, since at least the early 1950s, there has been a coordinated effort to debunk and discredit reports of this kind of unexplained phenomena. The message has long been that *reasonable people* don't believe in such things. Yet as credible journalists have explored the subject, they found that there is something more to these stories.[8] There is enough evidence to suggest that it is *unreasonable* to completely dismiss these claims, treating them as the fruit of overactive imaginations.

So what are they? As I've explored this subject to a *very* limited degree, including listening to former US government officials testifying before Congress, reading books and articles from those who have investigated these phenomena, and listening to the stories of those who have experienced them, it doesn't seem like we're dealing with anything benevolent. If anything, it sounds more like what people are encountering are demons.[9] And even that conclusion should be held with a relatively open hand because, the truth is, we don't *actually* know for sure. But what we do know is there is more to the world God created than we can explore with our limited perceptions. And we need to live with the tension that creates.

THE ONE SAVIOR WHO RULES US ALL

Exploring the question of whether we're alone shouldn't be left to the realm of speculative fiction. Christians know the answer to this— we are not alone. We live in a world where there is more than we can see. Where angels and demons are indeed among us. But they are nothing like the ideas we've picked up through centuries of storytelling and imaginings.

Angels are not huggable, cute, or controllable. They are not our deceased loved ones elevated to a new state of being. They are powerful servants of the Lord, carrying out his will in the world. Demons are not misunderstood, and they are not all-powerful beings. They are enemies of both God and humanity, whose sole aim is to harm as many as they can before they meet their end at the hands of Jesus, the One whom they fear (Luke 8:32). And all things, whether seen or unseen, explained or mysterious, obey him—the one Savior who rules us all.

REFLECT, EXPLORE, AND DISCUSS

1. What idea or concept stood out to you as you read this chapter? Why?

2. Read some of the Bible passages about angels and demons referenced in this chapter. How do these passages encourage or challenge you?

3. What new questions do these passages raise?

4. How comfortable are you with the idea that we live in a supernatural world? Why?

5. Imagine a friend discloses having had an encounter with some form of nonhuman intelligence. How would you encourage them based on what you've read in this chapter?

GOD MAKES

9

A WORLD WHERE GOD IS ALWAYS WORKING

The Seen and Unseen Works of God

You might not believe this, but *everyone* believes in a higher power. Seriously. Everyone. No exceptions.

No matter what beliefs they hold to, whether they are atheists, Buddhists, Scientologists, Muslims, Christians, or spiritual-but-not-religious, they believe there is some greater power at work in the world. They may not agree on what it is, or whether it has a personality of any kind—they might call that higher power karma, good vibes, or the universe—but they believe it exists. They *know* deep down that there's something else at work in the world. That, despite some of their arguments to the contrary, we are not meandering unguided through a meaningless existence.

And they are right, even if the *what* and *who* of that guidance are misunderstood.

Christians readily affirm that God is the power that everyone intuitively knows is at work in the world. After all, we believe God created the universe and rules over it. As its maker and ruler, God cares for his creation, and for us, deeply. He is intimately involved with it at every level. This is what the Bible tells us from its first word to its final one. But sometimes we are too quick to affirm that God is the one everyone intuitively knows is at work in the world without considering the questions it raises. For example, if God is at work in the world, *what* does that work look like? *Why* is he at work; what's the point? And does his work negate our choices—or do our choices negate his work?

These are good questions; *important* questions. And they are not questions God leaves entirely unanswered. But finding those answers begins by exploring the ways the Bible points to God working in the world. Which means it's time to start talking about how the impossible happens.

THE EXTRAORDINARY WORK OF GOD

The way most people think about God working in the world is through miracles. Instances that the most skeptical of us are tempted to reject because, well, miracles are violations of the natural operations of the world. So when they read about the stories of miraculous events in the Bible, they tend to jump to the conclusion that those stories must be entirely made up, or exaggerated explanations of natural phenomena that these less-enlightened people couldn't possibly have understood.[1] After all, seas and rivers don't part. Fire doesn't come down from heaven. People don't walk on water. No one could survive in the belly of a giant fish for three days. Voices can't be heard from burning bushes.

Reasonable people don't take such things seriously, because such things are impossible. And the impossible *does not* and *cannot* happen.

Which is true, from a certain point of view. You and I cannot make the impossible happen; it is not within our power to do so. But miracles do happen. And by miracles, I don't mean the improbable—events that are difficult to explain, but for which a natural explanation is possible, like when I find my car keys in my pocket when I'm running five minutes late for a meeting an hour's drive away. I mean the *impossible*. Things like an English-speaking pastor beginning to speak a foreign language they did not know while talking about Jesus. A woman who finds she no longer has epilepsy, nearly a decade after her diagnosis was first confirmed.[2] A teenage girl not only survives but completely *recovers* after being struck by a truck at high speed—an accident that should have killed her.

SO, WHAT IS A MIRACLE ANYWAY?

Miracles are supernatural acts of God intended to help us recognize who he is. The miracles we see in the Bible confirm the truth of God's message and the trustworthiness of his messengers. God performed signs and wonders through Moses not to exalt Moses, but so that people would know that he was sent by God (Exodus 4:5). He did the same with prophets we see in the Old Testament, such as Elijah, Elisha, and Isaiah.[3] Peter and the apostles also performed many signs and wonders as they went about proclaiming the gospel.[4]

And then there's Jesus himself, who performed signs and wonders everywhere he went. He healed the sick. Cast out demons. Raised the dead. Gave sight to the blind. Made the lame walk. Commanded nature. Fed thousands upon thousands with meager provisions. His miracles, like all the others, pointed to the truth of his message—not only that he was sent by God, but that he *is* God himself, walking amongst his people, there to lead them into truth and eternal life through faith in him.[5]

Jared Wilson tells us that miracles offer us a glimpse of a world that is "larger, more vivid, more real—more submissive to its Creator."[6] And when we begin to grasp this, we begin to see that the question of whether miracles happen at all isn't the question we should be asking.

I mean, the fact that we exist at all is miraculous. It is so unlikely for life to have come about in the universe that this is the only accurate description for it. That life exists is no accident. It is a miracle. And that alone should be enough to make every human being who ever lived stop and praise God (Romans 1:20).

But creation is not the only miracle we can point to right now. If you are a Christian, it is the result of a miracle—two miracles, actually. The first miracle is Jesus' resurrection. Though he was unquestionably dead, he rose again. And through that first miracle comes the second, as God raises the spiritually dead—we'll talk about what this means in chapter 18—to new and eternal life through faith in Jesus, complete with new desires, a new purpose, and a new future.

Life is a miracle. Our life through Christ is a greater miracle still.

THE EXTRAORDINARY WORK OF GOD

Miracles are real. They are extraordinary. They are *a* way God works in the world, but they are not the *only* way he works. They are not even the primary way he works. After all, miracles are, by definition, uncommon. Miracles do not happen every day; if they did, they would not be miracles. They would be ordinary. And if we think of miracles as the primary way God works, we might become disillusioned, if not jaded toward God because we haven't knowingly experienced such things.

Yet God is actively involved in the world daily (John 5:17). He is intimately involved in the minutest details. There is nothing too big or small for him to avoid his concerns. This active and ongoing rule over and care for all he has made is what Christians call *providence*.

WHAT IS PROVIDENCE?

Providence is the ordinary way God works in the world. It is his care for his people across time and space (the faithful—past, present, and future) as well as the whole of creation (the world and everything—and everyone—in it).[7] And it is these activities that we typically take for granted. After all, how many of us think about how the atoms that make up our bodies and everything around us hold together? Or why planet Earth continues in its orbit around the sun instead of just flying off into space? Or why gravity continues to hold us to the earth's surface? The sun shines. The rain falls. Seasons hold to a generally consistent cycle.[8] I rarely think about any of them. When I go to bed, I assume that the next day gravity will continue to work, that the earth will still be moving, and that my body is not going to suddenly disintegrate. Chances are, you probably don't give these a first or second thought either. Which is how it should be. If we spent our days worrying about *any* of these, we would not get a whole lot of anything done.

Scientific inquiry helps us understand how the natural forces of the world are intended to work and the mechanisms that are meant to keep them in check. But knowing the *what* and *how* does not explain the *why* or the *who* behind them. And the Bible gives us both. It says that these are all the work of God's unseen hand. He makes the sun shine and the rain fall (Matthew 5:45). He feeds the birds and "clothes" the flowers in beauty (Matthew 6:25-29). He holds everything he has made together (Colossians 1:17; Hebrews 1:3). He provides us with what we need, which is why Jesus himself said that we should not worry about what we will eat or drink or wear, or even about tomorrow because tomorrow will take care of itself (Matthew 6:31, 34). If that list of worries looks familiar, it's because it catalogs all the things practically everyone commonly worries about. We worry about making ends meet and having all that we need. We worry about the future, *a lot*.[9] But Jesus said, our "heavenly Father knows that [we] need them," and gives us all that we need to pursue his kingdom and righteousness—to live faithfully as people brought into his family through Jesus Christ's life, death, and resurrection (Matthew 6:32-33).

But providence isn't limited to providing for our daily needs. Every moment, God is working all the events of history together toward a specific end: the return of Christ and, with him, the coming of the new creation; this world restored to the perfection it had in the beginning, one where God and humanity live in perfect peace and harmony forever (Revelation 21:1-2). And that includes working all things together for good for *us* (Romans 8:28). To shape us into the kind of people who are representatives of that better world that is to come to the world we live in today. People who are different because of who we love, and because of who loves us (Matthew 5:3-11). People who celebrate and struggle differently because we know that nothing is truly purposeless. Who love those who hate us and pray for those who persecute us (Matthew 5:43-48). Who meet anger with kindness, counter cruelty with compassion, and live in the hope of what we believe but cannot see, and with endurance eagerly await the day when we will (Romans 8:25).

THE PRACTICAL PROBLEM WE HAVE WITH PROVIDENCE (AND MIRACLES TOO)

We also need to be honest: The truth that God works is easy to talk about in theory, but it is difficult to believe in practice. After all, unexplained tragedies strike and unspeakable acts of evil and injustice are committed every day. Our experiences seem to contradict the idea that God is doing anything in the world today. It leaves us to wonder if, at some point, he looked at all that he had made and said, "Carry on," or if he was ever involved in the world at all.[10] If he is here and he does care, why doesn't he take care of all the problems we see in the world? (Hold that thought for now—we'll return to it in the next chapter.)

Then there's the other significant consideration: What does God's providence mean for our ability to make real, meaningful choices?

Doesn't it reduce us to automatons—marionettes whose strings are pulled by a divine puppet master?

Christians of all traditions must be careful not to shrug off the practical problems and concerns some have with the idea of providence or give pat answers that dismiss anyone's doubts and concerns. People's questions are important and deserve to be treated that way. And part of handling those questions with the respect they deserve is acknowledging that there are limits to how much we can know about how providence works.

See, most of us gravitate to either/or options. We prefer to reduce complex choices and subjects to these options as often as possible. But the Bible doesn't allow for such reductionistic thinking. And when we try, we create problems for ourselves that the Bible doesn't. The Bible doesn't present God's providential rule, our ability to make real and meaningful choices, and the very visible ills of the world as being in opposition. We don't know exactly how the relationship between them works, only that they do (see Proverbs 19:21). Whereas we want an *either/or*, God gives us a *yes/and*.

THE GOOD NEWS OF GOD'S YES/AND

The yes/and relationship between God's providence, humans' free will, and the presence of evil in the world is a divine mystery, something God has not chosen to fully reveal to us. Instead, what God does reveal is that his plans for the world go forward *through* the actions and choices of human beings.

Joseph's story is the quintessential example that we see in the Bible. Joseph was hated by his brothers because of their father Jacob's favoritism toward him. They threw Joseph in a well and sold him into slavery, where he ended up becoming a servant to an Egyptian official. Though brought to Egypt as a slave, he was ultimately elevated to a position of supreme authority, which allowed him to save his family from starvation during a terrible famine (Genesis 37; 39–50). And where was God in all of this? Joseph told his brothers that what they meant for evil, God intended "for a good purpose" (Genesis 50:20). The brothers did what they wanted to do, and they were responsible for their choices. But what they wanted to do, wrong as it was, was the means through which God did what he intended—bringing Jacob's family to a land where they would grow from a small few to millions.

But Joseph is not the lone example of this. Throughout the Bible, we see example after example: Gideon, Samson, Saul, David, Solomon, and Daniel, to name but a few. Rulers, judges, and common people through whom God carried out his plans—including in their most vile acts.[11] Even Jesus' crucifixion, which was carried out by the evil desires and actions of humans, was intended by God as the means through which people's sins could be forgiven (Acts 2:23).

What we mean for harm, God intends for a good purpose.

BEHOLD THE WONDROUS MYSTERY

And so, God calls us to behold the wondrous mystery. To embrace that when we are speaking of divine mysteries, we should do so with humility, acknowledging that there is a limit to what we can know. But what we can know is this: While there are mysteries involved, the fact that God *is* working is not mysterious. He is always at work in ways that are seen and unseen.

And because we know God is at work, we can pray, knowing that he will hear us and that he will act according to his good purposes. We can talk about Jesus and do good works that demonstrate our faith, knowing that he gives people like you and me new life *through* people like you and me. And we live with hope instead of fear. We do not truly live in a world of uncertainty. We know God is actively engaged at every single moment, using the people he made—whether they love, hate, or are indifferent to him—as he moves history toward its intended conclusion. And because we know what that conclusion is, we have nothing to fear. There is nothing that can stop it. Nothing that can derail it. Not even us.

REFLECT, EXPLORE, AND DISCUSS

1. What idea or concept stood out to you as you read this chapter? Why?

2. Read some of the Bible passages about God's providential and miraculous work referenced in this chapter. How do these passages encourage or challenge you?

3. What new questions do these passages raise?

4. How are you most inclined to think about the relationship between God's actions and human agency?

5. Knowing that God is actively working in the world encourages us to live with hope, not fear. Do you agree or disagree? Why?

10

THE DIFFERENCE BETWEEN GOOD AND EVIL

Mysteries, Problems, and the Limits of Our Comprehension

I've loved mysteries and puzzles for as long as I can remember. There's something deeply satisfying about discovering the answer to a nagging question, or the aha moment that unlocks the plot of a novel. And don't get me started on the sense of triumph that is reached when finding the right spot for that one puzzle piece you've spent hours trying to place. But not every puzzle or mystery can be easily solved, or perhaps, solved at all. Some answers are elusive. The answers exist, but they remain fuzzy.

This probably explains why I think about evil so much. Evil is a mystery. Not in the sense of there being a lack of evidence of its existence, of course. There are abundant examples of evil for all of us to see. Human traffickers sexually exploit women, children, and men—and people pay to watch that exploitation.[1] Medical practitioners implement controversial (and potentially life-threatening) treatments because of profit potential.[2] Entire industries, including many multi-level marketing companies (MLMs) and payday loan businesses, are built upon preying on the most vulnerable in our societies.[3] Then there is the evil of sexual, physical, psychological, and spiritual abuse—many of which are interconnected—by those we are meant to trust who pervert that trust for their own ends, the evil of which is only compounded when churches and denominations defend abusers, resist accountability, and shift the blame to victims.[4]

These are examples of evil, and they hardly exhaust the wickedness that we see in the world. But why are these acts evil? What about them warrants that description? And this is where I start thinking (probably too much) about evil. We tend to look at evil and say, "We know it when we see it, but we can't explain it." We define it by examples. Or we use terms like *morally reprehensible, destructive,* or *harmful* as our definitions. But these terms only give us enough to say evil is bad, which is not terribly helpful.

This is why I say that evil is fuzzy. That there is a mystery to it. And it's one that has gnawed and nagged at humanity for as long as people have known good and evil (and not good alone). Philosophers and theologians have been searching for the answer since roughly half a second after mankind first realized evil was a thing. Some view good and evil as a duality, operating as opposite but equal forces in the world or the work of powers of equal but opposite intent. Others opt to reject the categories of good and evil altogether, seeing them as social constructs rooted in our culture or historical period (when it best suits their purposes).[5] But neither of these perspectives resolves the tension—the mystery at the heart of evil itself. They might lead to self-justification, self-indulgence, or self-help, but not to any lasting satisfaction.

So what do Christians think? Do we have a way to explain evil that isn't quite so fuzzy? Well, yes. And no. It's complicated. (Sort of.)

WHAT IS EVIL?

Christians have wrestled with this question since before we were first called Christians (Acts 11:26). We've looked at it from different angles, trying to grasp what we can of the mystery of evil. And one of the most consistent conclusions that Christians have agreed upon is that evil is *real*. I get that this might not seem terribly profound, but we also live in a world where some people think the Nazis weren't that bad. (They truly were bad.) Christians are not naïve about what humans are capable of because the Bible does not paint a naïvely optimistic picture of mankind. Murder, child sacrifice, rape, idolatry, abuse of power, coveting, stealing, gossiping, and lying are just a few of the nearly inexhaustible acts of evil people carry out in its pages.[6] When we look at all the evil that happens in the world, we are horrified (as we should be), but we are not surprised by it.[7]

But Christians also recognize that as real as evil is, we don't come to a better understanding of it by intently focusing on it. When we do this, we risk becoming hardened and desensitized to it. To develop callouses around our hearts and minds that leave us not only unsurprised by evil, but unhorrified by it.

Instead, we know that we can only understand evil in light of good. That's because evil, in its truest sense, exists only in contrast to good. Evil is not good's equal. Evil is a shade. It is a deviation and a counterfeit, a distortion and violation of all that is good, true, and beautiful.

This is one of the reasons the Bible encourages us to think deeply about all that is true, worthy of respect, just, pure, lovely, commendable, excellent, and praiseworthy (Philippians 4:8). And if we want to know what is good, we need to know God and his goodness. After all, God is not only good, he is also the source of all goodness (Psalm 16:2). He defines what is good and what is not (Genesis 1:4; 2:18). And he is the standard of good (Luke 18:19; 3 John 11). Also, because God is good, he does good to all people—those who love him and those who reject him—as he works providentially in the world.

Which sounds well and good. But doesn't evil's very existence challenge the notion that God is good? How can God be good and allow the evils that we see in the world to exist?

THE PROBLEM AND THE MYSTERY

This question, the problem of evil, has challenged humanity across cultures and worldviews for millennia, particularly in the idea that any good deity could be involved in the world, given how much evil exists. If an all-powerful, all-knowing, and benevolent deity were actively involved in the world, then surely evil would not be allowed to stand. But because evil exists, such a god is either unable to prevent evil, unwilling to stop it, or entirely uninvolved.[8]

In more recent times, the problem has broadened its focus not simply to evil's existence but to our lack of happiness. Or, more realistically, comfort. So if God were truly good and powerful, we would all be perfectly happy because that's what God would desire.[9] But pain, suffering, discomfort, and inconvenience all prevent our happiness. And we find ourselves back at our starting point once more: If we are unhappy or uncomfortable, it's because God is unable or unwilling to prevent it.

Through the centuries, Christian teachers have taken different approaches to answering this seeming contradiction—the paradoxical relationship between God's providence and the presence of evil. Some pushed the problem back to humanity, essentially saying that evil stems from our misuse and abuse of free will. Others made Satan out to be more powerful than he really is, elevating him to God's equal (a position that the father of lies would love for us all to believe he is in). Others still have tried to make the case that the existence of evil is part of the natural order; evil is a tragic possibility, not unlike an earthquake or tsunami. But none of these answers the problem of evil. They leave us in the exact same spot where we started. At best,

God is impotent. At worst, he is evil. But because he is neither, it's hard to take any of these solutions seriously.[10]

Another approach has been to focus on the greater purpose of evil, pain, and suffering. To lean on the truth that God has a purpose for evil, even if we cannot see it, as he takes what is meant for evil and uses it for good (Genesis 50:20). He uses pain and suffering to shape our character, making us more compassionate, steadfast, and peaceful (Hebrews 12:5-11; James 1:2-4). He uses pain to punish evildoers, demonstrating his good and just judgment of sin (Genesis 3:14-19; Romans 1:24-32). He uses pain to get the attention of those who reject him, drawing them toward repentance and faith in him (Luke 13:1-5; Romans 2:4). And while this perspective is true, it also doesn't satisfy the lingering *why* behind the existence of evil, pain, and suffering.

No matter how we look at it, the problem of evil leads us back to the mystery. And we cannot fully resolve it because the mystery is not something we can fully comprehend. It is *inscrutable*. And this is the way the Bible treats both evil's existence, and the problem that evil, pain, and suffering's existence presents. The Bible doesn't offer an account of evil's origin. It doesn't offer pat answers or blame humanity for evil's existence. And it certainly doesn't give the devil more credit than is due.

It gives us the book of Job.

JOB'S STRUGGLE WITH THE PROBLEM OF EVIL

Job was a righteous man whom God allowed the devil to test by taking away all he had: his wealth, his children, and his health (Job 1:6-20; 2:1-8). Yet when he lost everything, even as his wife was encouraging him to curse God and die, he refused, saying, "Should we receive what is good from God, and not also receive what is evil?" (Job 2:10).

Then his friends entered the picture. After they mourned together, having said nothing for a week, Job discussed his sorrows with his friends. He lamented that he was ever born (3:3). He longed for death, even as he defended his righteousness (3:20; 6:8). He had done nothing to deserve God's displeasure (34:5). From Job's point of view, God had wronged him—God was either not good, or God lacked the power to protect him from affliction. And as he voiced his complaint, Job sought comfort and compassion from his friends. Instead, they challenged his self-perception. If Job were truly as righteous as he claimed, surely God would not punish him in the way he so obviously was. After all, good comes to those who do good; those who do evil will reap what they sow (4:7-11; 8:20).

Through at least eight speeches from Job and eight rebuttals from his friends, they debated Job's circumstances and the rules by which God governs his creation. And even when one side or the other spoke the truth to some degree, they were still in error, as they spoke too confidently about that which they could only grasp in part. Job and his friends all looked at the world around them and came to different conclusions based on what they could observe and experience, but they left no room for what they couldn't know.[11]

Then God entered the fray, answering out of a whirlwind (38:1), ready to settle the matter. And in two speeches, God challenged the assumptions and assertions at the heart of Job's complaints.

"Where were you when I laid the foundations of the earth?" God asked as he confronted Job's understanding of how God governs the universe. "Have you ever in your life commanded the morning, or made the dawn know its place?...In what direction does light reside, and darkness, where is its place...?" (38:4, 12, 19).

In his first speech, God questioned Job more than 40 times; and when it was Job's time to respond, his opportunity to correct the Almighty (40:2), what could he say? Job realized the arrogance of his challenge. He did not know even half of what he thought he knew. Job relented, "Indeed, I am completely unworthy—how could I reply to you? I put my hand over my mouth to silence myself. I have spoken once, but I cannot answer; twice, but I will say no more" (40:4-5).

But God was not finished. With another speech, God questioned Job's contention that he was acting unjustly and described the power he exercises over all of creation (40:6–41:34). And again, Job's mouth was stopped. "I have declared without understanding things too wonderful for me to know," he said (42:3).

Job was satisfied with God's response to him in a way that is difficult for even the least cynical of us to understand. But why? God never actually gave Job the reason behind his suffering. The Lord did not reveal the details of the scene from his throne room and Satan's accusations against God and Job. Those answers, to our knowledge, never came. And if we are particularly jaded, there is a tendency to read God's responses as effectively saying, "I'm God; you're not. Be quiet." (Though, perhaps, not phrased quite so politely.) But that isn't what God did. What satisfied Job was that God was with him.

"The LORD answered Job out of the whirlwind" (38:1; 40:6 NKJV). Whenever we see "the LORD" in small caps like this, it signifies the use of God's covenant name: *YHWH* (which we usually pronounce *Yahweh*). The name that God gives to the people he calls his own (Exodus 3:14). God had not forsaken Job. He was present with Job in his pain and sorrow. His correction was not condemnation. It was an act of love—God's steadfast, loyal, unceasing love for Job (Hebrews 12:6).

EMBRACING THE LIMITS OF OUR COMPREHENSION

And that, ultimately, is God's answer to the problem of evil; it's the piece of the puzzle that gives us a better sense of the picture, even if we're still not sure what all we're looking at. Because, we must be honest: This is difficult to grasp. It stretches the limits of our comprehension. Yet this is the truth—this is the good news. We may never know why evil exists or why God allows it to persist. We may never fully understand his purposes for it—the greater good behind it all.

But we do know that God is good. We know God is the source of all that is good. We know he is good to this world and the beings he has created, showering grace and blessing upon us all. And we know that he is with us, even in those times when our pain and sorrow deceive us into thinking he has abandoned us.

And that is what allows us to carry on in the world without deserting ourselves to despair or anger. To live as people with hope, who know they can cry out to God and call on him to act (Habakkuk 1:1-4), who can pursue justice (Micah 6:8), even as we turn away from our own evil deeds and seek to make right what we have done wrong (Psalm 4:4). Evil is real, and God is completely good. Evil is real, and God is all-powerful. Evil is real, and God has a good purpose for it. Evil is real. But it won't last forever.

REFLECT, EXPLORE, AND DISCUSS

1. What idea or concept stood out to you as you read this chapter? Why?

2. Read some of the Bible passages about the existence of evil and suffering referenced in this chapter. How do these passages encourage or challenge you?

3. What new questions do these passages raise?

4. Do you agree with the following statement?: "Evil only exists in contrast to good." Why or why not?

5. When you see the evils of the world, are you most prone to anger or despair? How can what you've read in this chapter encourage you?

GOD JUDGES

11

THE EVIL THAT WE DO

Why Everything That's Wrong with the World Is Wrong with the World

I have a generally low opinion of humanity. Let me explain. While some might call me a pessimist, I prefer to see myself as a realist. Why? Because I have *reasons* for having a low opinion of us all. After all, I've been a user of social media since around the time the term was first coined.[1] This means I've been around long enough to see the rise of all kinds of platforms and services, all vying to be the next big movement that would unite the world. But no matter how strong their start, they inevitably all fall into disarray. Open expression of ideas devolves into groupthink as people become insulated. Questioning the group's established orthodoxy is met with anger, vulgarity, threats, and rejection.[2] Individuals, particularly men, use private and, eventually, public channels to harass others, often women.[3]

While every organization aims to limit the degree of harm caused, these kinds of issues truly are inevitable. Why? Because *people* use these platforms and services—including people who feel free to say *exactly* what's on their minds at any given moment. And often, what's on their minds are things that no one with a lick of common sense would want to share with anyone. But as much as I want to sit in judgment over these types of people, I also recognize that they're not all that different from the rest of us, except that they say they don't feel the constraints that most of us do in our darkest moments.

There's another issue as well: this example is only a symptom of a larger problem. It's a problem that extends beyond social media and affects every area of life: education, commerce, entertainment, government, and so on. And it's not a new problem either. This problem has plagued human societies for as long as we've had societies. Technology merely offers a new way to amplify it. There's a reason that the Bible warns against the power of the tongue, after all (Proverbs 18:21).

So why are humans like this? Why do we, left to our own devices, build up people only to tear them down? Why do we "bite and devour" one another when given the opportunity (Galatians 5:15)? As tempting as it is to say that the reason is because we're just bad people, that response is too simplistic, and it is also not entirely accurate either. Instead, if we want to understand why we are the way we are, we must dig deeper into an issue we began wrestling with in the previous chapter. This mystery and problem that plagues us all—the existence of evil in the world.

One of our struggles in understanding this mystery is that we don't know where evil came from. It doesn't have an origin story. Or if it does, God did not feel it necessary to inspire the authors of the Bible to write it down. Instead, from God's point of view it seems to be enough that even though evil is real, it does not exist independently. It is a shade—a distortion, perversion, and subversion of good. And in the Bible, another word is often used to describe this distorting, perverting, and subverting of good: *sin*.

A MULTIFACETED WORD FOR ALL KINDS OF EVIL

Sin is a strange word for many people in Western society. It's not entirely foreign to us. In fact, we use it regularly. But we typically use it as shorthand for violating a cultural taboo, subverting a societal norm instead of an objective standard. It's a mistake, a lapse in judgment, or a poor decision, but rarely is it used to describe something more serious than that. This also means that we frequently use the word *sin* ironically, when we cheekily describe something as being bad for being so good. For example, go to a bakery where cinnamon rolls have been cleverly named "sin-amon rolls" to describe their deliciousness. (It's not that clever.) But this irony, perhaps ironically, isn't ironic at all. It's just one more way people downplay sin's seriousness and complexity.

So what is sin? Sin isn't one thing. It is a multifaceted term describing all human activity that is contrary to God's will and commands. To sin is to fall short, or to miss the mark, of God's glory and standards for humanity by consciously defying him in thought, word, and action (Romans 3:23), which may explain why the Bible uses so many metaphors to describe it. Sin is a weight or burden (Leviticus 10:17), a debt (Leviticus 5:1; 24:15), an impurity or defilement (Psalm 51:7), and a sickness (Mark 2:17).[4] It is a transgression, a deliberate violation of God's commands (Romans 5:14; 1 Timothy 2:14).

But one of the Bible's most striking descriptions of sin is as the behavior of petulant children rebelling against a loving parent—a slap across the face of the One who made us and shows us the way of life (Isaiah 1:2). This image is so powerful because it goes beyond actions and addresses the heart behind sin. Sin is rebellion, which in this sense, is an act of selfishness. It is putting ourselves first rather than others (Philippians 2:3), working off the assumption that happiness comes from getting whatever we think we want rather than from obedience to God. And ultimately, that sort of selfishness goes by another name: *idolatry*, which means to worship someone or something other than God (Romans 1:18-25). To be selfish is to have self-interest rule our hearts (Matthew 15:10-20; James 4:1-10). But we are terrible gods, and inevitably, where the heart leads us is disappointment.

So that's what sin is, at least as far as the metaphors go that are used to describe it. But where did sin come from? Well, just as with the topic of evil, God does not give us the origin story of sin. We don't know how sin came into being in the first place. But we do know what happened when human beings first sinned. And it's a story that begins shortly after the beginning of everything.

THE GOODNESS WE ENJOYED AT THE BEGINNING OF THE WORLD

Let's think back to the creation story found in the first two chapters of Genesis. The creation story has a purpose: It establishes God's authority over the entire universe because he is its maker. Everything that exists, and everything that has the *potential* to exist, is his handiwork (Psalm 19:1). He made it all, including human beings, and he called everything he made good. But the humans were not just good—they were very good. They were beings made in his image, created to uniquely represent him in the created world both in what we do and *what we are*, including in our maleness and femaleness. Everything was good and perfect and holy and wonderful, just as God intended. It was in a word, *paradise*.

It was also a world with two simple commands, one positive and one negative. The positive: To care for and cultivate the world God made (Genesis 1:28), harnessing its resources—including the fruit of its trees—responsibly for the benefit of all humanity. The negative: To not eat the fruit of one specific tree, the Tree of the Knowledge of Good and Evil, which was placed in the garden's center. Of that tree, God said, "You must not eat…for when you eat from it you will surely die" (Genesis 2:17).

For a time—though we don't know exactly for how long—the humans kept both of these commands. The man and woman cared for the garden and ate its fruit. They did not eat the fruit of the tree at the center. They lived at peace and joy with one another, partners united in their purpose. They lived at peace with God, walking in the garden with him.

THE BEGINNING OF THE WORLD AS WE KNOW IT

Then we get to Genesis 3, where things become a little different. In verse 1, we meet the serpent, a being that was "more shrewd" (NET), "more crafty" (NIV, ESV), or more "cunning" (NKJV, CSB) than any other creature. And this serpent wasn't just cunning and crafty; it could *talk*. And talk it did as it slithered up to Eve, the first woman, who for some reason was hanging out near the tree in the middle of the garden. And Adam, the first man, was right there with her.

"Did God really say, 'You can't eat from any tree in the garden'?" the serpent asked (Genesis 3:1 CSB). That might appear to be an innocent question, but in truth, it was anything but. The serpent had an agenda—a plan to cast doubt on God's character and goodness. And because it was (and is) crafty, it knew that it couldn't do such a thing openly. It had to sow seeds of doubt. And the best way to do that was to ask a question the humans already knew the answer to.

So the woman replied, "We may eat the fruit from the trees in the garden. But about the fruit of the tree in the middle of the garden, God said, 'You must not eat it or touch it, or you will die'" (verses 2-3 CSB). So far, so good. While some might question her adding the prohibition against touching the fruit, her answer was right: Eating that tree's fruit would lead to their death. And it was her correct answer that gave the serpent the opportunity it needed.

"No! You will certainly not die," the serpent said to the woman. "In fact, God knows that when you eat it your eyes will be opened and you will be like God, knowing good and evil" (verses 4-5 CSB).

And with that, the seeds of doubt were sown.

This was the serpent's temptation, his ploy to lure the humans into violating God's single prohibition. It was with the promise of something that sounded like it would be good, while also undermining God's goodness. Eating the tree's fruit would not lead directly to death. It would lead to *enlightenment,* to gaining knowledge that God was apparently withholding from them—a sense of moral autonomy, the ability to decide for themselves what is good and what is evil.[5] Knowledge that would make the man and the woman *like* God. *But if God were willing to withhold that kind of knowledge, if he was preventing them from being like himself in that respect, was he really as good as he appeared to be?*

If that seems familiar, it is because it's what we all continue to experience today. We are all tempted by different experiences, cravings, and desires that seem good. (Some are questionably good under the right circumstances.) But when we actually get what we think we want, we find that it is not good—or it's not what is best.

While we aren't privy to the internal or external conversations the first humans had with each other in that moment, it seems clear that they didn't think through what the serpent was telling them. They didn't stop and consider how they were *already* like God. They were made in his image as moral, rational, and relational beings. They already had the ability to discern right from wrong, good from evil, because they already knew what was good by virtue of knowing the *source* of all goodness. They were being offered what they already had. And they took it.

The woman saw that the tree's fruit was "good for food and delightful to look at, and that it was desirable for obtaining wisdom" (verse 6 CSB). She took the fruit, and she ate it. Then she handed it to the man, and he did as well. And as they swallowed the fruit, "the eyes of both of them were opened," but instead of gaining a greater sense of wisdom, all they found was guilt and shame (verse 7 CSB). Realizing they were naked, they covered themselves with fig leaves as they hid from one another—and from God (verses 7-10). Partners became adversaries, jockeying for position against one another, as everything meant to be joyous became frustrating and futile (verses 11-13). And when it was all over, they found that they would die (verses 16-19).

Thus began the world as we know it. And as we've all experienced, we are not fine.

WE BROKE THE WORLD AND OURSELVES

Everything that's wrong in the world started at that moment when the man and woman put themselves at the center of their own existence, when they made themselves the arbiters of right and wrong. A moment when they chose to be like God in a way that they were never meant to be, and it ruined everything.

And by everything, I mean *everything*. The unity humans enjoyed in the beginning was replaced with discord. Sin corrupted our relationships with one another, disrupted our relationship with God, and distorted our relationship with the world around us as the desire to sin became the default mode of the human heart. In ways we can't fully comprehend, that first act of sin distorted not only the first humans' desires but the desires of everyone who came after them as "death spread to all people" (Romans 5:12 CSB). We became "dead" in our sin, lost and confused as we live under the dominion of the power of sin, indulging the desires of our hearts, no matter the cost or consequences (Ephesians 2:1-3).[6] And then, when sin's work is complete, it kills us (Romans 6:23).

Sin ruined how humans treat each other. This is why we turn one another into objects—*things*—to be used and then discarded rather than people to be loved, respected, and cared for. It's why we build people up as heroes and icons, only to tear them down when they no longer entertain or satisfy us. And it's why we manipulate one another, preying on and amplifying fear to have our own way.

Then there's what we do with God. Despite his existence being plain to us—obvious because of how his "power and divine nature" are clearly seen in what he has made (Romans 1:19-20 CSB), we reject him. We act as though he doesn't exist, reimagining religious belief as simply a rung on the intellectual evolutionary ladder to be moved beyond. We might embrace the idea of a god, as long as he makes no demands upon us, or he conforms to our ideals. We accept substitutes—wealth, sex, money, and possessions—and when we find no satisfaction in them, we seek out another (Ecclesiastes 1–2).

Finally, we consume rather than steward the people and provisions within our influence. We use each other as a means to accomplish our own ends. We are made in God's image and spend our lives trying to return the favor, creating gods of our own imagining to worship (Isaiah 44:15). We claim to be wise, but we are fools (Romans 1:22).

Now, does it make sense why I have such a low opinion of humanity?

But sin's presence doesn't simply help make sense of why we are the way we are. It also helps us make sense of the ways the world seems to be falling apart. Think about it this way: Sin is a foreign element, something that doesn't belong in the world God made. It is, effectively, a virus. When we are sick, our bodies immediately respond to the presence of the intruder, attacking the virus with everything our immune systems can throw at it.

The world responds in a similar way. Radiation from the sun puts us at risk of cancer. Water turns chaotic and deadly whenever a storm begins. Hurricanes ravage both coastal and inland cities. Tornadoes rip through small towns. Droughts cause meager crops to wither and die. Earthquakes level buildings. Tsunamis move islands. And these instances don't occur as a direct act of divine judgment. They are evidence of the "futility" everything has been subjected to because of the presence of sin in the world (Romans 8:20). Like antibodies trying to combat an invasive virus, they are the ways in which the world "groans," longing for deliverance and healing from sin's presence and effects (Romans 8:22).

GOOD NEWS FOR A BROKEN WORLD

I might be realistic about humanity, but I am not hopeless. After all, there is good news for this broken world and its equally broken inhabitants. Without exception, we "all have sinned and fall short of the glory of God" (Romans 3:23). We are all without excuse for refusing to acknowledge and honor him. After the first people sinned, God would be well within his rights to have wiped out humanity and started from scratch. But he didn't. Before he cast them out of the garden, he also gave them a promise along with the curse: that even though they disobeyed God and would experience the consequences of that disobedience, even though they would die, death wasn't the end of their story. One of their offspring would destroy the serpent who deceived them (Genesis 3:15).

God then clothed them in animal skins, replacing their roughly fashioned coverings of leaves (verse 21). He sent them away from the garden, but they left with the hope of returning in some way. Adam and Eve did not live to see that hope fulfilled. They had children, who had more children, who had more children. And with each generation that hope was passed along, even as the evil in their hearts grew to the point that "every inclination of the thoughts of their minds was only evil all the time" (Genesis 6:5). And although God sent a flood to cleanse the earth of evil, he still didn't wipe out all humankind. He spared one man and his family for humanity to begin anew, knowing that the evil that resided in their hearts would grow once more (Genesis 6:9–9:17).

But this wasn't some failure on God's part. It wasn't as if he were being thwarted in making all things better, moving from plan *A* to plan *B* to plan *Z*, as humanity descended further into madness. In some inscrutable way, he had a purpose for every act and intervention, as if to remind us that there is no way to heal the damage sin does to us and the world externally. Something needs to change in us. Something that we can't make happen on our own. Something only God can do.

And then, at just the right time, God did. He sent his Son Jesus into the world, to *die* for those who were helpless (Romans 5:12). To make the dead live in and through him (Ephesians 2:4-5). And although our bodies will still die, death is not the end for us or for this world. Instead, we live with the promise that death itself will die and that sin will be destroyed. And make no mistake: Jesus *will* indeed destroy the serpent and a new world will result (Revelation 20:7-10), one where suffering and sadness will be no more because the curse will be no more. A world that will come about because Jesus will make all things new (Revelation 21:1-5).

EMBRACING HOPEFUL REALISM

Talking about sin is complicated. No matter what perspective we're coming at it from—whether you're reading this book as a committed Christian, you're curious about what it is Christians believe, or you simply have questions—our understanding of sin is a significant barrier for many. After all, few of us would call ourselves *evil*. Most of us aren't walking around actively plotting ways to harm others. And again, let's be honest: We all know people who reject Christianity and are among the kindest and most compassionate people around. Before I was a Christian, I had problems with this too. But it wasn't the we're-inclined-to-do-evil part that was difficult for me. (Again, that whole being realistic/pessimistic thing.) It was that we couldn't (and can't) make ourselves better. It was that we need help.

And the complicated aspect of Christianity's view of sin is that it demands that we be both honest *and* hopeful. Its portrayal of the state of humanity is jarring, even shocking, because we all—including Christians—want to think that we aren't really all that bad. None of us are perfect. We're all growing and learning. We all make mistakes. And sure, that's true insofar as it goes, but it's dishonest to treat that as the whole story. When we do that, we wind up going through life defiantly like the Black Knight, treating our significant and literally life-threatening condition as just a flesh wound, trying to wage war without arms and legs.[7] It's naïve and, frankly, a little silly.

Western Christians especially can be guilty of this. Sometimes we minimize sin to the degree that it seems like nothing is off limits at all. Or we are so self-righteous, that we see ourselves as better than people who don't believe as we do (and if we're honest, better than most of the people who share our beliefs as well). We act like "good people" are inside the "true" church and "bad people" are outside. But there isn't any kind of room for this sort of posturing or self-righteousness within the Christian life because the whole point of Christianity is that we don't have any righteousness of our own to begin with! If we did, we wouldn't need Jesus. The Bible is honest enough to tell us that we are even worse than we think we are on even our worst days. It confronts us with just how ugly sin is.

As honest as Christianity is about sin, it doesn't leave us without hope. Christians should be the most hopeful people around because we know what God has done about sin. Hopeful realists, but hopeful nonetheless. Remember, God gave us Jesus to save us, so that everyone who believes in him will not perish but have eternal life (John 3:16). Jesus died so that death would lose its hold and sin would lose its grip; he died so that we could live. And he did it for the joy of seeing his people perfected and this world redeemed forevermore (Hebrews 12:2). Because of Jesus, sin doesn't have the final word—Jesus does. And because Jesus has the final word, we have good news to tell.

REFLECT, EXPLORE, AND DISCUSS

1. What idea or concept stood out to you as you read this chapter? Why?

2. Read some of the Bible passages about sin and its effects on the world referenced in this chapter. How do these passages encourage or challenge you?

3. What new questions do these passages raise?

4. Do you see yourself as more pessimistic or more optimistic about people and the world? Why?

5. How can you embrace the Bible's hopeful realism?

GOD JUDGES

12

PEOPLE WHO LOVE WHAT THEY SHOULD HATE

We Are Not as Free as We Were Meant to Be (But We Can Be)

When I moved to the United States from my native Canada in 2016, I was unprepared for how contentious discussions around the concept of freedom could be. And I suppose, there's a sense in which I would never be prepared. After all, "freedom" is the nation's driving cultural value in a way that is distinct from every other Western nation. And if you don't grow up in a context where freedom is upheld as a value in the way it is in the US, it's hard to understand. (And, despite all the years I've lived here, I still don't know that I fully understand.)

In some ways, this puts me at a disadvantage when exploring important societal issues with my American friends. But being an insider-outsider also has its advantages because it means I don't have the same kind of blind spots that others might. It's a bit easier for me to see where some of that contention stems from. And when it comes to the subject of freedom, the greatest source of conflict comes from a lack of agreement around what freedom means in relation to societal responsibility. If freedom means that we are not coerced or constrained when making one decision over another, do personal freedom and societal responsibility conflict? If they do, which one takes precedence, or should one take precedence over the other?

Despite what pundits and politicians proclaim on cable news and social media, there are no easy answers to these kinds of questions. (If there were, we wouldn't all be fighting about it, would we?) But there's another level of complexity that enters the discussion as soon as we start thinking about freedom and responsibility in connection to our faith. It is a difficult topic, but a necessary one to discuss, so here we go.

TIPTOEING INTO ONE OF THE GREAT DEBATES

Within Christian circles, these discussions revolve around the concept of free will. That is, the idea that if God is as all-knowing and all-powerful as he says he is, if he is working behind the scenes in a way that we cannot fully comprehend, are any of our decisions voluntary? Are they even our decisions at all? Do we have the freedom to make choices? While we covered some of this ground in chapter 9, let's remember that the Bible doesn't try to explain the relationship between humanity's ability to make meaningful choices and God's sovereignty over literally everything we can think of (and everything beyond that too). It presents both conditions as being equally true and equally valid simultaneously. And the Bible does not explain *how* they work together, only that they do. It does not try to reconcile friends because friends need not be reconciled.[1]

Although the Bible offers a resounding yes/and to the question of God's sovereignty versus human responsibility, we should also know that this is one of the great debates within Christian circles. Teachers and theologians have explored this issue for millennia, especially in regard to human sin.

In fact, it was at the heart of one of the great controversies in the early church. In the late fourth and early fifth centuries, a heresy called *Pelagianism* emerged that emphasized humanity's ability and need to obey God. That basic emphasis was itself not scandalous, as the Bible does stress the need for obedience (1 John 2:3-6; 5:2-3) and calls people to choose to believe the gospel without qualification (Mark 1:15; Romans 10:11-13). However, as this teaching developed, it moved beyond a radical call to obedience toward a rejection of sin's effect on our nature. Adherents argued that sin does not reshape our desires or the inclination of our hearts (a view that conflicts with Romans 5:12). Instead, they began to teach that it is possible for humanity to freely obey and follow God's commands of their own will and inclination in the same way that Adam and Eve exercised in the beginning. A person could take the most important and fundamental steps toward salvation without any help or intervention from God.[2]

And that is where the problem arose. Despite Pelagius' views gaining traction among portions of the early church, it was not left unopposed. A teacher named Augustine, who served as the Bishop of Hippo (a coastal town in North Africa) and who became one of the most influential Christian teachers across time and tradition, was arguably Pelagianism's most vocal opponent. Without dismissing the need for human beings to obey God, Augustine emphasized that obedience was impossible apart from an act of God's grace without his help and empowerment.

> It is not nature (which, sold under sin and wounded by corruption, desires a savior and redeemer), nor is it knowledge of the law (through which comes the recognition,

rather than the expulsion, of concupiscence) which delivers us "from the body of this death," but "the grace of God, by Jesus Christ our Lord" (Romans 7:24-25).[3]

Even though Pelagius's teaching was eventually condemned as heresy—as being entirely contrary to Scripture's instruction—the question he raised still lingers: Why do we choose to sin, and can we choose not to? Or maybe a better way to say it is this: Are we *really* as free as we think we are?

As a new Christian, I didn't know much about, well anything, when it came to how this works. But I knew enough to know that the best place to find the answer was in the Bible. I just didn't expect to find it in the place I did, John's Gospel.

WE ARE NOT AS FREE AS WE THINK WE ARE

John's Gospel holds a special place in the hearts of many Christians. After all, it is the book that contains the most well-known verse in the entire Bible. The verse that someone inevitably holds up on a sign during a sports event, John 3:16:

> For God so loved the world that He gave His only begotten Son, that whoever believes in Him should not perish but have everlasting life (NKJV).

John is the Gospel that Christians most often recommend for people to read if they want to know who Jesus is. After all, it's the one written for the purpose of revealing Jesus' deity and inviting readers to believe in him (John 20:30-31).

But John is also a very challenging book. It challenges our ideas of what Christians are to be known for (and it even does this to those of us who *are* Christians). It pushes back against notions of personal or subjective truth as Jesus declares that he *is* the Truth (John 14:6). But this book is also the place where the Bible provides the answer to our questions about freedom. In John 8:31-36, Jesus tells us just how free we really are.

This passage is one of many where Jesus challenged a group of Judeans who said they believed in him. He did this by telling them what it means to be one of his *disciples* (that means someone who follows his teaching). Disciples are people who know the Truth—they know Jesus—and would be set free by him (John 8:31-32). But what would they be freed from? At the time, the Jewish people weren't in bondage to another nation. (Although Judea was not exactly free to rule itself, as like most of the world at the time, it was occupied by the Roman Empire.) They had a degree of self-governance, albeit limited.

From a spiritual standpoint, the idea that they were in bondage must have seemed even more strange. After all, they were God's chosen people—the descendants of Abraham, the man through whose offspring the Lord promised the entire world would be blessed (Genesis 12:3; 22:18; 26:4). They had never been enslaved—so how could Jesus tell them they would become free (John 8:33)? Yet this is exactly what Jesus *did* say:

> I tell you the solemn truth, everyone who practices sin is a slave of sin. The slave does not remain in the family forever, but the son remains forever. So if the son sets you free, you will be really free (John 8:34-36).

When Jesus said that everyone who practices sin is a slave of sin, he was revealing another aspect of sin's effects on humanity. Remember in Genesis, God made creation "very good" (Genesis 1:31)? Part of that very goodness meant that people were free in a way that we can't imagine. The first humans could choose to obey God, to honor and love him. They could also choose not to—which is exactly what they did.

Genesis 3 tells the story of how it all happened, but the bigger question is *why?* Why did the man and the woman choose to reject God instead of trusting their Creator? Well, think back to the temptation we talked about in the previous chapter: The temptation the serpent offered was enlightenment, this idea that mankind could gain the ability to determine for themselves right and wrong. A sense of moral autonomy apart from God's. Although the temptation was based on a lie and Adam and Eve were deceived by it, their actions ultimately boiled down to this: They disobeyed because they wanted to. They chose to reject God. They were free to do so, and their use of that freedom doomed us all to bondage because human nature was twisted and distorted by Adam's sin (Romans 5:12). The freedom the first humans enjoyed, the freedom that we were meant to enjoy, was lost to us. Humanity toppled into a bottomless pit of ever-increasing evil; the intentions of our thoughts and minds are set upon it (Genesis 6:12; 8:21).

Again, we need to be careful. When the Bible talks about evil in this sense, it does not intend to conjure up the images of cartoonish super-villainy. Because evil and sin are synonymous, it means that sin, this desire we all share to do whatever is contrary to God's will, became the default mode of our hearts. So strong is this inclination that when presented with the choice to sin or not to sin, we will *always* choose to sin (Romans 6:16). We can't help it; we can't *not* do it. Why? Because we are enslaved to it, as Jesus said.

LOVING WHAT IS DESTROYING US

Today, using a word like *enslaved* is risky. For many in the United States, it calls to mind a wickedness that still haunts the nation to this day. But this word matters; it is not present for shock value. It is the word Jesus used to describe the state of our hearts. Again, if we're not careful, we can misunderstand what he's saying.

When the Bible describes people as being enslaved to sin, we might then be tempted to believe that we aren't responsible for the sins we commit. After all, if we can't help ourselves—if this is something we do unwillingly—then isn't it unreasonable of God to hold us accountable for things we don't have a choice to do, or that we don't *want* to do?

On the surface, this question's logic makes some sense. God would be unreasonable—even cruel—to punish human beings for doing something they have no control over or didn't really want to do in the first place. But this is where the question's logic comes to the end of its connection with reality, because if we followed it to its conclusion, it would lead us right back to Pelagius. But that's not what God does because that's not what *we* do. It's not simply that we sin because we can't do otherwise (though this is certainly true). We aren't victims forced to do what we don't want to do. When we sin, it's because we want to. More than that, we sin because it's what we *love*.

From the beginning, sin has had this consuming effect on people. It is pictured as an animal ready to pounce on its prey (Genesis 4:7) and a seductress who, with sweet and smooth words, leads those who follow her to their destruction (Proverbs 5:1-5). It consumes our thoughts; it fills our desires. This is why the prophet Jeremiah called the human heart "more deceitful than anything else, and incurable" (Jeremiah 17:9 CSB). And this is why Jesus said that out of the mouth, the heart speaks: "For out of the heart come evil ideas, murder, adultery, sexual immorality, theft, false testimony, slander"—all the things that defile and destroy a person (Matthew 15:18-19). Our hearts are in love with sin. We love "darkness"—evil in the sense of defiance of God's will, of being our own moral authorities—instead of light, the truth that comes from God (John 3:19). This is the basis of God's judgment of sin. It's not simply because we do evil, although we do; it's because we *love* evil.[4]

We sin and we keep on sinning because, ultimately, it's what we love to do most of all. We don't want to do what's right. We love nothing else like we love what's wrong in God's sight. This is the ugly truth the Bible reveals. We are not free the way we think we are. Sin enslaves us. And we love that which enslaves us.

THE HARD TRUTH WE NEED TO HEAR

This idea puts Christianity at odds with Western society in so many ways, especially when it comes to the way we value freedom. We are self-oriented. We are radically individualistic in every aspect of our lives. We're encouraged to listen to our hearts. To do what feels good, whatever makes us happy. Because if it *feels* good then it must be right.

We are so self-focused that we even seek to redefine the concept of truth itself. No matter the issue, whether we're talking about the divides we experience over politics or what makes a person a person, we do it because we think we are free to do so. And while it might be tempting to read this as though I'm pointing at people who don't believe the same things (or the same way) that I do, that's not the case. Christians are just as guilty of this. We do it all the time. We seek to redefine God's commands to make them less off-putting and we sand away the rougher edges of Scripture. We might pretty it up or justify what we are doing by saying that we're trying to break down barriers between us and people who don't know Jesus, but the truth is, we do it because we want to. People who believe that Jesus lived, died, and rose again to rescue us from sin still struggle with sin. We are still tempted toward it. We still feel the phantom pull of the chains that Jesus removed when he set us free.

We're all in the same boat.

If Jesus had only said that we were enslaved to sin, this would be really bad news. But he didn't. Instead, he gave us this great news: We might not be as free as we think we are, but true freedom exists. And true freedom is found only in Jesus. Through his life, death, and resurrection, Jesus offers all who turn to him the kind of freedom we desperately need—the kind of freedom many of us don't even know we need.

A freedom that requires a new heart, one with new desires. A freedom that breaks the chains sin creates around us and allows us to honor and obey Jesus. To trust in him as our only hope. And that's the good news that we need right now. No matter who we are, no matter our background, as we search for freedom Jesus is who we need. Jesus came to set us free—and those whom the Son sets free are truly free indeed.

REFLECT, EXPLORE, AND DISCUSS

1. What idea or concept stood out to you as you read this chapter? Why?

2. Read some of the Bible passages about our relationship with sin referenced in this chapter. How do these passages encourage or challenge you?

3. What new questions do these passages raise?

4. How does the language of captivity or enslavement to sin make you feel? Why?

5. In what ways do you see the love of sin playing out in your own life?

GOD RESCUES

13

ACCORDING TO A PLAN FOR THE WHOLE UNIVERSE

The Gospel Is Good News for You, Me, and Even Those Who Don't Believe It

If you could sit down and have a conversation with anyone, living or dead, of any background or language, who would it be? This isn't an easy choice for me to make. There are so many people who I think would be great to interact with. The three men I introduced at the beginning of this book—J.I. Packer, G.K. Chesterton, and C.S. Lewis—would absolutely be on this list. The same goes for Martin Luther, the German monk who kicked off the Protestant Reformation. (To call him interesting is an understatement.) I'd love talking about storytelling, pop music, and comic books with any number of my favorite writers too. For people who know me well, none of these suggestions are a surprise. But one choice that might surprise others, is that one of the people I most wish I could have a conversation with is the late Christopher Hitchens.

Hitchens was one of the most ardent proponents of not only atheism, but *antitheism*, of the early to mid-2000s. He didn't simply believe that there is no God. His view was that disbelieving in a higher power was a fundamentally good thing. He was openly hostile toward religion in general, and the Abrahamic faiths—Christianity, Judaism, and Islam—in particular. He saw the Bible as an instrument of evil, calling it a book put together by "crude, uncultured human mammals" that gave warrant for human trafficking, "for ethnic cleansing, for slavery, for bride-price, and for indiscriminate massacre."[1] (Is it any wonder he felt that no one was bound to follow anything it commands?) In Hitchens's view, religion had nothing to offer the world—any good that could be seen as incidental, and any virtues they taught or engendered were co-opted from our innate being.

As you can imagine, he and I would disagree on a lot. Like, pretty much everything.

But as hostile as he was toward religion and as strong a voice for unbelief as he appeared, he was also an advocate for rationality and intellectual honesty. He saw inconsistencies clearly and called those who made them to task, no matter what side of the debates they were on. And that's why I would love to have a conversation with him. It's not because I would want to debate with him; it's that I find honesty refreshing.

This is probably why one of my favorite Hitchens moments came in December 2009, when he was interviewed by Marilyn Sewell for *Portland Monthly*. Sewell, a Unitarian minister and self-described liberal Christian,[2] recognized Hitchens's tendency to cite what she described as "fundamentalist" sources in his books.[3] As one who doesn't take the stories of Scripture literally and doesn't believe in the doctrine of atonement (keep reading, we'll get there), she wanted to know if he distinguished between "fundamentalist faith and liberal religion." That is, in Hitchens's mind, was the problem all religion or just the dogmatic kind—and was his issue with all Christians or just the "fundamentalist" sort? His response was brief but breathtaking:

> I would say that if you don't believe that Jesus of Nazareth was the Christ and Messiah, and that he rose again from the dead and by his sacrifice our sins are forgiven, you're really not in any meaningful sense a Christian.[4]

Why would I call this *breathtaking*? After all, it reads a bit like he sidestepped Sewell's question. But really, he didn't. While Hitchens later described himself as having no quarrel with Sewell's brand of religion because both believe none of Christianity is true, he understood and could clearly explain the core message of Christianity. He knew the essential points of the gospel, even if he didn't believe it.

SKETCHING, DISTILLING, AND MIXING METAPHORS

Before I became a Christian, I didn't even have a sense of the essentials of the gospel. Hitchens knew those points far better than I did. It also wasn't a concern for me since I didn't care. Even as I began moving toward the faith, I was starting to get a sense of it, but that sense was fuzzy. It was more like a sketch on the back of a napkin than a fully realized illustration. The shape was there, but there were few details. Sometimes, how we typically describe the gospel—Jesus died and rose again—seems a bit like that. It's a sketch; what we're saying is true, but it can be a bit simplistic.

As I read the Bible and began to discover the expansiveness of the gospel and its effects, I started to see how important that expansiveness is. The scope of the gospel and its effects are cosmic, affecting everything, everywhere, throughout all time. It is a story, one that began before the "foundation of the world" (Ephesians 1:4), before God created anything that was, is, or will be. And this story runs throughout the entire Bible from beginning to end, as it describes this arc that moves from the creation of the world that we know to the coming of a new and better creation. A new heaven and a new earth where everything that is wrong in the world because of sin—death, suffering, guilt, shame, poverty, greed, racism, abuse, and every other ill that plagues us—will be no more (Isaiah 25:8; 2 Peter 3:13; Revelation 21:1). A renewed and restored world where God will live with his people forever. And the climax of this story, the moment that changes everything, centers on an event involving one man: the death and resurrection of Jesus of Nazareth.

But can you imagine what it would be like to start at the beginning of creation every time you wanted to talk about Jesus with someone? Or what it would be like to be the person listening? I don't think it would go well for anyone involved. Even the Bible itself doesn't do this. Instead, throughout the New Testament, the writers distill this message of good news. Writers focused on what was most essential for the moment and for the people they were writing to in a way that invited them to explore its depths for themselves.

That distillation can be as simple as a sentence, like John 3:16: "This is the way God loved the world: He gave his one and only Son, so that everyone who believes in him will not perish but have eternal life." The Bible can focus on how the gospel solves our sin problem in a more profound sense, with a picture of our hopeless state, as it does in Ephesians 2:4-5. It can also take a more personal, intimate approach, as in Galatians 2:20, where Paul wrote that he lived "because of the faithfulness of the Son of God, who loved me and gave himself for me."

THE ESSENTIAL GOSPEL

One of the best distillations might be 1 Corinthians 15:3-7, a passage written by a man named Paul to remind Christians in the city of Corinth what is of "first importance":

> Christ died for our sins according to the scriptures, and that he was buried, and that he was raised on the third day according to the scriptures, and that he appeared to Cephas, then to the twelve. Then he appeared to more than five hundred of the brothers and sisters at one time, most of whom are still alive, though some have fallen asleep. Then he appeared to James, then to all the apostles.

This is the passage we should turn to if we're looking for a clear picture of the gospel's essentials. In the first sentence alone, Paul captured the center of the core of the message—three points that comprise the traditional sketch of the gospel that many Christians can recite almost without thinking.

"Christ died." Despite how we might read it, *Christ* is not a last name. It is a title given to Jesus of Nazareth that is tied to promises and prophecies of an anointed one, a servant of God, that we'll look at in the coming chapters. But what Paul really wanted people to know is that Jesus died. He really, truly died (Matthew 27:50; John 19:30). After all, this is what crucifixion was designed to do—to kill a person. It was the punishment reserved for the worst of criminals. The way the Bible describes it, even the Romans, who specialized in making this death as drawn out and painful as possible, were surprised at how quickly Jesus died. They even pierced his side with a spear to make sure he was really dead before they took him down from the cross (John 19:34).

"He was buried." They didn't leave Jesus hanging on the cross or take his body down and throw it in a mass grave. His body was taken by his followers and placed in a proper tomb that belonged to a man named Joseph of Arimathea (Matthew 27:57-58; John 19:38-42). His body was wrapped in linen cloths and spices, which was part of Jewish custom at the time; a massive stone was rolled in front of the entrance to the tomb; officials stationed a guard to make sure no funny business occurred; and everyone thought that was the end of things (Matthew 27:59-66). And it was; until it wasn't.

"He was raised on the third day." Throughout the later days of his ministry, Jesus kept talking about being arrested, beaten, and then killed. But he always ended by saying, "On the third day, he will be raised" (Matthew 20:17-19; see also 16:21; 17:22-23). In saying this, Jesus was referring to Old Testament prophecies that, sometimes obliquely, hinted that death would not be the end of the story for God's anointed one (Psalm 16:9-10; Isaiah 53:10-12; Hosea 6:2). And on the third day, early in the morning, several women who followed Jesus went to the tomb and found the stone rolled away and his body gone (Luke 24:1-3), and the cloth that covered his face folded neatly on the slab on which he had been laid (John 20:7), as two angels told them, "He is not here" (Luke 24:4-7).

This declaration is truly what makes the gospel good news. The resurrection was the proof that all Jesus intended to do had been accomplished—that, as we'll see in chapter 16, the debt of sin has been paid. Death has been defeated, no longer having the last word, because Jesus is alive.

"Christ died…was buried…[and] was raised on the third day" truly is the purest distillation of the gospel message we can offer. It represents the defining truth that makes Christians *Christian*. It is the truth that we offer to the world as good news because we really do believe it is good news! It is the key to peace with God now and forever. It is the truth that brings hope and healing. And without it, we would be trapped forever vacillating between thumbing our noses at God and trying in vain to earn his approval. And we must understand that whatever else we might say about Jesus, whatever else we could say about his compassion and kindness, the wisdom of his teaching, or his uncompromising conviction, if we don't talk about his death, burial, and resurrection, we aren't talking about the gospel.

But Paul's distillation of the gospel didn't stop with those three points. He had two other elements that he considered vital, both of which invite us to explore the depths of what was of first importance.

"According to the scriptures." God did not keep Jesus' death and resurrection a secret, as though it was a birthday present hidden away until the big day arrived. Throughout the Old Testament, God revealed his plan to rescue the world through patterns, prophecies, signs, and symbols that we are encouraged to explore. Following his resurrection, Jesus himself even interpreted "the things written about himself in all the scriptures" as he walked with two disciples on the way to a town called Emmaus (Luke 24:27). Psalms 16; 22; 31; 118; and Isaiah 52:13–53:12, are just a few of the dozens of passages that help us to see how Jesus died and was raised again on the third day, according to the Scriptures.

"He appeared." Paul didn't simply say that Jesus rose from the dead. He named specific people who saw him. Jesus appeared to Cephas (also known as Peter), who was one of the first of Jesus' disciples and one of his closest friends. The rest of the 12 apostles, Jesus' closest companions in his three-year ministry in Judea, also saw him. One of them, Thomas, even refused to believe that Jesus had really returned until he saw him with his own eyes (Jesus did him one better and encouraged him to touch the wounds in his hands and side, see John 20:24-28). Throughout the 40 days between his resurrection and ascension (Acts 1:8), Jesus was seen by large groups of people. Even James, Jesus' brother[5] who eventually became a church leader in Jerusalem, saw him and believed that Jesus was the one God promised to send and restore his people.

Paul emphasized these two realities because he wanted people to know that the gospel wasn't something made up by him and others like him. The story of Jesus' death and resurrection wasn't some kind of fanciful imagining, or worse, a lie invented to take advantage of people. There were people that the Corinthians could speak with, people who were alive at that time, who had seen Jesus with their own eyes. These were people who had met Jesus face to face and could verify everything Paul wrote.

More than that, Paul wanted the Corinthians—and us today, 2,000 years removed from these events—to study the Scriptures for ourselves. He wanted us to see how the Bible does, in fact, testify about Jesus from beginning to end—not only in the New Testament, but in the Old Testament as well. That, "in the beginning," Jesus was present (Genesis 1:1; John 1:1). That the plan to rescue and redeem the world was not an afterthought or a last straw. It was God's intention from before the world was made (Ephesians 1:4). That the gospel changes the world because it changes people. Paul wanted us to look at Scripture this way because he knew that when we do, the Bible starts to make sense in a way that it never will without Jesus at its center—that it is a story of good news for the whole world.

THE STORY THAT MAKES THE BIBLE MAKE SENSE

For all that I admire about Christopher Hitchens and his desire for people to be intellectually honest, this is something he couldn't see. And because he couldn't see it, he couldn't deal with the Bible honestly. Despite knowing the sketch of the gospel event, he couldn't see the gospel story running through the pages of Scripture.

What he saw were commands, codes of conduct, and atrocities. He saw a book that, if followed, gave license to perpetuate evil in the world. And some have tried to use it this way, justifying horrible acts in the name of following God's commands.[6] But when we understand that the whole Bible leads us toward Jesus, we can see how it inspires us toward a life of devotion, to revel in God's glory and goodness. It inspires us to give thanks for the good news of what God has done to rescue us. We find our hope in the promises we have of a better world to come. We obey God's commands out of gratitude for it all. And we who believe have the privilege of sharing this good news with everyone.

Even if some of what we must share seems a little strange.

REFLECT, EXPLORE, AND DISCUSS

1. What idea or concept stood out to you as you read this chapter? Why?

2. Read some of the Bible passages about the gospel referenced in this chapter. How do these passages encourage or challenge you?

3. What new questions do these passages raise?

4. How would you explain the essential points of the gospel?

GOD RESCUES

14

BY BECOMING A HUMAN BEING

The Strangest Thing Christians Believe

There are many parts of Christianity that those of us who have been Christians for any significant amount of time can start to take for granted. I don't mean we ignore their importance (although we sometimes do that too). It's more that we forget how unusual they might seem to someone who is on the outside looking in. There are parts of our faith that, despite being true, seem downright strange. Maybe you've felt that way as you've read through one chapter or another in this book, leading up to now. The Trinity—God existing as three persons united in essence and will but distinct from one another—is one of those difficult truths that has caused more than one person to stumble into believing, and even promoting, heresy. The same is true of God's providential work, the inspiration of Scripture, and the mystery of the existence of evil.

Even the gospel itself can be a source of confusion for many. After all, the gospel is central to the Christian faith. In fact, there is no Christianity without the gospel—the truth that is summarized so beautifully in 1 Corinthians 15:3-4, "That Christ died for our sins according to the scriptures, and that he was buried, and that he was raised on the third day according to the scriptures." Much of that confusion centers around the one Paul called "Christ"—*Jesus*.

What is it about Jesus that causes confusion for some people? For a *very* small minority of vocal opponents of religion in general, it's a question of whether he existed at all.[1] For others, it's confusion about whether the claims of Christianity are a distortion or mythologizing of a real man, Jesus of Nazareth.[2] And then there are the questions from Christians themselves. Specifically, we look at Jesus in the four Gospels, and we can very clearly see that he is a human being. But we can also see that the Gospels (and the rest of the New Testament) assign him a divine status. So how can these two things be true if God is not a human being—if he is eternal, uncreated, without a physical body, and exists outside of space and time? How can Jesus be both divine and a human being?

THE TRUTH ABOUT JESUS' NATURE(S)

Before becoming a Christian, I didn't think about this too much (not that I thought about much of anything related to Christianity, of course). But that doesn't mean I didn't have assumptions about Jesus, as noncommittal as those assumptions might have been. A little over 2,000 years ago, was there a real person named Jesus from the town of Nazareth? I would have said, probably. But if he did exist, he likely was a normal guy whose followers made more of him than he actually was. That, or he was insane (or a cult leader, which is its own kind of insanity). Really, who can say? Whatever the case, the idea of Jesus being any kind of god was a nonstarter for me until I read the Bible for the first time. In those early days, I found that I couldn't avoid this question of who Jesus is.

First, Jesus is divine. Despite being difficult for most of us who lean toward skepticism to accept, the entire New Testament doesn't shy away from asserting Jesus' divinity. And by *divine*, I don't mean that the New Testament authors make him out to be some kind of demigod akin to mythical figures like Hercules, Orpheus, Achilles, or Maui. Jesus isn't a small-*g* god, either, as though he were a lesser being in a hierarchy of divine beings.

Instead, as you read in chapter 1, Jesus is the "exact expression of [God's] nature" (Hebrews 1:3 CSB). He is the Word who was "with God" and "was God" in the beginning, before anything else existed (John 1:1-3 CSB). He is the One through whom all things were created, and all things hold together (Colossians 1:15-17). Jesus does what only God can do, like forgive sins (Mark 2:5-12; John 10:28; 17:2). He is equal with God the Father in every way (Matthew 26:63-64; John 8:58; 10:30; 17:5; Philippians 2:6).

Second, Jesus is a human being. This might seem like a given, but it really isn't. Jesus' humanity has been central to some of the great controversies and heresies that plagued the early church. One of the most common heresies was that Jesus wasn't really human at all; he only *appeared* that way.[3]

But this is not the way the Gospels depict Jesus both before and after his resurrection. The Gospels describe him as being born in the same way people are—a real human being with a real human mother (Luke 2:1-7). And he didn't emerge from the womb as a fully grown human being. He was a baby who did all the things babies do, which means, despite what you might have heard in a well-known Christmas carol, there was at least *some* crying he made.[4]

Not only that, but Jesus also grew in the way children do. And even though he amazed the religious leaders in the temple when he was a child, he also learned the same way other children learn (Luke 2:41-52). He was hungry and thirsty (Mark 14:12-25; John 4:7; 19:28). He slept (Matthew 8:24). Jesus experienced pain, grief, and even temptation (Matthew 4:2; John 11:35). He was a real flesh-and-blood person who could be touched, hugged, leaned against, and even slapped (Matthew 26:67; 27:30; John 13:25). He still is. He understood the human condition because he is one of us—he can sympathize with our weakness because he has experienced it all (Hebrews 4:15).

The New Testament simultaneously holds up these two realities: that Jesus is a single person with two natures, one divine and one human, "without confusion, without change, without division, without separation."[5] The man Jesus of Nazareth is inseparable from God the Word, just as the Word is inseparable from the man. Jesus did not, at some point in his life, gain divine status or power. It was not granted to him when he was baptized in the Jordan and the Holy Spirit descended and rested upon him (Matthew 3:13-17). His divine nature is eternal—it is who he has been from before the beginning of everything. There was never a time when Jesus did not exist as the Word. But at a specific moment, the eternal Word *became* a human being.

Which, of all the things Christians believe that seem strange to those on the outside looking in, this might be the strangest thing of all.

WHY GOD BECAME A HUMAN

Jesus taking on human form, becoming one of us, is called the *incarnation*, a Latin word that means "to make flesh." Throughout the Old Testament, there were moments when different people had encounters with a being whom they recognized as God himself. Abraham and Sarah, who entertained the Lord (Genesis 18:1-33). Jacob, who wrestled with God in the night on the way to meet his brother Esau (Genesis 32:24-29). Joshua, who met with the commander of the Lord's armies (Joshua 5:13-15). Isaiah, who was given a vision of the Lord's throne room and saw the Lord in his splendor (Isaiah 6:1-13).

But Jesus' incarnation was not merely the appearance of God in human form. "The incarnation means that he who never began to be in his specific identity as Son of God, began to be what he eternally was not."[6] In his incarnation, God the Son, the second person of the Trinity, actually became one of us. He took on human flesh, looking like other humans and "sharing in human nature" (Philippians 2:7). But even as he was one of us, he was different from us: he was without sin. He was unencumbered by the chains that ensnare us; the ones that, left to our own devices, we love dearly.

Why did he do this? Why would God the Son leave his glorious state to become one of us? He did it so that he might rescue us—that sin would be "condemned...in the flesh" (Romans 8:3). He humbled himself to endure humiliation on our behalf, dying on a cross, becoming "sin for us, so that in him we might become the righteousness of God" (2 Corinthians 5:21 NIV). Jesus' humiliation would be turned into exaltation because of his resurrection from the dead in his defeat of sin and death, followed by his return to his glorious state at the right hand of the Father.

HOW GOD BECAME A HUMAN

While the idea of the incarnation might seem ridiculous today, it was hardly shocking in the earliest days of Christianity, especially as those first believers of the Way (Acts 9:2) interacted with Greek and Roman culture. For example, Greek mythology had a category for gods taking on human form, although the purpose of doing so was usually to have sex with someone (or something) that caught their eye. This was not the case with Jesus.

The details of Jesus' incarnation are different than anything else you might read about seemingly similar events, many of which emerged only centuries after Jesus was born, died, and rose again. And the difference wasn't only in the purpose behind Jesus' incarnation. The difference was in how it happened. And understanding that starts with a prophecy, several actually.

The first prophecy goes back to that day in the garden when the first humans sinned and were cast out. Embedded in the curse, the consequences of their sin, God gave Eve a promise: that there would be enmity—hostility—between her offspring and the offspring of the serpent. Eventually, one of the woman's offspring would come, and that enmity would reach its turning point. The serpent would harm him, but he would destroy it (Genesis 3:15).

As the centuries passed and humanity filled the earth, the promise stayed with them, if only lingering in the background. And as the Bible's narrative unfolded, the prophecy grew in clarity. This promised offspring would not be any person—he would be a king, the descendant of a king who was promised to have a son who would rule over a kingdom that would never end (2 Samuel 7:16). A descendant whom that king, David, would call Lord (Psalm 110:1). And this king would be called many names, including the Son of Man (Daniel 7:13-14), the Son of David (Isaiah 11:1), and the Son of God (2 Samuel 7:14; Psalm 2:7).[7] He was the *Messiah*, or the *Christ*, two titles meaning "anointed one."[8] And how would the people know that this son, this king—the Messiah—had arrived? "The Lord himself will give you a sign: See, the virgin will conceive, have a son, and name him Immanuel" (Isaiah 7:14 CSB; see also Micah 5:3).[9]

For roughly 700 years, God's people waited for this prophecy to be fulfilled, with many undoubtedly uncertain of what it could mean. Did Isaiah mean a young woman who would conceive and give birth to a child the way children are typically conceived and born? Or was this a young woman who was a virgin who would become pregnant with a child—one who had no biological father?

Would the Messiah's arrival be natural, or would it be a supernatural act of God?

And this is when the Gospels introduce us to a young woman, most likely a teenager, named Mary. One night as Mary prayed, something not heard of for centuries happened, an angel from the Lord—Gabriel—appeared.[10] "Greetings, favored one," the angel said, "the

Lord is with you" (Luke 1:28). Mary was confused and, no doubt, terrified. (Wouldn't you be if a supernatural being showed up in front of you?) What was happening? Why was this angel calling her "favored"? Mary was no one special. She wasn't well-known or important. She was ordinary. Nevertheless, the angel insisted that she had found favor with God, just as so many others who seemed unimportant or insignificant had done throughout history. And God's favor was going to be shown in a very specific way: She would become pregnant and give birth to a son, whom she was to name Jesus. He would be called "the Son of the Most High"—the Son of God—and he would be a king whose kingdom would never end (Luke 1:30-33).

We'll come back to this idea of Jesus being a king in the next chapter, so for the moment, let's focus on what the angel said was about to happen. Although Mary was engaged, she and her husband-to-be Joseph were not yet married. As a God-fearing Jewish couple, they had not yet consummated their relationship. So Mary being pregnant while still unmarried would raise some questions: Had she and Joseph gotten ahead of themselves? Had she been unfaithful to him? Would Joseph believe her?

And there would not just be the questions. The situation would have implications for how her life would unfold in a way that we might not grasp in our time and culture. Today, an unmarried woman, or even a teenager, becoming pregnant is not all that scandalous. It happens and is even expected in a society where marriage is uncommon. But for Mary, it would mean, at best, being ostracized—rejected—by her entire community. Things would only be worse if Joseph chose to end their relationship altogether. She would be left alone with a child to raise and have no support.

All of this must have been running through her mind as she asked, "How will this be, since I have not had sexual relations with a man?" (Luke 1:34). The angel explained that this would not be a normal pregnancy: Her child would be conceived through the power of God, he would be called the Son of God, and he would be holy—perfect, pure, and set apart—because he is God (Luke 1:35). The Word, God the Son, became the Son of God, as he took on flesh and dwelt among us (John 1:14).

While undoubtedly still confused and frightened, Mary trusted this was the Lord's will (Luke 1:38). Even Joseph, although he initially planned to end their relationship quietly when he learned what had happened, accepted that this was the Lord's work after the angel visited him as well (Matthew 1:18-25). The two were married but did not consummate their marriage until after the child, whom they named Jesus, was born in the town of Bethlehem, the home of Joseph's ancestor David, the great king of Israel (Luke 2:1-7).

IT'S OKAY TO EMBRACE THE STRANGE

Do you see why someone—maybe even *you*—might find all this a bit unusual, perhaps even strange? For a baby to be conceived without two people being involved in some capacity seems ridiculous to our sensibilities. And for two natures—human and divine—to exist within one person seems impossible.

So I can understand why someone might think the claims of Jesus' deity are a bit of mythologizing, the result of the stories of Jesus becoming sensationalized over time. It's the same reason I can understand why someone might prefer to believe that the whole story was borrowed from other religions entirely (even similar stories only appeared centuries after Christianity came onto the scene, or they require significant feats of mental gymnastics to draw a parallel).[11] I can even understand why someone might believe that the story of the virgin birth was an elaborate cover-up to hide that Mary had been unfaithful to Joseph, even if it does her an extreme disservice. These scenarios are easier to believe than to hold to the belief that Jesus is both fully God and fully human; one person with two natures. God in the flesh, born of a human woman, and with no human father.

But easy doesn't mean honest. And honest is what we all want to be, isn't it? For those of us who are Christians, being honest means admitting that there are parts of our faith that seem strange to anyone who doesn't believe it. What seems clear to us might be hard for someone else to understand and can even be frustrating for them in many ways. And if you're reading this and you feel that way, please know that I get it. I once was where you are now. What I now believe about Jesus didn't make sense to me before I believed it either. And even now, there are parts that are still a mystery—parts that I don't think anyone can ever fully understand.

These are things about which we can only know in part because we can only see them in part (1 Corinthians 13:9-12). But what I hope we all see clearly is that these things that sometimes seem so strange are really good news for the whole world. The man Jesus was a human being. The man Jesus is God in human form. And he came into this world to heal the divide between God and humanity.

REFLECT, EXPLORE, AND DISCUSS

1. What idea or concept stood out to you as you read this chapter? Why?

2. Read some of the Bible passages about Jesus' two natures referenced in this chapter. How do these passages encourage or challenge you?

3. What new questions do these passages raise?

4. Why is the virgin birth so important to Jesus' nature? What would change if it wasn't true?

5. What are the most challenging elements of Christianity for you to embrace? Why?

GOD RESCUES

15

AS A MEDIATOR WHO WILL NEVER FAIL

How Jesus Is Better Than the Best

Over our time as a couple, and especially as parents, my wife and I have become skilled in the art of mediation. I wouldn't send us in to resolve a global conflict or anything like that, but we do a solid job of creating, enhancing, and restoring peace in relationships by finding solutions that we can all either live with, or at the very least, all be equally unhappy with. This is something that you can only learn through years of practice.[1] And when people share lives and homes together, conflict is inevitable. Why? Because sometimes, even people who love one another deeply have moments when they love themselves just a little bit more.

Fights between our children. Arguments with one another. Arguments *with* our children. Most of the time, we're able to resolve these with face-to-face communication, which usually means a lot of open-ended questions. But there have been times, usually in conflicts between our kids, where we've had to serve as intermediaries. We act as go-betweens trying to bridge the resentment and communication gap between the two squabbling parties. Sometimes our efforts work, and peace is restored. Other times…well, we're working on it.

There has (almost) always been a need for mediators in person-to-person relationships, but mediators play an increasingly important role today in almost every part of modern society. Translators mediate messages across languages. Technology acts as a bridge over which people who live hundreds or thousands of miles away from each other can build extremely limited forms of relationships. Books allow authors to speak to and play a role in the lives of people they might never meet. (Thanks for reading this book, by the way.)

THE MEDIATORS TO PREPARE US

When it comes to God, we have mediators too, although we haven't always needed them. Remember that, in the beginning, the first people lived in the garden with God (Genesis 2:4-25). They spoke to one another face to face. They had an unfettered relationship with God. And that's important because, as his image bearers, it's what human beings were created for. We represent God to the world, yes, but we were also made to enjoy his presence. To *enjoy* him.

Then, the first people sinned and ruined everything. Their sin ruined—severed—their relationship with God (Isaiah 59:2). Their access had become inhibited, as it has been for every subsequent generation, as our love of what destroys us consumes us. Left to our own devices, we cannot have the relationship with our Creator that we were made for. But even though we don't want it naturally, we still need it. And even when we realize we do need it, we find out that we need help; the divide between us is too vast. We need a mediator, someone to stand between us and God, to bridge the chasm that sin created. So God provided these mediators in the form of prophets, priests, and kings.

Prophets: Communicators of God's Will

While not an official office—although some formally served as advisors to kings and officials—prophets were messengers sent to speak to God's people, some of whom also performed signs and wonders (miracles) meant to confirm that they really were sent from the Lord. We often think about prophets as offering visions of the future, which some most certainly did as they warned of the rise and fall of kings and kingdoms, what was then future judgment, and restoration. However, their primary purpose was to communicate God's will and commands in what was then, the present—to warn against sin and to encourage people toward ongoing faithfulness. It's no surprise then, that prophets played strategically significant roles within the Old Testament's overall narrative as the people struggled with fidelity and rushed headlong into idolatry.[2]

The greatest of the Old Testament prophets was Moses. He was a Hebrew, but he was raised as a member of the Egyptian pharaoh's family, after being adopted by Pharaoh's daughter when he was a baby. When he grew up, he saw a guard treating Hebrew workers cruelly. In anger, Moses killed the guard. Fearing for his life, he fled to the nearby land of Midian, where he remained for 40 years (Exodus 2). From a burning bush, God spoke to him, commanding Moses to return to Egypt and demand that Pharaoh free the Israelites from their bondage (Exodus 3). When Pharaoh refused (Exodus 5:1-5), God judged Egypt by sending ten plagues through Moses; each one intended to show God's power over the gods of Egypt (Exodus 12:12). Water turned to blood. Frogs, gnats, and flies swarmed. Livestock died. Boils erupted on the Egyptian people. Hail destroyed their crops. Locusts consumed what was left. Darkness covered the land. And finally, death came for the firstborn of every family (Exodus 7–12).

When the Israelites were free, Moses led them into the wilderness to prepare them to live as God's chosen people and toward the land they were meant to inherit (Exodus 19). It was through Moses that God established a covenant, a binding promise with the Israelites, and gave them the Law—the code of religious and civil conduct meant to identify the Israelites as God's people (Exodus 20:1-7; Deuteronomy 4:44). It was Moses who led the people to the promised land, and away from it when they were overcome by their fear (Numbers 13–14). Moses interceded for the people (Exodus 32:30-33). He spoke to God as a person speaks to their friends; he knew God face to face (Exodus 33:11; Deuteronomy 34:10). His face shone with the light of God's glory (Exodus 34:29-35). And when Moses died, it was God who buried him (Deuteronomy 34:5-6).

Priests: Representatives of God's People

But prophets were not the only mediators God provided. There were also priests. Priests were different than prophets (although some were also prophets), in that theirs was a formal office. Beginning with Moses' brother Aaron and the Levites (Exodus 28:1-4), the priests were responsible for teaching God's commands (Deuteronomy 33:10), maintaining the tabernacle (or tent of meeting) and later the temple (Numbers 3:21-26), and offering prayers and sacrifices on behalf of the people (Leviticus 1–7). They were intercessors, representing the people to God and God to his people, as they stood in the gap between both.

The most important of the priests under the Jewish sacrificial system was the high priest, who played a unique role in one of the most important festivals of Israel's worship calendar, the Day of Atonement. On that day—and that day only—the high priest entered the Holy of Holies, where God's presence resided in the temple, which was separated from the rest of the temple by a massive, thick, purple linen veil. After completing an elaborate set of cleansing rituals, symbolically purifying himself to be able to enter the presence of God, the high priest would present the blood of a sacrificial lamb to the Lord as atonement—payment or reparation—for the sins of the people (Leviticus 16).

But there was another, more mysterious priest about whom we know relatively little, but has been the source of endless speculation: Melchizedek. He was the king of Salem, later known as Jerusalem, and was also said to be a priest of "God Most High" (Genesis 14:18 CSB).[3] Abram (later known as Abraham) met Melchizedek as he was preparing to meet with the king of Sodom. Melchizedek blessed Abram, and Abram gave him a tenth of all he had as a gift (Genesis 14:19-20). Nowhere else in the *narrative* of Scripture does Melchizedek appear again. This is what makes him such an enigma. He has no background and no genealogy. There is no explanation of how he came to be a priest of God. He simply was, and then, was not. The mystery around his background led to much speculation about his identity, with him gradually taking on the characteristics of a semi-divine Messianic figure.[4] Whatever the case, Melchizedek is a priest of a different sort, of a higher order than the priests of the Mosaic law, from an eternal priesthood that would endure forever. An order fit for a righteous king (Psalm 110:4).

Kings: Administrators of God's Justice

Finally, there were kings who served as mediators of a different sort. Where prophets communicated God's word and priests interceded for the people, kings were meant to be administrators of order and justice and representatives of the Lord (1 Samuel 10:1). Unlike how the rulers of other nations might have been perceived, the authority was limited and prescribed by God himself (1 Samuel 10:25). They were to rule as those living under authority themselves—kings for whom the Lord was *their* king (Psalm 110:1).

There were two kings who, to some degree, represented the best of what a king was meant to be. The first was David, the poet-warrior-shepherd king. Although he was far from sinless—in fact, at least one series of sins was shockingly vile (2 Samuel 11)[5]—his main desire was to please God in all he did, so much so that he was characterized as being a man "after [God's] heart" (1 Samuel 13:14; Acts 13:22 CSB). He was humble and loyal to the Lord, trusting God's wisdom over his own (1 Samuel 17:47; Psalms 23; 51). It was to him that God made the promises of an eternal kingdom, a covenant that would last forever (2 Samuel 7).

The second great king was Solomon, who succeeded his father David (1 Kings 2–3). God spoke to Solomon in a dream, telling him to ask for anything that he desired, and it would be granted to him (1 Kings 3:5). Solomon, already wise beyond his years, asked for the one thing he knew he needed most: not wealth or possessions, but wisdom. "Give your servant a discerning mind," he said (1 Kings 3:9). Solomon knew he needed wisdom to judge God's people and discern right from wrong, determine good from evil. His request pleased the Lord, so much so that God gave Solomon wisdom as well as all that he did not ask for—riches and the honor to be the greatest king of his generation (1 Kings 3:13). For the majority of his reign, Solomon's kingdom was one of peace and prosperity. It was during his reign that the temple was built, a place not only for the Israelites to worship, but also as a place for those from other lands to gather in as well (1 Kings 8:41-45).

MEDIATORS WHO ALL FELL SHORT

But there was a problem with these mediators, even the best of them: None of them were perfect. They were human beings, prone to the same sinful tendencies and the same weaknesses that we all are. Moses resisted taking on his role due to his apparent slowness of speech (Exodus 4:10-12). He became so angry with God over the stubbornness of the Israelites that he was forbidden from entering the promised land itself (Numbers 20; Deuteronomy 32:51-52).

David's reign was filled with strife as his son Absalom led an insurrection against him (2 Samuel 15–19). Despite loving the Lord and despite all his wisdom, Solomon's heart was drawn away into idolatry by the allure of wealth, possessions, and his many—*many*—wives (1 Kings 11:1-8). And even the office of the kings was something of a concession to the stubbornness of the Israelites. Theirs was to be a nation with one king, God. But the people wanted kings like the other nations around them, a human one (1 Samuel 8:1-9). And God gave them what they wanted, especially as Solomon's successors tore the kingdom apart and the people were eventually sent into exile as captives of Babylon for 70 years (1 Kings 12:1-16; 2 Chronicles 36:15-21).

And as for the high priests? Their weakness was shown in the unceasing nature of their task, as they brought another sacrifice for the people—and themselves—before the Lord, year after year, until they died.

SIGNPOSTS POINTING TO SOMEONE GREATER

In their form and function, prophets, priests, and kings were signposts. They were offices and authorities that pointed to someone greater who was coming later. A better mediator, one who would be superior to even the greatest prophet, the most faithful priest, or the wisest king. This mediator would be the prophet Moses promised would someday come as he prepared the Israelites to enter their new homeland (Deuteronomy 18:15). He would be the long-awaited king, the son of David, to rule over an eternal kingdom (Isaiah 9:7; Daniel 7:13-14). He would be the priest who would offer a once-for-all sacrifice for the people (Hebrews 10:14).

As prophet, priest, and king, Jesus was the mediator all the others pointed to. He was the substance of their shadow. But how could it be that Jesus fulfilled any of these roles, let alone all of them?

Jesus, the Great Prophet. As a prophet, Jesus came preaching a message of repentance and renewal for God's people—the gospel of the kingdom of God (Mark 1:15; Matthew 4:17, 23; 9:35). He initiated a new covenant, an unconditional, eternal covenant that would never be broken and never end (Hebrews 7:22; 8–10). But unlike the prophets who came before him, Jesus was not merely a messenger sent to speak the word of God. He is the Word of God made flesh, the ultimate revelation of God, and the exact expression of his nature (John 1:14; Hebrews 1:1-3). Jesus is "the way, the truth, and the life" (John 14:6 NKJV), the one of whom the Father commanded from heaven, "Listen to him" (Matthew 17:5).

Jesus, the Great High Priest. Jesus is not a priest like the descendants of Aaron and the Levites. He is not a priest because of his family line; he is a priest of a different order—a priest of the order of Melchizedek (Psalm 110:4; Hebrews 7:17). He is the perfect priest, "holy, innocent, undefiled, separate from sinners, and exalted above the heavens," who has no need of offering sacrifices for his own sins before making an offering for the sins of the people because he had no sin to atone for (Hebrews 7:26-27). And the sacrifice he offered was wholly unique as well, because he did not offer the blood of a lamb to make atonement. He *was* the sacrifice, "offering himself once for all" (Hebrews 7:27; see also Philippians 2:8). For this is why he came into the world, to be the atoning sacrifice for our sins (1 John 2:2; 4:10). And even now, he continues as our priest, interceding for us as he sits at the right hand of the Father (Romans 8:34; Hebrews 7:25; 9:24). Able to sympathize with our weakness because he was tempted in every way that we are (Hebrews 4:15). He knows our weakness and frailty. He knows our struggles and temptations. He understands our deepest needs and longings. And no matter how often we fail and fall short, he will not abandon us. He is with us, interceding for us, until the end of the age (Matthew 28:20).

Jesus, the Righteous King. From the beginning of Matthew's, Luke's, and John's Gospels, Jesus is identified as the long-awaited king of Israel, the true son of David (Matthew 1:1-17; Luke 1:32-33; 3:23-38; John 1:49). But he rarely referred to himself in this way or affirmed anyone's speculation (John 4:25-26). It was only when the time had come for him to be crucified that he openly affirmed his kingship because his kingdom is not like those of this world (John 18:36). And after his resurrection, he confirmed that all authority had been given to him, as he commissioned his followers to go into all the world making disciples (Matthew 28:18-20; 1 Corinthians 15:20-28). And even now, he rules and reigns righteously over all the universe—he is the King of kings and Lord of lords, the first and the last, who holds all things together by the word of his power (Colossians 1:13-20; 1 Timothy 6:13-15; Revelation 19:12, 16).

THE MEDIATOR WE CAN COUNT ON

Until the end of the age comes, we will always need a mediator. Fortunately, Jesus will always be there. He will never let us down. He will never grow tired of our confessing our sins and failures, or of us coming to him when we are struggling and overwhelmed. He invites us to "confidently approach the throne of grace to receive mercy and find grace whenever we need help" (Hebrews 4:16). And "whenever" really does mean *whenever*. Every time we need help, he is there. Every time we sin, he is ready to hear our confession, and he invites us to confess without fear of rejection. We don't have to pretend that Jesus doesn't know these things or understand what they are like because he absolutely does (Hebrews 4:15).

But he doesn't just know, he has overcome them all through his sacrifice. There is nothing more that needs to be done. When Jesus said, "It is finished" (John 19:30 CSB), he meant it. In his death and resurrection, Jesus healed the divide between God and humanity. And by faith, he invites us to cross the chasm and enjoy peace and healing forever.

REFLECT, EXPLORE, AND DISCUSS

1. What idea or concept stood out to you as you read this chapter? Why?

2. Read some of the Bible passages about Jesus fulfilling every mediator's role referenced in this chapter. How do these passages encourage or challenge you?

3. What new questions do these passages raise?

4. How does knowing that every human mediator falls short affect how you see leaders in the church and in society?

5. Where do you need to embrace Jesus as your mediator more fully?

GOD RESCUES

16

THROUGH THE STRANGE BEAUTY OF DEATH

A Sacrifice That Satisfied

One of my all-time favorite verses in the Bible is found near the end of the first chapter of John's Gospel. It's one that is essential to the story John is telling in his book. But if we read it too quickly, it can almost seem like an aside.

After opening his Gospel with this grand vision of the eternal Word who in the beginning was with God and was God, who came and dwelt among us (John 1:1-18), the scene shifts and introduces us to a man named John (John 1:19-28). John was a prophet whose life was devoted to preparing the people for the coming of the Messiah—the promised rescuer, the long-awaited king to sit on David's throne. He was "the voice of one shouting in the wilderness: 'Prepare the way for the Lord, make his paths straight'" (Luke 3:4; see also Isaiah 40:3).

Everything John said caused a stir, not only among the people but among the religious leaders of the time as well. He kept warning people to flee from "the coming wrath," and to "produce fruit that proves [their] repentance"—to be content with what they had, to share with those in need, and for officials not to extort money from the people (Luke 3:7-14). And as he preached, people came to him asking to be baptized, a ritual meant to symbolize their repentance—their desire to turn to the Lord and be cleansed. As more and more people came, John's fame grew, as did his list of enemies (including Herod, the tetrarch who ruled as king under the authority of the Roman Empire). But John did not care for fame, nor did it bother him how much his message angered the powerful. He had a mission to complete.

Then one day, John saw him. The one John had been waiting for—who he was preparing the way for. Jesus was there at the Jordan River, and he was coming toward John. And then, with the power of a dam bursting, John shouted,

> Behold! The Lamb of God who takes away the sin of the world! (John 1:29 NKJV).

This might seem like an odd choice of wording to announce the arrival of God's promised rescuer. And certainly to us, it does. After all, if we were in John's place, we would probably be more inclined to opt for a more heroic declaration. "Look, the king is here!" or "There he is, the Messiah!" Why would he opt for referring to Jesus as a lamb, as something weak and helpless? After all, a lamb was something to be sacrificed. It was something meant to die.

Which was exactly John's point.

Despite how peculiar it might seem to our ears, John's declaration was good news. He was pointing to something good and beautiful—something that would come from death.

HOW CAN ANYTHING GOOD COME FROM DEATH?

But how can there be anything beautiful that comes from death? How can these two things go together at all? After all, death is ugly. It is dark. It is unnatural. There is something about it, even when a person dies after having lived a long and full life, that makes us want to cry out, "This is wrong; it shouldn't be!" When loved ones are diagnosed with a terminal illness, we respond with anger. When people die, we often recast or reframe our relationships in order to avoid speaking ill of the dead. We offer well-meaning platitudes about being in better places and God needing another angel to comfort the grieving.

When we're not confronted by death, we do what we can to avoid thinking about it altogether. We hate death, even if it shapes so much of our experience of life. And we should hate it. After all, death was never meant to be. It is a constant reminder of the brokenness of this world—of the mess we made of everything.

Which takes us back to the *why* of it all. Why would John announce Jesus, the long-awaited Messiah, by calling him something that is meant to die? Because that's why Jesus came into the world—he came to die. He was meant to be an atoning sacrifice.

SACRIFICES, SUBSTITUTES, AND SHADOWS

Like so many words that appear in the Bible and Christian teaching, atonement is not one that we typically use in everyday life. To atone means to pay back or make reparations with the goal of reconciliation.[1] In Christian teaching, atonement focuses on the relationship between God and humanity—how to heal the divide between God and mankind that sin created. Following the events of Genesis 3, atonement is one of the core themes of the Bible, in part because Genesis 3 also made death one of the Bible's core themes.

Despite being told that eating the fruit of the tree of the knowledge of good and evil would bring death, the first humans didn't die immediately, at least not physically. But even though physical death didn't come to them the moment they took that first bite of the fruit, death *did* come. From Genesis 4 onward, beginning with Cain's murder of his brother Abel (Genesis 4:1-16), a veritable parade of death marches through the descendants of Adam as, with person after person, we read, "he died."[2] Where it was once impossible, death became inevitable, an unstoppable force that taunts us to this day.

But even as death had its way with humanity, some people began to "call on the name of the LORD" (Genesis 4:26 NKJV). They worshiped him with prayers, and it seems, with sacrifices. Perhaps it was the story of Abel's sacrifice of the firstborn sheep of his flock that inspired them, a sacrifice offered in faith that pleased the Lord (Genesis 4:3-5; Hebrews 11:4).[3] Perhaps it was something deeper, a knowledge etched into their hearts though they had not the words to express it (Romans 2:15). Whatever the cause, in times of praise and times of repentance, those who worshiped the Lord did so with sacrifices (Genesis 8:20). When reconciliation needed to be made or when peace was to be restored, whether people hoped for children or a good harvest, a sacrifice was made.

This practice continued for millennia, as worshipers offered sacrifices to God. Over time, some people began wrongly sacrificing to *other* false gods, the "powers" and "principalities" that act as the rulers of this world (Ephesians 6:12). Some sacrificed animals. Others sacrificed other human beings—and even themselves—to gods without voices (Psalm 115:5).[4]

While many of the examples of sacrifices in Genesis seem unguided by any explicit command, from Exodus forward, the story changes. After delivering the Israelites from Egypt, God established an elaborate sacrificial system, one that would mark them as his people. This system, like the Law itself, was a guidepost, a guardian helping the people experience reconciliation. So with every festival and gathering, sacrifices were made. Some were signs of peace and thanksgiving for the Lord's kindness and provision. Others addressed the people's ongoing infractions of God's law (Leviticus 2–4). But the most important sacrifices were the sacrifices offered during the Passover and the Day of Atonement.

A REMINDER OF REDEMPTION

The Passover was held in memory of the final plague sent upon Egypt, during which God spared the firstborn males of every household who painted their doorposts with the blood of a one-year-old male lamb, free from any physical defect or deformity. Death literally passed over these houses (hence the celebration's name), and the Israelites were freed from their bondage to Egypt as a result (Exodus 12:1-32, 42-51). Every year, the Israelites were to sacrifice a male lamb at midnight, essentially reenacting that night so they would not forget what the Lord had done for them.

A SYMBOL OF FORGIVENESS

The Day of Atonement was a different affair, unique among all the sacrifices of the Israelites. This sacrifice could only be offered by the high priest on behalf of the people, who could enter the sanctuary with "a young bull for a sin offering and a ram for a burnt offering" (Leviticus 16:3).[5] But these offerings weren't for the people as a whole; the bull was sacrificed to make atonement for the high priest himself and his household (Leviticus 16:6). That's why he also came with another sin offering, two male goats taken "from the congregation of the Israelites," and with these came another ram for a burnt offering (Leviticus 16:5). Why two goats? One was to be a sacrifice to the Lord, offered in the place of the people. As for the other, it was meant for "Azazel," and was not to be killed.[6] Instead, the high priest would take this goat and banish it into the wilderness, a scapegoat symbolically carrying away the people's sin as it went to its fate (Leviticus 16:10).

The sacrifices brought peace between God and his people. But that peace was fleeting because the people continued to sin; their need for atonement, for reconciliation, only grew. So the sacrifices were offered again and again, year after year, by priests who themselves required forgiveness. It's tempting to read this and think the system failed. But the system was never the point. It could not take away the people's sins because it never could (Hebrews 10:11). The sacrifices were never meant to. For all their symbolic power, the sacrifices were just that: *symbols*. They were a preview, a shadow, of something greater to come. A perfect once-for-all sacrifice that could never again be repeated.

But to truly grasp that, there is still one other sacrifice to consider. It's one that many struggle to understand because it's one that makes no sense apart from Jesus: A father tasked with sacrificing his beloved son.

THE PREVIEW OF A PROMISE

In Genesis 22, hundreds of years before the Israelite sacrificial system was ever established, God said to Abraham, "Take your son—your only son, whom you love, Isaac—and go to the land of Moriah! Offer him up there as a burnt offering on one of the mountains which I will indicate to you" (Genesis 22:2).

(I wasn't kidding when I said this is a sacrifice many of us struggle to understand.)

The natural instinct for most of us (hopefully) would be to refuse this command—to say no as emphatically as possible! After all, as we know from later in the Bible, human sacrifice is detestable to God (Leviticus 20:1-5; Micah 6:6-7). He *hate*s it; it is evil. Yet the Lord told Abraham to do this. And what's more, Abraham saddled up his donkey in the early morning, took two of his servants with him, along with his son Isaac, and wood for the offering, and off he went (Genesis 22:3).

For three days, Abraham and Isaac traveled but what they said to one another is unknown to us. Perhaps it was three days in silence, with Abraham praying, trying to understand why the Lord was asking this of him. After all, Isaac was a child of promise, a child born to his wife Sarah when she and Abraham were already 100 years old (Genesis 21:5). It was through Isaac that Abraham's family would continue—and the one through whom the world would be blessed (Genesis 15:4).

As for Isaac, who can say what he was thinking? It was not as if he were a small child. He was old enough and strong enough to carry a heavy load of wood.[7] Meanwhile, his father was an elderly man. So if escape had been on his mind, it would have been possible. But Isaac stayed. And when they arrived at the mountain, Abraham said to his servants, "You two stay here with the donkey while the boy and I go up there. We will worship and then return to you" (Genesis 22:5).

Up the mountain, Abraham and Isaac went. As they walked, Isaac asked, "Where is the lamb for the burnt offering?" Abraham replied, "God will provide for himself the lamb for the burnt offering, my son" (Genesis 22:7-8). When they arrived to the place the Lord showed him, Abraham built the altar. He tied up Isaac and placed him on top of the wood. Isaac, for his part, allowed him to do so (Genesis 22:9-10). Even as Abraham took his knife and prepared to sacrifice his son, those words, "God will provide," must have been ringing in both their ears. And before the knife came down, the angel of the Lord—the mysterious being who may have been the Lord himself—called to Abraham, commanding him to stop.

"Do not do anything to him, for now I know that you fear God because you did not withhold your son, your only son, from me" (Genesis 22:12). The test was over, a test not borne of any uncertainty on God's part about Abraham's faith, but one to *demonstrate* Abraham's faith. He would not hold back the one through whom God's promises to him would eventually be fulfilled. "He was fully convinced that what God promised he was also able to do" (Romans 4:21). He trusted the Lord more than his circumstances—and somehow knew that, even if the Lord did not stay his hand, Isaac would return with him from the mountain. Abraham believed, and his faith was credited to him as righteousness (Genesis 15:6; Romans 4:22). And that's when Abraham saw it, a ram caught in the bushes. A ram provided by God himself as the burnt offering (Genesis 22:12-13).

WHEN SHADOWS GAVE WAY TO SUBSTANCE

All of this—not just the sacrificial system, but Abraham and Isaac's sacrifice—loomed large over John's declaration: "Behold! The Lamb of God who takes away the sin of the world." His words have this feeling of release—of one saying, "Finally!" when something long anticipated is finally realized. Because that's exactly what was happening.

Jesus the Messiah had come. And the Messiah was not only a mediator between God and humanity—he was more than a king to rule over God's people and God's world, a prophet to reveal God's word and will, and a priest to make intercession for the people. He was the Lamb Abraham *knew* God would provide. Jesus was (and is) the perfect Son of God, who obeyed his Father in everything, who needed to offer no sacrifice for his sins because he had no sins to atone for (Hebrews 4:15). He was the Son the Father did not spare, but instead was "pleased" to crush (Isaiah 53:10 CSB), not out of any sort of malice, but because it was through Jesus that the cycle of death would be broken. And because of him, many brothers and sisters would be welcomed into God's family (Romans 8:29).

Jesus is our substitute, sacrificed for our sin. He provides forgiveness for the sin and disobedience of all who believe in him, forever making peace between God and his people (John 3:16; Romans 3:26). He is the substance of which all the sacrifices the Law commanded were but a shadow. And as the shadows gave way to substance, the need for sacrifices came to its end. "It is finished," Jesus said (John 19:30 CSB), and he meant it. How do we know? Because Jesus is not dead. He is alive.

THE MULTIFACETED LOVE OF GOD ON DISPLAY

The death and resurrection of Jesus is the most powerful way that God demonstrates his love for us. No longer do we fear judgment. No longer does guilt hang over us. No longer do we face the wrath of God. Why? Because God did not spare his Son (Romans 8:32). This kind of language makes many people uncomfortable. And not just uncomfortable. Some read it and take it to mean God is some kind of moral monster guilty of child abuse on a cosmic scale.[8] But this kind of thinking misunderstands the gospel itself.

The gospel puts the multifaceted love of God on display because the concept of atonement itself is multifaceted; some aspects are more preeminent than others, but all add to a fuller understanding. Christ's death was a ransom, paying the debt our sin incurred (Mark 10:45; 1 Timothy 2:6).[9] Christ's death satisfies the need for justice against the offense of sin.[10] Jesus was victorious over sin and death; indeed death has been "swallowed up in victory" (1 Corinthians 15:54; see also Isaiah 25:8).[11] And as our substitute, he was the sacrifice to end all sacrifices, the One who "destroyed" (NET) or "canceled" (CSB) the record of our debt—the insurmountable debt incurred by our sin—taking it away by nailing it to the cross (Colossians 2:14). He took upon himself the wrath of God on our behalf, "suffered once for sin, the just for the unjust, to bring [us] to God" (1 Peter 3:18).[12] It is through this atoning sacrifice that God perfectly demonstrated his love, for "in this is love: not that we have loved God, but that he loved us and sent his Son to be the atoning sacrifice for our sins" (1 John 4:10).

WHY THE GOOD NEWS IS GOOD

This is what makes Jesus' death a thing of beauty. It is why we can call Jesus' atoning sacrifice good news. As John Stott states, "Divine love triumphed over the divine wrath by divine self-sacrifice."[13] Jesus the

Redeemer has come. The sacrifice has been made, and it never needs to be offered again. The chains of sin are broken. Our debt is paid. Our punishment has passed over us, taken by another. Death itself is defeated; its sting removed (Hosea 13:14; 1 Corinthians 15:55). Is it any wonder why multitudes sing, "Worthy is the lamb who was killed to receive power and wealth and wisdom and might and honor and glory and praise!" (Revelation 5:12)?

Someday, you and I, if we believe this, will be there among them. But we're not there yet. For now, we wait in anticipation. And while we wait, as our anticipation builds, we can have confidence as we behold the Lamb who takes away the sin of the world.

REFLECT, EXPLORE, AND DISCUSS

1. What idea or concept stood out to you as you read this chapter? Why?

2. Read some of the Bible passages about Jesus' atoning death referenced in this chapter. How do these passages encourage or challenge you?

3. What new questions do these passages raise?

4. How might considering the purpose of Jesus' death affect your prayer life, your worship, and your witness in the world?

GOD RESCUES

17

THROUGH AN EMPTY TOMB

Our Only Hope in Life, Death, and Everything That Comes After

Before I was a Christian, I used to say a lot of ignorant things about Christianity. Okay, not just Christianity, but about the idea of faith itself. It wasn't because I was some kind of ardent atheist or anything like that. (I was too apathetic for that.) My go-to, like so many others who don't really know what they're talking about, was to make accusations about blind faith; to say that what people believed about God (no matter what god we were talking about) was basically wishful thinking.

Then, I became a Christian and was proven wrong. And also, right. Here's what I mean: As a new Christian, I saw a lot of the exact things I was afraid of in people that I was getting to know. There were some for whom their faith was an emotional experience. They didn't worry too much about facts or theology or anything like that. They simply believed, and that was enough for them. But I also met *more* people who were the exact opposite. Men and women who had reasons for the hope they had (1 Peter 3:15). They recognized that our faith isn't rooted in emotion, but in reality. In events that happened and that matter.

So far, that's what we've looked at as we've explored God's plan to rescue the whole world—the whole universe—from the curse of sin and death. We've looked at how Jesus, the promised rescuer, was both fully God and fully human, like us in every way but without sin. How Jesus is the mediator to whom all others pointed, and his sacrifice was the substance of which all others were mere shadows. But there's one other aspect of this plan that we need to embrace, one upon which our entire faith stands or falls: the resurrection of Jesus.

PREVIEWS AND PROMISES OF THE RESURRECTION

The concept of resurrection itself is one that, at first glance, appears to be absent from the Old Testament. But sometimes appearances are deceiving. Even though it doesn't appear explicitly, it seems to be a concept that developed over the Israelites' history. As he longed for release from his present suffering, Job asked, "If a man dies, will he live again?" (Job 14:14). Later Job said, "As for me, I know that my Redeemer lives, and that as the last he will stand upon the earth. And after my skin has been destroyed, yet in my flesh I will see God" (Job 19:25-26). While it's not wise to leap to conclusions, Job's words encourage us to wonder if, perhaps, there is more to life and death than we understand.

In the Psalms, there seems to be an increased awareness of the inescapable presence of God. There is nowhere we can go, whether to heaven or into the pit of *Sheol*, the place of the dead, where God will not be with us (Psalm 139:8). Through the prophets, there are potential hints of a resurrection, as in Isaiah's declaration that the Lord will swallow up death (Isaiah 25:8), Hosea's words promising rescue by the Lord (Hosea 6:1-3), and the same prophet's borderline mockery of death itself (Hosea 13:14), but it's still veiled. You could even look at Jonah's being vomited out of the giant fish that swallowed him as a symbolic resurrection (Jonah 2:10), with an emphasis on *symbolic* (and we'll come back to this in a moment).

Later, in the book of Daniel, we have the first unmistakable picture of resurrection, as "many of those who sleep in the dusty ground will awake—some to everlasting life, and others to shame and everlasting abhorrence" (Daniel 12:2).[1] And then there's Isaiah's suffering servant, who despite being crushed by the Lord, would "see descendants and enjoy long life, and the LORD's purpose will be accomplished through him. Having suffered, he will reflect on his work, he will be satisfied when he understands what he has done" (Isaiah 53:10-11). Despite being killed (Isaiah 53:9), this servant would live again. Death was not the end for him.

But in all of this, there was no clearly defined understanding of resurrection—neither of God's people as a whole and certainly not of the promised Messiah. There were hints, questions, and symbols, but little else.

JESUS AND THE RESURRECTION

By the time of Jesus, the Jews had developed an understanding of a resurrection on the long-awaited Day of the Lord, the day when God would come to judge his people (Micah 4). The dead would rise, some to everlasting life and others to everlasting judgment. But their understanding was still limited, especially when it came to the Messiah. They saw this promised figure as a powerful human ruler, a king to lead them into victory over their enemies and restore the kingdom as it had been during the reign of David. But when the Messiah actually showed up, he was a humble man about whom there was seemingly nothing special, at least as far as outward appearances were concerned.

But his teaching was different; he taught with authority (Matthew 7:29). When he spoke, people had to listen. And as Jesus taught his disciples, he kept talking about how he was going to be arrested and then killed. "The Son of Man...will be handed over to the Gentiles; he will be mocked, mistreated, and spat on. They will flog him severely and kill him" (Luke 18:31-33). But death wouldn't be the end for the Son of Man, Jesus. Instead, "on the third day he will rise again" (verse 33).[2] But they didn't understand what Jesus was talking about. Even the teachers of the Law, those who were supposed experts in the Scriptures, couldn't quite grasp what he was talking about. When they demanded a sign from him, Jesus answered:

> An evil and adulterous generation asks for a sign, but no sign will be given to it except the sign of the prophet Jonah. For just as Jonah was in the belly of the huge fish for three days and three nights, so the Son of Man will be in the heart of the earth for three days and three nights (Matthew 12:39-40).

Jonah's experience in the giant fish *was* a symbol, but it was a symbol of something else: Jesus being killed and returning once again. Matthew didn't indicate whether Jesus' listeners understood him or not in the moment. It's probably safe to say that they remained in the dark. It wasn't until after Jesus had been killed that anyone started to understand, when on the first day of the week following his death—the third day—the tomb was found empty (Matthew 28:1-10; Mark 16:1-8; Luke 24:1-12; John 20:1-9). Jesus' body was gone. As the day went on, the news spread quickly, though almost no one was quite sure what it meant. Had the body been stolen? Had Jesus' followers gone to the wrong place? But as people kept talking, and as more of his disciples *saw* him, the truth was undeniable: Jesus had risen from the grave, just as he said he would, and according to the Scriptures (Luke 24:27).

The Holy Spirit's influence aside, it is because of people talking about the resurrection that we know any of this happened at all. People who saw Jesus after his resurrection. People who touched the wounds in his hands (John 20:24-31), hugged him (John 20:10-18), and ate meals with him (Luke 24:30-31, 42). But we wouldn't know about any of it were it not for a group of Jesus' female followers.

THE FIRST WITNESSES

As the week began, a group of women—Mary Magdalene, Joanna, Mary the mother of James, and Salome—came to properly prepare Jesus' body after the hasty preparation it received before the Sabbath. But when they arrived to his grave, they found the stone that sealed the tomb had been rolled away, and inside the place where Jesus' body had been laid was an angel of the Lord (Matthew 28:2).

"Why do you look for the living among the dead?" the angel said (Luke 24:5). "I know that you are looking for Jesus, who was crucified. He is not here, for he has been raised, just as he said. Then go quickly and tell his disciples, 'He has been raised from the dead. He is going ahead of you into Galilee. You will see him there'" (Matthew 28:5-7).

That final command from the angel—to go and tell the disciples—probably seems innocuous to you (and it should). But at the time, this may have been even more shocking than the tomb itself being empty. In the first century, women were not permitted to testify in court; they were not seen as reliable witnesses.[3] Yet Matthew, Mark, Luke, and John all credit women, by name, as the first to see the empty tomb; and not just the first to see that Jesus' body was no longer there, but to be the first to speak of what happened. All these women were well-known among Jesus' followers. One—Mary, the mother of James—was also Jesus' mother.[4]

So why would the Gospel writers credit these women as the first witnesses to the resurrection if it was a cultural taboo? Because it's what happened; it was the truth. More than that, it was an invitation: If you don't believe this written account, go and ask them. And not only them, for Paul wrote to the Corinthian church that there were hundreds of people who saw Jesus after his resurrection, and most of them were still alive at the time of Paul's writing (1 Corinthians 15:6).

OKAY, BUT WHAT IF JESUS *DIDN'T*?

But let's say, for example, that none of this was true. That despite the scrutiny crediting women as witnesses would bring to the story, it was all a bit of fanciful imagining and that Paul was just wrong about how many people saw Jesus. How would you prove that? All it would have taken to disprove Christianity would be to disprove the resurrection.[5] And to do that, you'd have to find Jesus' body, wherever it might be. But despite all the efforts over the centuries, and the location of Joseph of Arimathea's tomb was never a guarded secret, the body remains undiscovered.[6] Even when explorers and filmmakers claim to find his tomb, they come up short.[7] (Not surprisingly, Jesus was a common name.[8]) That said, failing to find the body has not prevented people from putting forward alternative theories in order to reject Jesus' resurrection. The three most common being:

- the disciples stole the body
- the disciples were overcome by grief
- Jesus didn't actually die from his injuries

The Conspiracy Theory: Jesus' Disciples Stole the Body

The oldest and most common alternative amounts to a conspiracy theory on the part of Jesus' disciples. Rather than being resurrected, the tomb was empty because the disciples overpowered the guards, rolled away the massive boulder that sealed it, and took the body. After that, they began to spread the lie that Jesus had risen from the grave as he said he would, even though they had his body. The earliest version of this is surprisingly recorded in the Bible itself:

> While they were going, some of the guard went into the city and told the chief priests everything that had happened. After they had assembled with the elders and formed a plan, they gave a large sum of money to the soldiers, telling them, "You are to say, 'His disciples came at night and stole his body while we were asleep.' If this matter is heard before the governor, we will satisfy him and keep you out of trouble." So they took the money and did as they were instructed. And this story is told among the Jews to this day (Matthew 28:11-15).

The conspiracy theory, while among the oldest alternatives to the resurrection, is also among the easiest to debunk. Why? It has more plot holes than a Michael Bay movie. Think about this: How would a small group of fishermen, one of whom feared a servant girl (John 18:15-18), overpower the highly trained Roman soldiers stationed at the tomb (Matthew 27:62-66)? Also, who was it who told the religious leaders about the tomb being empty? Those very same soldiers! Wouldn't that suggest they knew what happened, especially since the religious leaders bribed them to say the body was stolen? And when you consider the sincerity the disciples showed in the face of persecution, imprisonment, and death (Acts 12:1-3), is it likely that any of them would have endured torture and death for something they knew was a lie?[9]

The Mass Hallucination Theory: Jesus' Disciples Had a Shared Mental Break

A second alternative is one that doesn't openly aim to impugn the character of Jesus' disciples, although it does, effectively, question their sanity. This view is that the grief-stricken disciples were so overcome by the loss of Jesus that after he died, they began to see him even though he remained in the tomb. They were collectively hallucinating.

Like the conspiracy theory, the problems here are numerous. After all, hallucinations tend to be the product of a single mind, not a shared event. And hallucinations also don't tend to embolden those experiencing them. If anything, they further weaken a person. Yet the resurrection motivated the disciples to boldly proclaim the gospel throughout the Roman Empire, even at the cost of their own lives. As Adrian Warnock observes, for a hallucination to have that effect "is completely inconsistent with the results of hallucinations as described in any medical textbook."[10]

But for the sake of argument, let's imagine that the disciples were, in fact, all having a shared hallucination, and that shared hallucination motivated them to risk their lives to share the gospel. If Christ had not been raised, but his body was still in its tomb—a location that was known at the time (John 19:38), all the Romans and the Jewish leaders needed to do was unseal it.

Again, Christianity hinges on the resurrection. To stamp it out, all anyone had to do was show the body. But they didn't. Why? Because the tomb was empty.

The Swoon Theory: Jesus Didn't Really Die on the Cross

A final alternative puts forward the idea that Jesus didn't really die on the cross at all. He only appeared that way, when in fact, he was only very badly injured and *swooned*, or fainted, rather than died. This theory always reminds me of Dr. Evil's henchman, Mustafa, moaning in agony after being dropped into a fiery pit and exclaiming he still was alive, only badly burned.[11] Why? Because this theory is as realistic as a James Bond parody.

Remember, Jesus was crucified, not placed on a fainting couch. Crucifixion was an instrument of supreme torture, one reserved for the worst of criminals, designed to kill those experiencing it slowly, painfully, and humiliatingly. The condemned were forced to carry the wooden beam to the place where they would be nailed to it. Large spikes were driven through their hands and feet. And as they hung in place, they gasped for air, slowly suffocating while onlookers mocked and spit upon them. And all of this was after they had been beaten, whipped, and scourged by their captors, prior actions that were often enough to kill the condemned.

Jesus experienced all of this as he was reviled and rejected by those he came to save (Mark 14:64; 15:15-32). And after he used his last breath to say, "Father, into your hands I commit my spirit" (Luke 23:46) and died, a soldier "pierced his side with a spear, and blood and water flowed out immediately" (John 19:34). After he was taken down from the cross, he was declared dead, wrapped in burial clothes and more than a hundred pounds of spices, and then laid to rest in a tomb until the first day of the week (John 19:39-42; 20:1).

He was unquestionably and irreversibly dead. But even if he had somehow survived all of that and was only seriously wounded, he surely would have died while trapped in the tomb without food, water, or medical intervention. To think that he was otherwise—or that he could have gone for a seven-mile hike to a town called Emmaus afterward (Luke 24:13)—stretches credulity.

THE TRUTH UPON WHICH OUR FAITH STANDS

Despite the incredulity of these alternatives, the idea of a literal, bodily resurrection is hard to take for many. They might agree that Jesus really did die, but they will then argue that Christians are missing the point when we insist that he actually rose from the dead. Some would argue that instead of a physical resurrection, it was a spiritual one. Despite being dead, Jesus lived on in the hearts of his disciples, inspiring them to love and good works (Hebrews 10:24).[12]

But again, this misses the point of what the New Testament teaches. Christianity is not a philosophy designed to teach us to live more compassionately (although it certainly does equip us to do so). It is a faith built upon the truth that Jesus Christ died, was buried, and rose again (1 Corinthians 15:3-8). Without the resurrection, we have nothing worth believing in or sharing with the world. Instead, we should be pitied more than anyone if the resurrection were not true. Why? Because we would have believed a lie. The apostle Paul put it this way:

> If Christ is being preached as raised from the dead, how can some of you say there is no resurrection of the dead? But if there is no resurrection of the dead, then not even Christ has been raised. And if Christ has not been raised, then our preaching is futile and your faith is empty. Also, we are found to be false witnesses about God, because we have testified against God that he raised Christ from the dead, when in reality he did not raise him, if indeed the dead are not raised. For if the dead are not raised, then not even Christ has been raised. And if Christ has not been raised, your faith is useless; you are still in your sins. Furthermore, those who have fallen asleep in Christ have also perished. For if only in this life we have hope in Christ, we should be pitied more than anyone (1 Corinthians 15:12-19).

If Jesus' body were found, it would mean that he was never raised from the dead. And if Jesus was not raised from the dead, Christianity would be meaningless. It wouldn't be true. A resurrectionless faith is an empty faith. It is useless, without substance. To proclaim such faith would be to lie about God, leaving us in the same place where we started before we believed: lost, condemned in our sins. Without the resurrection, "all is vanity" (Ecclesiastes 1:2 NKJV). Better to go "eat and drink, for tomorrow we die" (1 Corinthians 15:32).

OUR LIVING HOPE

But the good news is that Jesus is alive. Jesus' death was the atoning sacrifice needed to pay for our sins (1 John 4:10). His resurrection is the proof that he actually did it—that he saves "completely those who come to God through him" because he is alive (Hebrews 7:25).

Jesus is the "firstfruits of those who have fallen asleep," the first raised from the dead, and all who believe will one day be raised like him (1 Corinthians 15:20). He is ruling and reigning over all creation, seated at the right hand of God the Father (Ephesians 1:20; Hebrews 8:1), interceding on our behalf. Jesus is the Lord of the dead and the living (Romans 14:9). All his enemies—sin, Satan, and even death itself—are subject to him (1 Corinthians 15:25-27). And there is a day coming when he will bring them all to their end (Revelation 20:13-14; 21:4).

Because Jesus is alive, sin no longer has the last word. Because Jesus is alive, death has no sting (1 Corinthians 15:55). Because Jesus is alive, God makes all who believe alive in him—through a "new birth into a living hope through the resurrection of Jesus Christ from the dead" (1 Peter 1:3).

REFLECT, EXPLORE, AND DISCUSS

1. What idea or concept stood out to you as you read this chapter? Why?

2. Read some of the Bible passages about Jesus' resurrection referenced in this chapter. How do these passages encourage or challenge you?

3. What new questions do these passages raise?

4. How important do you believe the resurrection is? Why?

5. What does Paul say your life would look like if Jesus hadn't risen from the dead?

GOD RESCUES

18

BY MAKING THE DEAD LIVE

What It Means to Be Born Again

Years ago, I read a story about a man named George Whitefield, a preacher and evangelist from the eighteenth century who was one of the founders of the original Methodist movement and a one-time partner of John and Charles Wesley.[1] He was said to have preached some 18,000 sermons, which as a preacher myself, I can tell you is a *lot* of preaching. With so many sermons, some repetition and revisiting would be inevitable. But there was one subject on which no less than 3,000 of all his sermons were devoted. A subject that can be summarized in five words: You must be born again.

Whitefield's preaching resonated in the hearts of many who heard it, and they became Christians. But there were also some people who were confused, even frustrated, by his frequent declarations that they needed to be born again. Finally, after hearing one such message, a man decided to confront Whitefield on the matter. "Why do you keep preaching that we must be born again?" the man asked. And without missing a beat, the preacher replied, "Because, sir, you must be born again."[2]

The term *born again* didn't mean much to me before I became a Christian. Because I didn't grow up in or around the faith, it wasn't something that came up in conversation at all. If I heard it at all, it was through a news report about elections in the United States. So I thought "born-again Christian" was a political designation; a voting bloc. I didn't realize that it meant something that had nothing to do with political affiliations, and everything to do with the gospel. But what exactly does it mean to be born again—and how can it happen?

I know now that I was not alone in asking this question. And if you've found yourself asking this, neither are you. It's a question that's been asked since a meeting one night between Jesus and a man named Nicodemus, about 2,000 years ago.

WHAT IS THE NEW BIRTH?

Nicodemus was a devout Jewish teacher, a member of the Pharisees. The Pharisees were deeply committed to studying the Scriptures (John 5:39), seeking to obey them as carefully as possible. They wanted to be holy, to be free from sin, and the only way they thought they could do that was to keep the Law.[3] And because they were diligent in their study, they knew about all the promises of a coming Messiah. They knew the signs to look for. And when Jesus arrived in Judea, teaching and performing miracles (John 2:23; 20:30), they became curious. But Nicodemus's fascination went beyond mere curiosity. He *knew* that Jesus had come from God, even if he didn't entirely know what that meant (John 3:2). So he went to speak to him—to find out who this man was. But instead of telling Nicodemus who he was, Jesus said, "Truly I tell you, unless someone is born again, he cannot see the kingdom of God" (John 3:3 csb).

At first glance, Jesus' statement might seem like a non sequitur. After all, Nicodemus didn't ask how to see or enter the kingdom of God. He wanted to know who Jesus was. But Jesus was answering the question behind Nicodemus's question, the one that really mattered. Nicodemus, for all his devotion to the Scriptures and his earnest adherence to the Law, truly wanted to know how he could find the peace with God that all his obedience to the Law couldn't provide. Jesus knew this because he knew (and knows) the hearts of people (John 2:24), and this is why his answer was, "You must be born again."

Yet Nicodemus didn't understand. How could that happen? After all, it isn't as though a person can re-enter his or her mother's womb to be born a second time (John 3:4). But Jesus expected that Nicodemus would understand what he was talking about. "Are you a teacher of Israel and don't know these things?" Jesus said (John 3:10 csb). But why would Jesus have this expectation? Because Nicodemus was such a devout student of the Scriptures and God had revealed this in the Scriptures. This is why he said again, "Truly I tell you, unless someone is born of *water* and the *Spirit*, he cannot enter the kingdom of God" (John 3:5 csb, emphasis added).

Jesus' reference to water and the Spirit did not come out of nowhere. He was pointing Nicodemus to two important prophecies that Nicodemus would be familiar with. Two prophecies that provided some understanding of what it meant to be born again. The first prophecy, found in Isaiah 44:3-5, was a promise of renewal for God's people, where the Lord described how he would pour out his Spirit on future generations. And just as water heals parched and cracked soil, the people would be restored. They would be the Lord's. The second prophecy, Ezekiel 36:25-27, was even more overt, where together, water and spirit signify a cleansing from spiritual impurity and a transformation that would enable people to wholeheartedly follow God.[4]

These promises of renewal and restoration pointed to a supernatural work of God, to what happens in the new birth, or *regeneration*: The Holy Spirit causes people who are "dead in [their] trespasses and sins" to live once more (Ephesians 2:1, 4-5 csb). And that is what we all need. Sin has left us with "heart[s] of stone" (Ezekiel 36:26), stubborn and unresponsive to God's Word and the Holy Spirit. We have no love for God; no desire to listen or obey. We're inclined toward sin, loving darkness rather than the light (John 3:19). We can't self-actualize our way out of our sin problem. We cannot will ourselves to stop loving sin. Only God can. And in regenerating us, God cleanses us, saving us by "the washing of regeneration and renewal by the Holy Spirit" (Titus 3:5 CSB). Our hearts of stone are replaced with "heart[s] of flesh" (Ezekiel 36:26) no longer in bondage to sin, free to love God as we were always meant to. It's a transformation so powerful that it can only be called a new birth, as the Holy Spirit works, as D. Martin Llyod-Jones observes, "Down in the very depths of the personality, and put there a new principle of life, something absolutely new, so that there is the 'new man.'"[5]

In proclaiming the new birth, Jesus was saying that if anyone is going to enter the kingdom of God, if anyone is going to be saved, it would take a miracle. And that is exactly what regeneration is.

THE NEW BIRTH AND OUR NEW LIVES

To be born again is to begin a new life—our life with Christ (Colossians 2:13). It doesn't mean that our external reality changes, but everything about who we are at our deepest level does. Our name and circumstances don't change, but who we are deep down does. Or to put it another way, "You're still the same you, but you are not the same you that you were before."[6] And from that newness of being—this new birth with a new heart—comes new desires, a new purpose, a new identity, and a new future:

- New desires—You *want* the things God wants (Psalm 37:4; Philippians 2:13).
- A new purpose—Your whole life is meant to be about

honoring, enjoying, and serving God (Psalm 73:24-26; John 17:22, 24; 1 Corinthians 10:31; Romans 11:36).

- A new identity—You are a beloved child, adopted into the family of God, and your Father is God himself (Romans 8:15; Ephesians 1:5; Galatians 4:5).

- A new future—You are destined to live forever with God in a renewed and restored world (Revelation 21:1–22:5).

All this, and so much more that we'll explore in the next chapter, is ours through the new birth. There is no magic formula that grants this to us, nor is there any task for us to perform. There is nothing to earn. It is all freely given, a gift of God's grace—his unmerited favor—toward those he loves. The only thing God asks of us? To "repent and believe" (Mark 1:15).

The kind of belief, or faith, I'm talking about here is way different than wishful thinking, which is what I remember thinking before I believed the gospel. It is also something far different than offering mental assent to historical facts. The faith that the gospel creates within people is a genuine, heartfelt recognition of the truth of the gospel (John 1:10-13). To know it is true deep down in the core of our being, even if we don't fully understand it. And that leads us to confess that Jesus is the Son of God (1 John 4:13-16). And out of that confession comes a desire—a *need*—to *repent*, which is a word that carries this idea of turning and returning (Acts 3:19-21). We experience a heartfelt recognition of our own sinfulness (Luke 5:8), but instead of running away from God and either futilely attempting to do better or trying to convince ourselves that sin is good (Isaiah 5:20), we turn to Christ. We ask him to forgive us of our sins because he is "faithful and righteous to forgive us our sins and to cleanse us from all unrighteousness" (1 John 1:9 CSB).

INTERTWINING EXPERIENCES OF GRACE

Regeneration, faith, and repentance are these intertwining experiences of grace, inseparable from one another while still being distinct from one another. If that statement seems a bit challenging to wrap your mind around, try thinking about the relationship between regeneration, faith, and repentance as the earliest first moments of life.[7] To be born again is, in a sense, like entering into the world as a brand-new baby. What does a healthy baby do after being born? The baby takes his or her first breath outside the womb and almost immediately begins to cry. The same is true when we are born again. When the Spirit gives us new life, we instinctually respond in faith and repentance. It's as natural as breathing. (And sometimes involves crying too.)

And if we extend that analogy further, what usually happens with children after they are born? They grow up. The same is true with those who are born again. We begin as spiritual newborns. But eventually, we discover our arms and legs. Soon we're crawling, then toddling, then walking, and eventually running toward a life of holiness—one where we become more like Jesus as our faith in him grows (Hebrews 12:1). That's the process Christians call *sanctification*, which is our gradually becoming more and more like Jesus through the power of the Holy Spirit—living out our new desires, becoming who God says we already are because of the new birth. And that process continues up until the day that we stand before Jesus, when we see the kingdom of God with our own eyes and are welcomed into Jesus' presence, to experience the rest he provides (Matthew 11:28; Hebrews 4:1-16).

GOOD NEWS FOR THE WHOLE WORLD

Whatever else we could say about it, we need to recognize that to be born again—regeneration—is inseparable from being a Christian. In fact, from a divine perspective, they are synonymous. To be a

Christian is to be born again. And to be born again is to be a Christian. Why? Because "unless one is born again, he cannot see the kingdom of God" (John 3:3 NKJV).

This means that regeneration is good news, and not just for those of us who believe that Jesus loved us and gave himself for us (Galatians 2:20). It is good news for the whole world. It means that God is doing what he has always done: He is saving sinners (1 Timothy 1:15). The Holy Spirit goes where he wills, bringing new life to some of the most unexpected people (John 3:8). And wherever people who love Jesus talk about Jesus, whether in a conversation at home, in a coffee shop, at work, at school, or even over a text message, the Spirit is at work. He is drawing people to Jesus, replacing stone hearts with hearts of flesh. He is making the dead live. And he will keep doing it until the day all things are made new.

REFLECT, EXPLORE, AND DISCUSS

1. What idea or concept stood out to you as you read this chapter? Why?

2. Read some of the Bible passages about the new birth referenced in this chapter. How do these passages encourage or challenge you?

3. What new questions do these passages raise?

4. Have you been born again?

GOD RESCUES

19

WITH A GOAL IN MIND

*How the Holy Spirit
Makes Us More Like Jesus*

I spent most of my early years as a Christian confused about the Holy Spirit. In that sense, I was not unique. Many people—even professing Christians—are confused about him, especially his divine nature and his personhood. Some aren't even sure he is real at all![1] But my confusion wasn't related to his divinity or personhood. That I got. I could see from Scripture that the Holy Spirit is God and acts accordingly. What I didn't know was what it meant for the Spirit to be at work in my life.

I didn't entirely understand what he does.

Ironically, I was also a member of a church that placed a high emphasis on the Spirit. But this emphasis had more to do with specific gifts they believed were signs of his presence, to be experienced by all Christians. Gifts I did not experience and felt no need to (although I felt some pressure to fake it at times). Because I don't do well with confusion, I did what made the most sense: Starting with the Scriptures, I sought to understand the Spirit's role in our lives, and whether I was missing out on anything. What I discovered is that the Holy Spirit is involved in every aspect of the Christian life to the degree that it can be called the Spirit-filled life.

WHAT IS A SPIRIT-FILLED LIFE?

To be Spirit-filled means to have the Holy Spirit living within you. At a fundamental level, it is synonymous with being a Christian in the same way to be regenerate—born again—is to be a Christian. "If Christ is in you…the Spirit is your life" (Romans 8:10), or to "have the Spirit is to have Christ; to have Christ is to have the Spirit."[2]

Because the Spirit lives within us, we are people who walk "according to the Spirit" (Romans 8:4). Our outlook on life is shaped by his presence and his work in our lives (Romans 8:6). We no longer want to live in hostility with God, but to pursue life and peace with him and with one another (Romans 8:7). We want to please him in all that we do, and because the Spirit is with us, we actually can.

The Spirit's presence is an all-encompassing reality, a transformative experience for us into the image of Christ "from one degree of glory to another, which is from the Lord, who is the Spirit" (2 Corinthians 3:18). This experience stretches back to before the world as we know it came into being and continues into the world that is still to come. It encompasses the entirety of God's saving work through Christ, because in a sense, the work of Christ is also the work of the Spirit.

THE SPIRIT AND OUR SALVATION

In saying this, I don't mean that the Spirit died on the cross with Christ or anything like that. (Remember, heresy is bad.) What I'm talking about is the Spirit's involvement in our salvation from its beginning through to its completion, purposing and applying the work of Christ to us, and empowering us as we seek to live faithfully as one of the beloved children of God.

Think about Romans 8:29-30, which falls near the end of a larger exploration of the Holy Spirit's work and our relationship to him. There, Paul wrote:

> Those whom he foreknew he also predestined to be conformed to the image of his Son, that his Son would be the firstborn among many brothers and sisters. And those he predestined, he also called; and those he called, he also justified; and those he justified, he also glorified (Romans 8:29-30).

In isolation, the relative succinctness of these two verses can be deceptive. But in them, Paul summarized everything that came before, not just in this chapter of Romans but in the previous seven, helping us to understand the unfolding work of salvation to the degree that we are able. Christians have likened this passage to a golden chain, with the Spirit at work in all of them as God *foreknew* and *predestined*, *called*, *justified*, and *glorified* those he saves.

THOSE HE FOREKNEW AND PREDESTINED

On their own, these two terms are profound. To *foreknow* means to "know beforehand," in the sense of God setting his affections or love upon a person (John 15:16; 1 John 4:19). Meanwhile, *predestined* speaks to God's predetermined plans and purposes; it reminds us that God is the author of our salvation, from beginning to end.[3] Together, these two relate to one of the most humbling, awe-inspiring, and misunderstood doctrines of the Christian faith: *election*—God's gracious, wise, and holy will in saving sinners by faith in Jesus Christ (Ephesians 1:4-6).

If you're anything like me, that statement raises several questions. How does God choose? Does he use some sort of specific criteria?

Why does he save some people and not others? And after 20 years of study, here's what I can say: I don't know. More than that, no one knows. (And anyone who says otherwise is selling you something.)

We can't know because God doesn't tell us. These are mysteries, and their answers belong to him alone. They are profound truths that are simply too big for us to grasp. But here's what I do know: God calls all people, everywhere, to repent and believe the gospel because we all share the same dire spiritual condition. And what's amazing is some people actually *do*. In fact, everyone who calls on the name of the Lord will be saved (Romans 10:13)—and their number is so vast it cannot be counted (Revelation 7:9).

For some, the Spirit's presence is most difficult to see in this aspect of salvation. But as a member of the Trinity, he is integral to all that goes on "behind the veil" (Hebrews 6:19 NKJV). He was there before the foundations of the world as the plan of salvation was formed, loving us as the Father and Son love us before we could ever love him, purposing to draw the hearts of sinners to himself (Ephesians 1:4-5).

HE ALSO CALLED

This is not an external call in the sense of an encouragement to respond to the gospel message. It is an internal work of the Holy Spirit in the hearts of sinners, drawing sinners to himself (2 Timothy 1:8-10). This calling leads to our *regeneration*—to being born again as we move from spiritual death to life, replacing our hearts of stone, and giving us hearts of flesh that desire to love and please God (Psalm 104:30; Ezekiel 36:26; John 3:5-7; Acts 11:18; Philippians 1:29).

HE ALSO JUSTIFIED

Justification is a term that means to acquit. It is a declaration of innocence in the eyes of God or society. Every religion and worldview has a concept of justification built into it, and without exception, their approach is the same: Justification is performance-based. We earn it, or at least maintain it, through our actions. But Christianity's perspective is unique because justification is not something we can earn. We are justified by faith (Romans 8:33-34). Through faith in Jesus' death and resurrection, we are declared righteous—innocent—by God. We believe, and our faith is credited as righteousness (Genesis 15:6; Romans 4:3).

But understanding justification merely as a legal declaration undersells its great value. It is disappointing in the same way a chocolate bunny that looks solid, but in reality is actually hollow, is disappointing. The righteousness we have is not merely declared; it is Christ's righteousness, given to us—applied by the Spirit—in exchange for our sin (Romans 5:17; 1 Corinthians 1:30).[4] And what's more, Jesus did not simply exchange our sin for his righteousness. Jesus, the one who was without sin, *became* "sin for us, so that in him we would become the righteousness of God" (2 Corinthians 5:21). All condemnation became his. All blessings became ours as those justified apart from works (Romans 4:6).

And the righteousness we have by faith propels our growth in righteousness as the Holy Spirit transforms our hearts, minds, and character to reflect Christ to greater degrees every day of our lives (Galatians 5:16-26; 2 Thessalonians 2:13). He leads us to pursue righteousness as we have been declared righteous, empowering us to overcome sin and temptation, and interceding for us as he carries our prayers to the Father, and prays for us when we are weak and ignorant of what to pray (Romans 8:26-27). He teaches and reminds us of what Christ commanded (John 14:26; 1 Corinthians 2:10-11). He counsels and comforts us (2 Corinthians 1:4). And the Spirit sends and equips us according to his purposes, empowering us with gifts to testify to the truth of the gospel and build one another up in the faith (Acts 13:2; Romans 14:19; 1 Corinthians 12–14).

HE ALSO GLORIFIED

The great chain culminates in a promise, in its end goal. There will come a day when our pursuit of righteousness will reach its end. Either at our death or when Christ returns to rule and reign over the earth, the Holy Spirit's work in us will be complete (Philippians 1:9-11; Colossians 1:22). On that day, we will be *glorified*, free from the presence and stain of sin in our lives, with perfect physical bodies upon our resurrection and a fuller knowledge and understanding of God—fully knowing as we are fully known (1 Corinthians 13:12; Philippians 3:20-21).

And in this, the Spirit is present as well. His presence is the seal and proof—the down payment—that God will do what he says (2 Corinthians 1:21-22; 5:5; Ephesians 1:13-14). If we belong to Jesus, we have the Holy Spirit and we are his forever (John 14:16).

BE FILLED WITH JOY AND THE HOLY SPIRIT

This is what I wish I had known early on in my faith in Christ, because the Spirit's role in our lives is not cause for confusion, but celebration. The Holy Spirit loved us from before the beginning of the world. He draws us to Christ and grants us new life by faith in Jesus. He justifies us, replacing condemnation with Christ's righteousness. He lives within us, empowering us to pursue holiness here and now (1 Peter 1:16). And he will never, ever leave or forsake us.

Because the Spirit is with us, we should strive for a greater awareness of his power and presence. We should desire to know him better and to be led by him; to be "filled with joy and the Holy Spirit" (Acts 13:52 CSB). So what does that look like?

Practically, it means seeking to be people who live out of a surplus of his fruit in our lives (Galatians 5:22-23). So we invest in the Word, listening for the Spirit to "speak" to us through the pages of Scripture. To reveal his will to us in the words he inspired because the more we meditate on the Word, the deeper our relationship becomes. We commit ourselves to serving the body of believers because this is how the world will know that we belong to Christ, when they see the Spirit's power at work in our love for one another (John 13:35). We live faithfully in the world, where we will experience the power of the Holy Spirit—that we will be filled to a greater degree according to his purposes. That we will testify to the goodness of the gospel, trusting him to give us the right words to speak, and counting on him to bring good out of our mistakes.

That's the life we're called to. That's the life that is ours through the gospel—the life that is ours because the Spirit is our life.

REFLECT, EXPLORE, AND DISCUSS

1. What idea or concept stood out to you as you read this chapter? Why?

2. Read some of the Bible passages about the Holy Spirit's work in our lives referenced in this chapter. How do these passages encourage or challenge you?

3. What new questions do these passages raise?

4. If you are a Christian, how have you seen the Holy Spirit at work in your life?

5. Where do you need his help to a greater degree?

GOD RESTORES

20

A UNITED PEOPLE

Many Metaphors and One Reality

As a new believer, I began a quest to know everything I could about my new faith and the object of my faith, Jesus. I read everything I could get my hands on. I read about prayer, evangelism, suffering, salvation, grace, and Scripture (and I was reading the Bible too). It wasn't until I reached one specific subject that I hit a wall: the church.

Before I became a Christian, I had no clue what purpose a church served or even what it really was. Like most Western people, I assumed that a church was a type of building. As for what went on there, based on what I heard from the very few people I knew who had any interaction with it at all, it didn't sound like anything I would be interested in. Church was a lot of kneeling, standing, droning recitations, and maybe had some incense. Pop culture only cemented my belief that the church and whatever went on inside those buildings was a downer.

Once I became a believer, I saw that my impressions weren't exactly on the mark. And I wanted to correct that. So I read everything I could get my hands on. The problem was, of course, that almost everything I read seemed just as jaded and confused as everything I'd absorbed through grumpy friends and pop culture. Most of the popular works at the time focused on analyzing what church is or what it should be. *Incarnational, organic, authentic,* and *missional* were among the more common descriptors and buzzwords. But for all my reading, I didn't have a greater sense of what makes the church *the church*.

So I went to where I probably should have started. I began studying my Bible—and even dipped my toes into the ancient creeds—to get a sense of how it described this thing we call *church*. And what I found was liberating.

UNITED IN OUR TIME AND PLACE

The Bible doesn't describe the church the way we often do in the West. It doesn't describe the church as a specific location or event.[1] Instead, in virtually every instance, the church refers to God's people (Matthew 18:17; Acts 5:11; 8:1, 3; Colossians 1:9). More specifically, the church is the assembly of God's people, in one place and time, to celebrate and proclaim the gospel in word and deed.

Through the gospel, we are united together, one as Jesus and the Father are one (John 17:11, 21). This oneness is not the erasure of all that makes us unique and distinct. It is to be of like mind—united in desire and intent—and working toward a shared purpose as people who have experienced the all-encompassing love and compassion of the Father, Son, and Holy Spirit (Philippians 2:1-2). Whether we gather in a dedicated building, a school cafeteria, or in a field, if we are God's people, we are the church (Romans 16:16, 2 Corinthians 8:1, and Galatians 1:2).

UNITED ACROSS TIME AND SPACE

While the church is a time- and location-bound reality, it is also a *universal* one. Universal describes how the nature of the church does not have any boundaries. Language, ethnicity, nationality, and moment in history mean nothing to the gospel (John 10:16; 17:20; Acts 10:34-43; Galatians 3:28; Revelation 7:9). All people who have ever believed—and *will* ever believe—the gospel are united to one another in Jesus. We are all a part of his great assembly whose names are recorded in heaven (Hebrews 12:18-24).

UNITED IN OUR COMMITMENT TO THE TRUTH

The church—God's people—is not united by temporary causes and concerns (even if these often matter a great deal). Our unity is based in a commitment to the truth, "built on the foundation of the apostles and prophets, with Christ Jesus himself as the cornerstone" (Ephesians 2:20 CSB).

The church holds to the message handed down to us, the message available to us today in the Bible, the story of God's plan to rescue and redeem people through Jesus' life, death, and resurrection. And this truth that unites us motivates us to pursue holiness—to live as reflections of Christ, as a people set apart for his possession (1 Peter 1:16; 2:9; 2 Peter 3:11). It encourages us to embrace our role in declaring the good news of the gospel to people from every nation and people group. And it grounds us in a sure home—a firm conviction—of the world that is to come, one free from the presence and effects of sin, where we will enjoy his presence forever (Revelation 21:1-27).

UNITED EVEN WHEN WE DISAGREE

Whatever else we want to say about the church, this understanding must be our first priority. The people of God are the church (2 Corinthians 6:16). *Together.*

But unity in the gospel doesn't mean we agree on everything. We do have disagreements on what some might call secondary matters.

That is, matters of faith and practice that are not essential for salvation. We can still be united in the gospel and disagree on different issues. Such as approaches to baptism, who can or cannot be a pastor or elder in a local church, and beliefs about specific spiritual gifts. Also, we can be united when the world around us pressures the church to adopt opportunities to divide, such as political preferences, ethnicity, socio-economic status, nationality, and language. These things *should* not, and *must* not, be allowed to divide us in our essential unity.

Instead, we need to hold fast to the Bible's image of the church: God's people, uniquely and wonderfully made individuals, united in the gospel as a reflection of the oneness of the Trinity, living as witnesses to God's kingdom here and now, and throughout all time (Matthew 28:18-20; John 17:20-23).

THE MANY METAPHORS THAT UNITE US

The Bible deepens this understanding by using several different metaphors that reflect our unity. The church is a body, a bride, a temple, and a priesthood. Each metaphor highlights our unity, while also reminding us of our diversity.

As the *body of Christ*, we are Christ's representatives here on earth, under his authority as the head of the body (Colossians 1:18). Every believer is an equally valuable, yet different, part of the body, playing a role in building each other up in our faith, and in our mission to make Christ known (1 Corinthians 12).

As the *bride of Christ*, we are united with Christ, submitting ourselves with joy to the One who sacrificed all for us (Ephesians 5:22-31). The church is the one for whom Christ died to present to the Father holy and blameless (Ephesians 5:27), distinct from, yet joyfully bound in a lasting covenant to Christ, our bridegroom (Revelation 19:7; 21:2, 9; 22:17).

As the *temple of the Holy Spirit*, we are indwelt both individually and corporately, empowered for encouragement and mission, given gifts that are unique to the Spirit's purposes for us, and bear the fruit that can only be the result of the Spirit's presence in our lives (1 Corinthians 3:16-17; 12:12-13; 13; Galatians 5:22-23).

And as a *holy priesthood*, we enjoy unrestricted access to God and offering spiritual sacrifices acceptable to God through Christ (1 Peter 2:5). We are free to approach God with boldness because we have been redeemed by Christ (Romans 5:1-5; Hebrews 4:14-16).

This diversity is what allows the church's mission to make disciples possible. All of us are equally empowered for the task. All of us share the same inexhaustible power of the Spirit. All of us have the same gospel to proclaim. But we are all called to do so in different contexts and with different gifts to meet the needs of the time and place in which God has called us to make disciples.

THE MOST IMPORTANT METAPHOR OF ALL

But the Bible uses one other metaphor to describe the church: a family. Through the gospel, we are adopted by God and named his sons and daughters (Ephesians 1:5). We are beloved children and coheirs with Christ (Romans 8:17). We have a Father who loves us with the most powerful love imaginable—a "Never-Stopping, Never Giving Up, Unbreaking, Always and Forever Love."[2] Our Father gives good gifts to his children (Matthew 7:11) and is always working out all things for their ultimate good (Romans 8:28).

On one level, this metaphor is easy to understand. We understand family relationships, at least in theory. But its apparent ease doesn't diminish its importance. This is a metaphor that crosses into reality—it's not that God is *like* a Father to us. He really is our Father, and we are his children through faith in Christ.

But this is also what makes it a challenging image for so many. Many of us have experienced profound brokenness in our families of origin—divorce, abuse, neglect, abandonment, and countless other sins besides. And sadly, many of us have found similar pain in our experiences with other Christians. We all sin against one another in different ways, often unintentionally. But sometimes, those sins *are* intentional—and of a great evil. As a result, this metaphor is prone to misuse and abuse, especially when unqualified, manipulative, and abusive people are in positions of influence.

EMBRACING THE MOST CHALLENGING METAPHOR

Even though it might be tempting to abandon this image of the church because of misuse and abuse, we need to embrace it. More than that, we need to pursue to live as a healthy family.

To be safe places, where people can be vulnerable without fear of reprisal, judgment, or manipulation. For the church to be safe, it means that we need to be compassionate toward those whose experience of family falls far short of God's desire and standard, especially within the context of the church. Because if we truly believe that when one suffers, all suffer together, we need to live like it (1 Corinthians 12:26).

To be places where everyone belongs. Being compassionate also means helping people see that they belong. That whatever they've experienced doesn't make them some kind of "other" or outcast. The weary, brokenhearted, and downcast all need our love. Those who have experienced real hurt and pain at the hands of other professing Christians that has left their faith hanging on by a thread. A healthy church, one that embraces this metaphor, needs to be a place that welcomes them in and says, "You belong here."

To be places that take their time. And in all of this, the reality is that it takes time. Hurt people don't feel safe instantly. And they don't feel like they belong overnight. They may even lash out at times because they're waiting for the other shoe to drop. But a healthy church is going to recognize and embrace the challenges that come with being patient with people. Praying for them. Loving them in the ways they can receive.

Ultimately, this is a way that we are expressing our belief in the gospel. Jesus died for us, not just to save us from our sins, but to make us a part of his family. And that is the key—the family is his. None of us are fathers or mothers (or weird uncles I hope). God is our Father, and Jesus is our coheir who shows us the way, and who calls us to love one another because this is how the world will know that we are his (John 13:34-35).

That is what the world needs to see. That is what people who have been hurt in many ways need to experience. To see that the metaphor isn't *just* a metaphor—that, because of Jesus, it is real.

A BETTER ANSWER THAN I EVER EXPECTED

This is not the understanding of the church I expected to find when I asked, *What is the church?*, all those years ago. But it's the understanding I need, a better answer to my question than I expected I would find. An answer that satisfies and inspires me to give my life to its cause.

The church is people here and now, across space and time, and from every nation and people group, united in Jesus. The church is a body and a bride. A temple and a priesthood. The church is a family, the family of God, where all who put their hope in Christ are welcome and none are turned away.

That's the church as it should be, as the Bible describes it. That's the church as it will be, when all things are made new. And that's the church we are called to be while we wait for that day to come, as we love one another and declare the good news of Jesus together.

REFLECT, EXPLORE, AND DISCUSS

1. What idea or concept stood out to you as you read this chapter? Why?

2. Read some of the Bible passages about the church referenced in this chapter. How do these passages encourage or challenge you?

3. What new questions do these passages raise?

4. Think about your church experience. How can you help nurture the unity described in this chapter?

GOD RESTORES

21

OUR RELATIONSHIPS WITH ONE ANOTHER

How the Gospel Makes Us Safe

When we look back on the first 25 years of this century, trying to figure out how to characterize them, what do you think people will say? There are so many significant events to choose from that will shape our thoughts. The destruction of the World Trade Center's twin towers, and the ongoing effects of the 9/11 terrorist attacks. The rapid rise of social media platforms that were intended to democratize information and connect the world. The invention of smartphones and other technology that was meant to simplify our lives. The erosion of public confidence in the institutions we have—such as the media, our governments, and the church—if not entirely distrusted, at least less well respected.

Personally, I think we'll look back on those 25 years and see a relational crisis; an epidemic on an unimaginable scale affecting every aspect of our lives. The platforms meant to connect the world divide us, sequestering us into algorithm-designed echo chambers.[1] The technology meant to simplify life brings more complexity, destroying our ability to rest and focus. Mistrust and suspicion characterize the way we see the world, causing us to question everything we hear, read, and see as we assume some kind of nefarious ulterior motive.

We don't know how to be husbands or wives. We don't know how to be friends. We don't know how to be vulnerable. We are not safe.

This should not surprise us, really. Relational discord is a consequence of sin (Genesis 3:8-16). And what we see in the world is the result of people—including many Christians—unquestioningly embracing tools that make us anxious and gullible as they feed our sinful desires.

But it doesn't need to be this way. Because the gospel transforms people, making us new people with new desires, it also gives us the ability to overcome the relational discord that ravages the world. Through the power of the Holy Spirit living inside of us, we can be husbands, wives, mothers, fathers, children, friends, and neighbors who love one another and those around us in ways that reflect the beauty of God's love for us in Jesus—ways that glorify him. But possible doesn't mean *easy*.

MORE RADICAL THAN REINVENTIONS

Let's think about marriage first. It is rare for any media outlet or self-declared influencer to say anything positive about marriage. (Although it does happen on occasion.[2]) You're far more likely to find articles bearing headlines like "The Sexist and Racist History of Marriage That No One Talks About,"[3] "How Did Polyamory Become So Popular?"[4] and "Is an Open Marriage a Happier Marriage?"[5]

Despite the headlines, as well as the oft-repeated doom-and-gloom statistics about divorce rates, it's an oversimplification to say that Western society is opposed to marriage. It isn't. Our society is actually *pro*marriage. It only wants to define it on its own terms. This explains the widespread acceptance of same-sex marriage as much as it does further redefinitions, such as polygamous, polyamorous, and open marriages. But it also explains why the average person can't describe what marriage is or is intended to be. Some see it as a vehicle for companionship and personal fulfillment. While others see it as nothing more than a social construct, a contractual arrangement that has no more benefit to society than cohabitation.

But Christianity's take on marriage is far more radical than any redefinition or reinvention of it. Remember that when God created the world, he called everything good except for one thing: "It is not good for the man to be alone" (Genesis 2:18). So God created a companion for him—one like him and distinct from him, to represent and reflect God alongside him. Fundamentally, that is God's intended design for marriage: A lifelong covenant between one man and one woman, who partner and colabor for one another's good (Genesis 2:21-25).

Marriage, as God intends it, allows us to experience intimate companionship, of relational and emotional intimacy—to be fully known without fear of judgment or shame. Marriage is the context for healthy sexual expression, physical intimacy overflowing from relational intimacy (Hebrews 13:4). It is the natural home for children to come into being and be raised in love and safety, as men and women multiply in a unique expression of our nature and calling as image bearers of God (Genesis 1:28). But there is more to marriage than all of this. A deeper meaning that, in a sense, makes the gospel visible through the relationship between husbands and wives.

WIVES ARE NOT SECOND-CLASS CITIZENS

In Ephesians 5:22-23, Paul charged wives to "submit to your husbands as to the Lord" and to do so because "the husband is the head of the wife as Christ is the head of the church" (CSB). This language is jarring for modern readers. It can read as though Paul were advocating for a kind of *subservience* as though the husband is the superior or better of his wife. This has led some to charge Paul with misogyny, looking upon his writing with suspicion. And that suspicion is further compounded as Paul continues, "[Christ] is the Savior of the body. Now as the church submits to Christ, so also wives are to submit to their husbands in everything" (verses 23-24 csb).

While the word *submit* does carry a sense of obedience, Paul was not advocating for a kind of master-servant relationship between husbands and wives. Women are not second-class citizens of God's kingdom. Unfortunately, men can too easily forget this, which leads to a lot of posturing, chest-thumping, and men demanding their own way as they hold their wives (and themselves) up to arbitrary or culturally conditioned standards of what is expected of husbands and wives.[6]

Appearances to the contrary, Paul wasn't declaring husbands to be in charge, as you'll see in a moment. He was dealing with our heart postures, our dispositions toward one another in relationship to Christ. And Paul could urge wives to "submit to their husbands in everything" because of his command to husbands.

HUSBANDS ARE NOT MICROMANAGERS

As though anticipating suspicion and the distortion of his command to wives, Paul made it clear what it means for a husband to be the head of his wife:

> Husbands, love your wives, just as Christ loved the church and gave himself for her to make her holy, cleansing her with the washing of water by the word. He did this to present the church to himself in splendor, without spot or wrinkle or anything like that, but holy and blameless. In the same way, husbands are to love their wives as their own bodies. He who loves his wife loves himself. For no

one ever hates his own flesh but provides and cares for it, just as Christ does for the church, since we are members of his body (Ephesians 5:25-30 CSB).

Far from being a microsovereign reigning over a personal kingdom, a husband is not called to be a leader, but a servant. He is called to sacrifice himself for his wife. To consider her needs ahead of his own, as being more significant than his (Philippians 2:3-4), and to do so out of reverence for Christ. If he is to lead in anything, it is to be in fostering a culture within his family where his wife can flourish. Where she has the freedom to discover and express her gifts to the fullest, and to grow in holiness and Christlikeness. He is to create an environment where his wife is safe in every respect—emotionally, physically, and spiritually—because he is submitting himself to Christ as a member of *Christ's* body.

WORSHIP THROUGH RELATIONSHIP

What Paul describes might best be understood as an expression of worship through relationship—an expression that reveals the profound mystery of the gospel. That Christ, though existing "in the form of God, did not consider equality with God as something to be exploited" (Philippians 2:6 CSB). Instead:

> He emptied himself by assuming the form of a servant, taking on the likeness of humanity. And when he had come as a man, he humbled himself by becoming obedient to the point of death—even to death on a cross (Philippians 2:7-8 CSB).

In humility, Jesus sacrificed himself, saving his body, the church. Husbands and wives are called to reflect this in their relationships with one another, as they submit to one another in reverence to Christ (Ephesians 5:21). They are united in will and purpose, united as one flesh (Ephesians 5:31), distinct but inseparable partners walking side by side as they reflect Christ in ways that honor their distinctiveness.

This is God's design for marriage. It is what makes marriage make sense—the "profound mystery" of marriage reflecting Christ and the church (Ephesians 5:32). As Timothy and Kathy Keller state, "If God had the gospel of Jesus's salvation in mind when he established marriage, then marriage only 'works' to the degree that approximates the pattern of God's self-giving love in Christ."[7]

WHERE WE FIND SAFETY FOR EVERY RELATIONSHIP

All this talk about the meaning of marriage might be encouraging for those of us who are married. But what about everyone else? If you're not married—whether widowed, divorced, or have never been—reading about marriage can feel discouraging, as though you're being left out of something important. While marriage does display the mystery of the gospel in a unique way, our other relationships do as well.

We are all called to live as imitators of God, walking "in love, as Christ also loved us and gave himself for us" (Ephesians 5:2 CSB). To walk as "children of light—for the fruit of the light consists of all goodness, righteousness, and truth—testing what is pleasing to the Lord" (Ephesians 5:8-10 CSB). To speak to one another in "psalms, hymns, and spiritual songs, singing and making music with your heart to the Lord, giving thanks always for everything to God the Father in the name of our Lord Jesus Christ, submitting to one another in the fear of Christ" (Ephesians 5:19-21 CSB). To reflect the humility of Christ as we move through life together.

Humility is not to think of ourselves as less important than others; it is to recognize that the needs of others often surpass our own. In a sense, humility is love in practice as we pursue to *out-love* one another, seeking one another's best because of the love we have experienced in the gospel. In humility, we are "devoted to one another with mutual love, showing eagerness in honoring one another" (Romans 12:10).

And this kind of humility, this kind of love, creates relationships where we can experience genuine openness and vulnerability; to live as people who weep with those who weep and rejoice with those who rejoice (Romans 12:15). It makes it safe to let our guard down and to be honest about the fact that we are messed-up people who need a *lot* of help. Humility makes it safe to invite people into our mess, not only to help us but also to learn from our experiences as we bear one another's burdens and seek to truly encourage and spur one another on to love and good deeds.

No fear. No shame. No judgment. The gospel makes us safe (1 John 4:18).

TAKE ALL THE TIME YOU NEED

All of this is easy to say, but hard to live out. No matter our backgrounds, no matter our histories, we've all been hurt by other people. At some point, likely many, our trust has been violated. We don't feel safe.

And these violations are not overcome quickly or easily, especially when other Christians are the ones who hurt us. And there can be a temptation for us to rush those who have been hurt to get better. We do it to ourselves too. But the safety we have in the gospel means we do not need to hurry. People are not projects or problems to solve. They are people to love. So we want our relationships to be saturated in the gospel, praying and trusting that the Holy Spirit will work in them according to his timeline, not our own.

If we want to overcome the relational crisis that has marked the beginning of the twenty-first century, it's going to take time. If we want to overcome the mistrust and suspicion that have become so deeply ingrained, it's going to take time. If we want to be people who walk in the light, it's going to take time. If we want to be husbands and wives who reflect the goodness of the gospel, it's going to take time. If we want to be friends who spur one another on to love and good works, it's going to take time. If we want to feel and experience safety, it is going to take time.

Take all the time you need.

REFLECT, EXPLORE, AND DISCUSS

1. What idea or concept stood out to you as you read this chapter? Why?

2. Read some of the Bible passages about the gospel and relationships referenced in this chapter. How do these passages encourage or challenge you?

3. What new questions do these passages raise?

4. Think about your relationships. How do they reflect the vision shared in this chapter?

5. What, if anything, might need to change to better reflect God's design for us?

GOD RESTORES

22

OUR GREATER PURPOSE

Worshiping in Songs, Sacraments, and Every Part of Our Lives

On May 21, 2005, David Foster Wallace took his place at the podium at Kenyon College in Gambier, Ohio. Considered one of the most influential writers of the 1990s and early 2000s, Wallace had been called upon to impart a few words of wisdom to the graduating class of the private liberal arts school. His commencement address was a masterclass in deconstruction as he poked fun at the tropes of commencement speeches while exploring notions of truth, certainty, and what matters most in life. And as he approached his conclusion, he made what might be the most provocative statement in a message filled with them: "In the day-to-day trenches of adult life, there is actually no such thing as atheism."

> There is no such thing as not worshipping. Everybody worships. The only choice we get is what to worship. And an outstanding reason for choosing some sort of god or spiritual-type thing to worship—be it J.C. or Allah, be it

Yahweh or the Wiccan mother-goddess or the Four Noble Truths or some infrangible set of ethical principles—is that pretty much anything else you worship will eat you alive.[1]

I didn't hear this speech until I had been a Christian for several years, but when I did, I was blown away. See, before I believed, I would have outright rejected the idea that I worshiped anything. Like I've said before, it wasn't because I was a deeply convinced atheist. I just didn't care enough to care. But after coming to faith, I could see how that was the case. I didn't worship a god, but what I did care about—what, in a very practical sense, I worshiped—was money, reputation, and achievement.

Maybe the same is true for you. Whether you're a Christian or not, you might read Wallace's words and find them hitting home in a way you didn't expect. That's because there's a truth to them that goes deeper than even he fully understood. Because he was right. We are all worshipers. We all worship something. The question is: What are we worshiping?

But first, let's back up a second and ask a question that you may not even realize we need to ask: What does *worship* mean?

GIVING THE LORD HIS DUE IN EVERYTHING

Many Christians in the Western world tend to think about worship as music, which makes sense given how we typically use the word as shorthand for congregational singing. And while this isn't wrong, it is incomplete. The words we typically see translated as worship in the Bible describe an act of deference or reverence, of bowing or kneeling. This is not accidental; it signifies that worship is a heart posture, expressing devotion, reverence, and adoration to someone or something.

Worship is hardwired into who and what we are as human beings.

We cannot help ourselves (Romans 1:18-22). We will worship anything: animals, nature, and even other human beings. But the only one worthy of this sort of reverence is the Lord himself. So to worship God is to give him all the praise he is due as our Creator and Savior. To live in the "fear," or reverence, "of the Lord," which is the beginning of wisdom and knowledge (Proverbs 1:7). Worship, as the Bible describes it, isn't limited to one act or situation. It is not a synonym for singing. Worship encompasses every aspect of our lives.

And yes, that includes singing.

RAISING OUR VOICES IN WORSHIP

Even though it is wrong to reduce worship to singing, Scripture is absolutely clear that singing is a part of what it means to worship. All throughout the Bible, from beginning to end, singing is tied to worship:

- "I will sing to the Lord, for He has triumphed gloriously!" (Exodus 15:1 NKJV).
- "I will sing praise to the Lord God of Israel" (Judges 5:3 NKJV).
- "I will give thanks to You, O Lord…and sing praises to Your name" (2 Samuel 22:50 NKJV).
- "I…will sing praise to the name of the Lord Most High" (Psalm 7:17 NKJV).
- "I will sing with the spirit, and I will also sing with the understanding" (1 Corinthians 14:15 NKJV).
- "Be filled with the Spirit, speaking to one another in psalms and hymns and spiritual songs, singing and making melody in your heart to the Lord" (Ephesians 5:18-19 NKJV).

- Admonish "one another in psalms and hymns and spiritual songs, singing with grace in your hearts to the Lord" (Colossians 3:16 NKJV).

I could quote more verses, but I think you get the point. A biblical view of worship is more than singing songs of praise, but it certainly isn't less. Singing is an act of worship, and we should take every opportunity to encourage one another to raise our voices and declare the greatness of God together.

CELEBRATING WITH SACRAMENTS

A *sacrament* or *ordinance* is a practice or ritual that serves as a sign or symbol of a spiritual reality.[2] While traditions vary in terms of how many they observe, two are embraced by all branches of Christianity: baptism and the Lord's Supper.

Baptism. Instituted by Jesus when he issued the great commission—to make disciples in the name of the Father, Son, and Holy Spirit (Matthew 28:19; Acts 2:38), this sacrament is meant to be a sign and a symbol of our faith in Christ as our crucified, buried, and risen Savior. Baptism does not grant new life in Christ, although in some mysterious way, it assures us of our union with Christ. The early church saw baptism as one element of a three-fold initiation rite along with faith and repentance.[3] It was a declaration that the one baptized was part of God's covenant family and a beneficiary of God's promises by symbolizing their death to sin when plunged into the water, the burial of their old selves while below the surface, and their resurrection to new life when they reemerge from the water.[4]

Many church traditions continue to practice baptism in a similar fashion today, with new Christians baptized by immersion as an act of obedience to the Lord.[5] But some years into the second century, another form emerged that over time took prominence: infant baptism. Typically conducted with a sprinkling of water, infant baptism is less of a symbol of the faith of the person being baptized and is understood more as a covenant promise—that the child may come to possess genuine faith as they experience life within the covenant community of God, functioning effectively as a new covenant parallel to the old covenant sign of circumcision.

While Christians remain in good faith disagreement about which practice is most faithful to Scripture, both sides in the debate agree that baptism is an act of worship. It is a sign that we believe that salvation belongs to the Lord (Jonah 2:9) and that all who call on the name of the Lord will be saved (Acts 2:21).

The Lord's Supper. Also called *communion* or *the Eucharist*, the Lord's Supper is a sacrament meant for all who believe, all who have been saved through faith in Jesus' death and resurrection. Instituted during Jesus' last meal with his disciples before his crucifixion, it is a powerful and multisensory reminder of the gospel. It is typically practiced by taking and eating a small piece of bread, representing Christ's body broken for us, and drinking a small amount of wine or grape juice, representing Christ's blood that was shed for us. We are to approach this rite in a worthy manner, to treat it with great care because of all it represents (1 Corinthians 11:27-32) because it is an act of worship.

In a way that we cannot fully comprehend, Christ is spiritually present in this symbol. No miracles occur to transform the bread and wine into something other than bread and wine, of course. The bread and wine are bread and wine.[6] (Or juice, depending on your convictions.) Yet Christ is also there with them, feeding our souls as the bread and wine feed our bodies.[7] It reminds us of our union with Christ, that the life we now live we live by faith in the Son of God, who loved us and gave himself for us (Galatians 2:20). It creates a sense of hope as we wait expectantly for the day when he returns, we will see him face to face, and fully know as we are fully known (1 Corinthians 13:12). And we are encouraged to love one another as Christ loved us (John 13:34-35).

WORSHIPING AS CARETAKERS AND CULTIVATORS

We raise our voices in worship as we sing God's praises. We worship God as we celebrate the sacraments of baptism and the Lord's Supper. We also worship through *stewardship*. This word calls us back to God's intention in creating humanity, to serve as caretakers and cultivators of creation (Genesis 1:28; 1 Corinthians 4:1-2). As worshipers, we steward everything God has given us—our time, talents, and treasures (Matthew 25:14-30)—in order to glorify him.

Time. As created beings, we are called to make the most of each day, using our time well for God's glory. We work hard as though we are working for the Lord (Colossians 3:23), but we also rest. We take the time necessary to care for ourselves, acknowledging our limitations as created beings because even they are a gift from God—a reminder that we are not him.

Talents. God gifts each of us with unique abilities, both spiritual gifts and natural talents, which we are called to use in service of others as "good stewards of the varied grace of God" (1 Peter 4:10 CSB). As long as we live, we are to develop and use these talents to their fullest extent to the glory of God.

Treasures. We are to manage, according to God's purposes, the finances and material possessions he provides us with. This means striving to live within our means and regularly, sacrificially, joyfully, and prayerfully giving our finances toward God's kingdom work out of a desire to see him glorified in the world (Proverbs 3:9; Matthew 6:1-4; Mark 12:41-44; 1 Corinthians 16:2; 2 Corinthians 9:6-7).[8]

PURSUING JUSTICE AND MERCY

Worshiping as cultivators and caretakers extends beyond our time, talents, and treasures and into our presence in the world. We are called to pursue human flourishing, working for the good of all people without compromising our loyalty to Christ and to the truth. We are to do as the Lord requires of us: "to do justly, to love mercy, and to walk humbly with [our] God" (Micah 6:8 NKJV).

The early church's faith was not a quietly pietistic one that left society to fend for itself. The first Christians were compelled to pursue the good of others. They had a profound—and profoundly good—moral, social, and spiritual influence in "daily life and manners…in the elevation of Womanhood…and in the gradual abolition of Slavery, and in the ransoming of Captives, and in acts of mercy and love to the sick and dying in Hospitals, and in times of Plagues, Pestilences, and Famines."[9]

The First Council of Nicaea even decreed that wherever a church or cathedral was built, a hospital would be also. These hospitals would welcome the poor, the working class, the elderly, and the infirm without qualification. All who needed care would receive it. The early church's witness was a witness that "won for it a thousand hearts."[10]

This legacy continues today. Painfully, while there are too many examples of Christians acting contrary to their faith and even opposing biblical justice—as in the barbaric practice of chattel slavery in the eighteenth and nineteenth centuries, and the segregation laws that characterized much of the twentieth—there have also always been Christians who refused to compromise or capitulate. Christians who recognized that their faith called them to pursue the good of all people.

So we actively oppose racism and celebrate ethnic diversity because humanity was created by a God who loves diversity and will be worshiped by a "vast multitude from every nation, tribe, people, and language" in the new creation (Revelation 7:9 CSB). We defend the sanctity of human life from conception to natural death. We protect the right for human beings to be born, give families to orphans, promote education, and help those in need through acts of compassion and generosity because all human beings are valued by God and have the right to flourish. We uphold God's good design for humanity, as male and female, not out of a spirit of fear or hatred, but because they *are* God's good design for humanity.

We are to defend the weak, protect the innocent, and oppose the proud, while refusing to allow wolves among us who seek to destroy and devour us. We are to be concerned about the moral character of leaders, to be engaged in the public square, and oppose greed, selfishness, and every other vice that threatens to harm those made in God's image.

TO LIVE IS TO WORSHIP

David Foster Wallace was right that everybody worships. Humans don't have the ability not to. Because worship, as Scripture describes it, is not a segmented activity or a special hour in our lives. Worship *is* our lives.

To live is to worship. Every moment of every day, in the most significant decisions and the most seemingly mundane moments, we are worshiping. We are revealing what matters most to us. Every moment is holy, and an opportunity to pursue righteousness, truth, and love for the good of all and to the glory of God. To be people who give God his due, revering him and making his greatness known in our work and rest, our celebrating and sorrow, and our care and cultivating.

And even in our singing.

REFLECT, EXPLORE, AND DISCUSS

1. What idea or concept stood out to you as you read this chapter? Why?

2. Read some of the Bible passages about worship referenced in this chapter. How do these passages encourage or challenge you?

3. What new questions do these passages raise?

4. In what area of your life is there an opportunity to worship Christ to a greater extent?

GOD RESTORES

23

OUR GREAT COMMISSION

Good News Worth Sharing in Word and Works

It was October 1999, just a couple of months into my first year of college, when I met Emily. Two of our mutual friends were dating, and they decided it would be a good idea for us to meet. I was socially awkward and angsty. She was (and is) the perfect combination of really smart and really pretty. (She's also one of the most naturally funny people I know. But I didn't find that out until our third conversation.) Clearly, we were a match made in heaven, despite me not knowing if heaven even existed at the time.

She was also a Bahá'í, which is a religion I'd never heard of before meeting her. But I was a quick study. This religion, which has its roots in Islam, was founded in the nineteenth century. The Bahá'ís are all about the essential oneness of humanity: nationally, ethnically, and spiritually.[1] This is why they teach that every major religion is one part of a long chain of progressive revelation, with each religion's central figure being an equal "manifestation of God,"—an authoritative representative for the eras in which he lived.[2]

They also reject *proselytizing*. Kind of. They are highly engaged in humanitarian efforts around the world and actively encourage members to talk about their faith, but only in ways that won't make hearers feel as though they're being encouraged to convert. Instead, Bahá'ís want people to see the value of the principle of oneness, to see how it changes the world, and to make that principle their own.

So *proselytizing*. But super low-key about it.

THE PROBLEM WITH PROSELYTIZING

I'm not seeking to poke fun at the Bahá'ís, or anyone else for that matter. I get that as a term, *proselytizing* comes with baggage. We associate it with manipulation or coercion, especially in a religious context. But proselytizing is simply about persuasion. It is encouraging a person to join a cause, a mission, or a way of life. And it is impossible for us to *not* proselytize. All people, everywhere, do it all the time. Whether we're talking about religion, politics, technology, coffee, cars, cinematic universes, or graham crackers, we're trying to convince others to see our perspective, and usually, agree with us. It is acting as an advocate, ambassador, or evangelist for what we care most deeply about.

CHRISTIANS HAVE A GREAT COMMISSION

This idea of being advocates or ambassadors is not foreign to Christianity. In fact, it is an essential component of our calling in the world, which Jesus himself issued before he ascended to the Father:

> All authority has been given to me in heaven and on earth. Go, therefore, and make disciples of all nations, baptizing them in the name of the Father and of the Son and of the Holy Spirit, teaching them to observe everything I have commanded you. And remember, I am with you always, to the end of the age (Matthew 28:18-20 csb).

This is what Christians call the Great Commission. Under Jesus' authority as king of the universe and as his representatives (2 Corinthians 5:20), we proclaim the good news of what Jesus has done to rescue the world, which is the heart of *evangelism*. And along with that, we help one another grow into mature followers of Jesus, which is what we call *discipleship*.

In one sense, this calling should be as natural as breathing for all of us. But whether it's because we feel the weight of the subheads in our Bibles or because we've been pummeled by poor, and sometimes, manipulative teaching, many Christians struggle to talk about Jesus with anyone—even with other Christians! As for discipleship? That feels like something for professionals, people with at *least* a bachelor's degree in the Bible, doesn't it? Despite whatever external pressures and fears push us away from either, every Christian is called to play a role in helping people know Jesus and grow as one of his followers.

EVANGELISM: WORSHIPING JESUS BY TELLING PEOPLE ABOUT HIM

I sometimes describe myself as one of the world's most timid evangelists. I even joke that God was so serious about me sharing the gospel with people that he once gave me a job with "gospel" in the title. And I say it this way because of the stereotype of a street preacher that still permeates the American consciousness—the man standing on a soapbox on a street corner with a loudspeaker, shouting about people being sinners destined for hell. I'm not that guy. Neither are the street preachers I know. (Although I have seen one or two of these types out in downtown Nashville over the years.)

But in truth, I'm only timid in the sense that I am concerned about talking about Jesus and the gospel naturally. I don't want to sound like I'm following a script like the Jehovah's Witnesses I talked about back in chapter 1. So I don't shoehorn Jesus into a discussion about a great meal, a fun movie, or a good book, for example.[3] I talk about Jesus and the gospel as a part of what I talk about regularly, and the ways I do so are contextually appropriate.

And that's what I want to encourage you with as well: If you are a Christian, no matter who you are—no matter your gifts, strengths, weaknesses, your personality type, or your confidence level—you can do this too. You are called to share the good news that Jesus lived perfectly on our behalf, died in our place, and rose again from the dead.

See? It's that easy. (*Says the guy writing the book.*)

EMBRACING THE DELIGHT OF EVANGELISM

But don't read what I just said above with a sense of becoming obligated. While there is a command present, evangelism is not simply a duty. It is intended to be a *delight*. Sharing the gospel is an act of worship; it is something we do as an expression of our love for Jesus. We share out of thankfulness for the grace we have received from him, and from a desire for others to receive this grace as well. Evangelism is an invitation to experience the new life that Jesus offers in the gospel.

At this point in the book, you probably don't need me to retread the familiar territory of what the gospel is (and if you do, go back and read chapter 13). So rather than repeating myself, I want to encourage you to see evangelism as a delight, as an act of worship, and not merely an obligation.

Your story matters. If you're a Christian, the way God worked in your life to bring you to faith is worth celebrating. Maybe you grew up in a family that loved Jesus and following him seemed the most natural thing in the world. Or maybe you grew up in that same kind of home, but you wrestled with faith and rejected it for years before finally seeing that Jesus is who he says he is. Or like me, you didn't grow up around Christianity at all and you became a Christian as an adult. No matter how you came to faith, it is a gift, and it is worth celebrating and sharing with others.

But we also need to remember that sharing our story is not the same as sharing the gospel. They are connected, but different. Your story is how you came to believe the gospel and be saved through it. The life, death, and resurrection of Jesus is the gospel. And "your story can provide a natural opening to sharing the most important message about the most important person in the universe."[4] So don't be afraid to share your story, no matter how seemingly ordinary or extraordinary it might appear to be.

You don't need to be perfect, only faithful. Maybe you hesitate to share the gospel because you don't seem to have it all together. You still struggle with sins. Your prayer life could use some work. You've never heard of Obadiah, let alone read his book. What I love about Christianity is that it doesn't require us to be perfect before we talk to people about Jesus. If that were the case, the gospel would never have left Jerusalem.

Remember this: the apostles included a denier (Peter), a doubter (Thomas), a Roman collaborator (Matthew), and a terrorist (Simon). Paul persecuted Christians before becoming one (Acts 9:1-31). They were a mess. And everyone else who has ever believed in the gospel has also been a mess. And that's exactly the point. "God saves messed-up people through Jesus. And God makes Jesus known to messed-up people using the messed-up people he saves."[5] So don't freak out. You don't need to be perfect. You only need to be faithful.

What happens is not up to you. In my experience, it is rare for a person to respond to the gospel immediately after hearing it. It's much more common to see someone not openly respond at all, at least initially. And that's okay because you don't know what the Holy Spirit is doing in that person's life. The words you speak might seem to bounce off the person you are sharing with, but they can also be finding their way deep down into your listener's heart—growing like a plant, slowly underground before breaking ground (Luke 8:4-15). We might sow a seed, and we might water it, but it's God who causes it to grow (1 Corinthians 3:6-9). So don't worry about whether a person responds. Only be faithful to share and be an encouragement to those who believe and want their faith to grow.

DISCIPLESHIP: WORSHIPING JESUS BY GROWING TOGETHER

When we read the Great Commission, we can mistakenly read it as a call to evangelize, to proclaim the gospel message. And while that is part of Christ's commission to us, it is only a portion of it. To make disciples is to teach and train our fellow believers to become mature followers of Jesus. To help them "observe everything [Jesus] commanded" us (Matthew 28:20), as they grow in their knowledge of, obedience to, and love for the Lord.

But growing in spiritual maturity isn't one task. It is the culmination of all the formal and informal instruction, guidance, and encouragement we receive in all times and places, and in every area of life (Deuteronomy 6:4-9; Acts 20:17-24). The best word to describe this is *edification* (1 Corinthians 10:23; Ephesians 4:16), a word that conveys the idea of building one another up, of helping one another mature in our faith.

LIFE AS A (HEALTHY) GROUP PROJECT

I sometimes struggle with the "one another" aspect of discipleship. It feels a bit too much like group projects in school, which were always the worst because I usually ended up doing all the work, while my partners got to reap the benefits. I'm much more comfortable thinking about spiritual growth from an individual perspective. And I know I'm not alone in this. Many of us think about spiritual disciplines—practices that help us grow in our faith—in this way. We gravitate to what we can on our own. So when we read and study the Bible, pray, read books like this one, listen to podcasts, journal, or do anything else we might do regularly to grow in our faith, we do it alone.

There is a place for solitary activities—for time alone with God. Jesus modeled this, especially in prayer (Matthew 14:23; Mark 1:35; 6:46; Luke 6:12). Careful contemplation and reflection often require solitude. But solitary activities alone are not enough to grow us into the image of Christ. Discipleship is not fully experienced individually because it is not possible to edify yourself. Edification requires *community*. It requires the church, the people of God, working together to build one another up in the gospel (Romans 14:19; 15:2; Ephesians 4:29; 1 Thessalonians 5:11).

Discipleship is a (healthy) group project. No one person is required to do all the work. We all have a part to play and we all benefit. So we learn together through preaching and teaching (Ephesians 4:11-13) and Bible studies. In prayer, we bring one another's needs to God. We explore, discuss, and apply books together. We serve our communities together. As we watch one another's lives, we learn by example what it means to follow Jesus (1 Corinthians 11:1). We learn to rejoice with those who rejoice and weep with those who weep (Romans 12:15). We learn to faithfully walk through suffering, grief, and hardship—things only experience can teach.

This is discipleship in its truest sense. It is life *together*, worshiping Jesus by growing together. Because when we are together, we can consider how to spur one another on to love and good works (Hebrews 10:24-25). We build one another up and encourage one another in relationship (1 Corinthians 12:26; Galatians 6:2). We grow deeper in our understanding of our identity as believers—as people who are new creations in Christ, created for good works (2 Corinthians 5:17; Ephesians 2:10).

OUR PERSUASIVE PROMISE AND WAY OF LIFE

When we think about proselytizing, about persuasion, we need to remember that its power comes from promises. That's what Christianity has to offer. Its message is persuasive because its promise is powerful: We are rescued from our sins through the life, death, and resurrection of Jesus. A new life with new desires, a new identity, a new purpose, and a new future. Peace with God now, and forevermore. All this is given to us by faith in Jesus. That's a promise worth sharing. So let's not be afraid to talk about it.

But the power doesn't only come from the promise of the future; it includes how it changes people today. Because of the gospel, we experience the world differently. We live as people with hope, even when hope seems to be in short supply. We live as people who experience true community and seek one another's best, loving one another as Christ first loved us (John 13:35). This is a promise worth *experiencing*. Let's invite others into this glorious promise.

REFLECT, EXPLORE, AND DISCUSS

1. What idea or concept stood out to you as you read this chapter? Why?

2. Read some of the Bible passages about evangelism and edification referenced in this chapter. How do these passages encourage or challenge you?

3. What new questions do these passages raise?

4. How comfortable are you sharing the gospel with others? Why?

5. In what ways can you more fully embrace the "one another" experience of discipleship?

GOD REIGNS

24

OVER LIFE *AFTER* DEATH

The Question Everyone's Asking (Even When They Don't Realize It)

Outside of the particularly morbid, few people like to think about death. Most of us like to avoid it as much as possible. We fear it almost as much as we fear public speaking. But what about the topic of what happens *after* we die? Well, that's another story.

Before I became a Christian, I didn't really give the afterlife much thought at all. Like in so many other matters, I didn't have a strong opinion. For the most part, I saw it as a pop culture plot device:

- Spock sacrifices himself to save the USS Enterprise? Cool. He transfers his immortal soul into Dr. McCoy's head until it can be returned to Spock's regenerated body.[1]

- Bill and Ted are killed by evil robot versions of themselves? No problem. They beat the Grim Reaper in a game of Twister to come back to life and save the day.[2]

- Buffy the Vampire Slayer dies saving the world again? She'll be back next season.[3]

While it's tempting to look at the prevalence of life-after-death plots as examples of lazy storytelling (especially in *Buffy*'s case), there's a reason storytellers keep returning to this particular well. These stories resonate with us. They touch on something deep within us that senses that, perhaps, death isn't the end it seems to be, even if we can't agree on what it means.[4]

WHAT DIFFERENT RELIGIONS BELIEVE ABOUT WHAT HAPPENS AFTER WE DIE

While there is a very small, but very *loud*, group of people who confidently assert that death is the end (we cease to be and are little more than worm food, as an atheist friend once put it), their perspective seems to be out of step with the majority of humanity across time and space. Instead, because human beings are irrepressibly religious, virtually every religion offers an answer to the question of what happens after we die.

Buddhists, Hindus, and Sikhs, for example, generally believe that death leads to rebirth; we are reincarnated into another form, as higher or lesser beings, as we seek the spiritual insights that lead to liberation—our becoming one with the universe.[5] Norse paganism, also known as *asatro,* had, and *has,* a more complicated view of the afterlife.[6] Historically, this religion has believed in three different realms, two of which were reserved for those given entrance by Odin (Valhalla) and Freyja (Fólkvangr), while the majority entered the realm of Hel.[7] The Mormons believe that when we die, we enter an intermediary state, a "spirit prison." We remain there until the resurrection from the dead, where we will then gain entrance into one of three heavenly kingdoms based on our faithfulness to the Mormon version of Jesus and our moral uprightness: the *celestial, terrestrial,* and *telestial* kingdoms.[8]

But perhaps the most common view in the West, certainly in North

America, is what we'll call American folk religion. This view believes that when we die, we go to heaven. There, we are reunited with our loved ones, including our beloved pets. God might be there too, but Americans aren't all that committed either way. In fact, they're not even sure about how you get there, or who is allowed in. They just know: You die, and you go to heaven.[9]

Despite my lack of a strong opinion before I became a Christian, if pressed, I probably would have offered something close to the view of American folk religion. Generally, if you die, you get to enjoy some kind of heaven. Unless you were Hitler, of course. If there was a hell at all, that was certainly where you'd find him. And probably someone else that I didn't much care for. But that's about it.

However, after becoming a Christian, I began to explore the subject really for the first time. I wanted to understand what my newfound faith taught—what I was going to believe. And what I found is that Christianity has a lot to say about life, death, and everything that happens afterward. It answers the question we're all asking.

THE GOOD NEWS (FOR CHRISTIANS) ABOUT DEATH NOT BEING THE END

As with virtually every other religion, Christianity agrees that death is not the end—for anyone. This is true no matter if a person loves Jesus, hates him, or is publicly ambivalent toward him. All people, everywhere, across space and time, have a future awaiting them following their physical death. But unlike American folk religion, death isn't instant access to a vaguely defined heaven, nor does it begin a new cycle of existence, as in reincarnation. It is the beginning of an eternal existence.

Christians understand death to be the beginning of eternal life for those who believe the gospel. When a Christian dies, he or she immediately enters the presence of the Lord (2 Corinthians 5:8). When Jesus told the thief who was crucified beside him that the thief would join him where he was going, Jesus called this place "paradise," not because of what this place is like, but because of who is present—Christ, God himself (Luke 23:43). But even this is not the end. It is something of an intermediate state, which is why the New Testament authors metaphorically refer to faithful believers who have died as merely being asleep. It is a precursor to our final state, the bodily resurrection that all will experience when Christ returns at the end of all things (1 Corinthians 15:50-57).

For some, the term "intermediate state" might seem reminiscent of the Roman Catholic doctrine of *purgatory*, or even the Mormon spirit prison, but they are nothing alike. In Catholic teaching, purgatory is an intermediary state where the dead are purged of whatever sin remains before they are allowed to enter heaven. (Mormonism's spirit prison serves a similar function.) But despite attempts to equate it with the Old Testament concept of *Sheol* (Deuteronomy 32:22; Job 14:13; Psalm 30:3)—the realm of the dead in Jewish thought—purgatory, neither in form or function, is found in the Bible itself.[10] When death comes, the work is finished. The race is won and we have completed the fight of faith (2 Timothy 4:7). Christians do not need additional purification before we can be welcomed into Christ's presence. "To be absent from the body" is "to be present with the Lord" (2 Corinthians 5:8 NKJV). When Christians die, we are with him. And Jesus says to all who enter, "Welcome."

OUR RESURRECTION AND OUR PERFECT SELVES

This will be our existence until the time of our bodily resurrection (Revelation 20:5-6). But the bodies we will inhabit when we rise won't be like our current ones. They will be new, glorified bodies, perfected and free from the effects of sin that plague us today (Roman 8:22-23; Philippians 3:20-21).

There are many mysteries around our glorified bodies that we cannot know until we experience them for ourselves. For example, we don't know how old or young we will appear, whether we will experience the passage of time, if we will need sleep, or if we will need to use the bathroom. (Everything my children used to ask when they were small.) But that doesn't mean we're left entirely clueless. Scripture gives hints of what we might experience, some of which come from looking at what Jesus could do following his resurrection. He could eat. He could be touched and hugged. All who knew him before his death, knew him after his resurrection.

It will be similar for us. We will be able to feast on the finest food and drink without shame or fear of overindulgence. We will have new and redeemed desires. We will have identities uncompromised by status-seeking and sin. We will work, and it will be a delight rather than drudgery. We will never again experience sickness or sadness. We will never die. But most importantly, in these bodies, we will live in the presence of Jesus, whom we will see face to face for the first time and who will live with us forever (Luke 22:18; Revelation 21).

That's just a little hint of what awaits the Christian. But what about those who reject him? What awaits them?

THE BAD NEWS (FOR NON-CHRISTIANS) ABOUT DEATH NOT BEING THE END

For those who don't believe the gospel, to die is to enter an afterlife marked by judgment. The condemnation that their sins bring remains upon them (John 3:36). So to die is to experience the consequences of a lifetime of sin, as people who loved darkness rather than light (John 3:19).

Like the souls of Christians, the souls of non-Christians enter a sort of intermediate state upon death. But rather than experiencing the presence of the Lord while awaiting their resurrection from the dead, non-Christians experience judgment while they await a final judgment—one of both body and soul (Matthew 10:28; Revelation 20:14). And the realm of this judgment is called hell (Matthew 5:22), the "lake of fire" (Revelation 19:20), and the "second death" (Revelation 21:8).

The word most frequently used for *hell* in the Bible is *gehenna*. This word finds its origins in a real place, the valley of Hinnom. This was a place infamous for the evils the Israelites committed there, as they turned from the Lord and worshiped false gods—even sacrificing their children to one named Molech (2 Kings 16:3; 23:10). For all the abominable acts carried out there, for all the evil committed in that place, the prophet Jeremiah declared that this valley would be a place of judgment; there, the Lord's wrath, his holy anger toward evil, would fall (Jeremiah 19:6-9).

Because of this, the valley carried a symbolic weight, with the prophets' condemnations serving as a warning of what would happen on the Day of the Lord, the day when God would wipe away all evil from the face of the earth (Zephaniah 1:14-18; 3:8-10). Those who rejected God to the end, who were obstinate in their rebellion, would be cast into a place where the "worm does not die, and their fire is not quenched" (Isaiah 66:24 NKJV)—a place of unquenchable fire (Mark 9:43) and everlasting destruction (Matthew 25:41; 2 Thessalonians 1:9), consciously experienced by those who are condemned to it (Luke 16:19-31).

No one was more urgent in his warnings about avoiding hell than Jesus. No one spoke as frequently of this judgment (Matthew 5:29; 18:9; Mark 9:43-47). Why? Because "it is appointed for men to die once, but after this the judgment" (Hebrews 9:27 NKJV). There are no second chances. Death apart from Christ means there is no hope of forgiveness, no further opportunity for repentance. Our sins remain, and with them, the consequences that Jesus bore for all who believe. Rather than paradise, all that awaits is conscious eternal punishment in the lake of fire. And far from being eager to see people meet this fate, Jesus was compelled to warn us to flee the wrath to come (Ezekiel 33:10-11).

ALTERNATIVES AND THE EMOTIONAL WEIGHT OF ETERNAL PUNISHMENT

For centuries, Christians (and many non-Christians) have tried to wrap our heads around what hell will be like, specifically what is a human's experience in hell? Many Christians understand hell to be the state of conscious eternal punishment described above, where all who die rejecting Christ will knowingly experience the full consequences of their sin. In fact, this has been the majority perspective throughout history.[11] But it hasn't been the only view to emerge over the centuries. One such view is *conditional immortality*, or *annihilationism*.[12] This perspective teaches that eternal life awaits all who repent and believe the gospel. But rather than any sort of ongoing punishment, the judgment of those who reject Christ ends in the complete destruction of body and soul in the second death.

A second view, *universal reconciliation,* teaches that because God desires that all will be saved (2 Peter 3:9), he will save *everyone*. His love is so great that, ultimately, no one can possibly reject it forever. Hell, which was made for the devil and his angels (Matthew 25:41), will at most, house *only* the devil and his angels in the end (and maybe not even them).

I see the emotional appeal of both arguments, but I don't believe either does justice to the Bible's teaching on hell and eternal judgment. At the same time, I'm painfully aware of the weightiness of this teaching because the weight *is* real. There is a reason that C.S. Lewis once wrote, "There is no doctrine I would more willingly remove from Christianity than [hell], if it lay in my power…I would pay any price to be able to say truthfully: 'All will be saved.'"[13]

Some who wrestle with this doctrine struggle with it so deeply that they see it as an outsized reaction, perhaps even an act of casual cruelty, for simply not believing that Jesus lived, died, and rose again. To those who feel this way, eternal judgment is "psychologically crushing…terrifying and traumatizing and unbearable," according to author and former pastor Rob Bell.[14]

But that's not what makes judgment so weighty from my perspective. It is not that innocent people will go to hell, it's that in giving people over to judgment, God gives them what they want. Human beings spend their lives raising a clenched fist (and possibly other defiant gestures) at their Maker. They reject him at every turn, and some of those who do even claim to be Christians. And when they do experience judgment, their hatred of God and their love of darkness outweighs their anguish. And if the gates of hell were thrown open, they would still choose to remain there, preferring their suffering to the presence of God.

IF WE LOVE PEOPLE, WE HAVE TO TELL THE TRUTH

The emotional weight of judgment made Lewis long to do away with it. But he couldn't. He saw that it had "the full support of Scripture and, specially, of our Lord's own words; it has always been held by Christendom; and it has the support of reason."[15]

But that didn't mean he liked it. We should be challenged by the weight of this doctrine. It means we're emotionally healthy people if we wish that no one experiences eternal judgment. But we also don't want that weight to lead us to downplay the circumstances—to hold hell at arm's length because it's too difficult to bear, or to sand off its edges because we don't want to be seen as uncaring fear-mongers. If we downplay or distance ourselves from the parts of our faith that make us uncomfortable, we risk diminishing the gospel that we say we believe. And a diminished gospel is no gospel at all.

It is not loving to downplay, reject, or redefine the nature of hell. Of course, we want to be wise about when and where we share with others. A eulogy may not be the wisest choice, for example. But even so, the reality of eternal judgment should serve as a motivator. It helps us to recognize that every breath we take is a gift from God, an opportunity for people to experience God's reconciling love on *his* terms by embracing the one way any person can be saved—by turning to Christ in faith and repentance. We know a day is coming when the opportunities will be no more. When reconciliation, as J.C. Ryle puts it, "will not always be accessible: the way to it will one day be barred, and there will remain nothing but the lake that burns with fire and brimstone."[16]

So if people we love are far from Christ, we need to tell them the truth about the good news, and also the bad news that makes the good news better. We need to pray for them regularly until one of us dies, or we reach the day they repent and turn to Jesus. To make the most of the time we have while the day remains open. And when someone we love dies, and we're not sure where they stood, we need to trust the Lord to do what is right, whatever that may be (Genesis 18:25).

REFLECT, EXPLORE, AND DISCUSS

1. What idea or concept stood out to you as you read this chapter? Why?

2. Read some of the Bible passages about the life after death referenced in this chapter. How do these passages encourage or challenge you?

3. What new questions do these passages raise?

4. Ask someone you know about what he or she believes will happen after we die. What did you learn from this person's response?

5. How might what you learned from this person help you to talk about Jesus with others?

GOD REIGNS

25

OVER A NEW CREATION

And a World We Can't Imagine

At this point, you've probably picked up that I am a big fan of science fiction and fantasy. In part, this is because I have always been a giant nerd. I fell in love with comic books because of an issue of Marvel's *What If?* featuring Conan the Barbarian. Every Sunday morning, I would watch *Star Trek* repeats on the CBC (Canada's national broadcasting network). I read The Lord of the Rings trilogy in its entirety shortly after I turned 11 years old.

I still love to explore these genres, but once you become familiar with them, their tropes—the overused themes and plot devices—become obvious. One of the most prominent has to do with the sort of world in which the stories take place. Most often, science fiction and fantasy stories take place in either a utopian fantasy or a dystopian nightmare. A utopian fantasy is the world as we would like it to be—one in which humanity has evolved out of its propensity toward conflict, where there is no suffering, pain, or sorrow. Where all people, everywhere, seem to have everything they need. This is the vision of humanity's future that guides much of *Star Trek*, as humanity spreads a message of peace, tolerance, and currency-free economics throughout the galaxy.

A dystopian nightmare, as the name suggests, is the exact opposite. They are our worst fears brought to life, alternative worlds without hope. These are the settings for books and films like *The Hunger Games*, *The Handmaid's Tale*, *1984,* and the timeline where Biff Tannen has taken over Hill Valley in *Back to the Future Part II*.

As a reader and writer, I actually prefer dystopian stories. They are more satisfying; more engaging. I could make all kinds of arguments about this being because dystopias lend themselves to more dramatic storytelling, as conflict is baked into the premise. But that's not why I like them. I prefer dystopias because I find our imagined utopias to be too small.

THE SMALL STORIES THAT EASILY AMUSE US

Think about *Star Trek* for a minute: While its storytelling is at its best when it is self-aware enough to recognize that humans are still broken messes, its whole premise is built upon the notion that humanity has evolved beyond the interpersonal disputes that currently plague us, including our need to believe in a higher power. It is the idealized humanist vision of the future. Earth is the center of galactic politics and humanity has an important lesson to share with the more primitive species out amongst the stars, complete with an inspiring and self-righteous monologue—when they are ready, of course.

But despite all its fantastical trappings, *Star Trek*'s vision is far too small. All utopian visions are. They are mudpies with which we content ourselves because we are, as C.S. Lewis said, "far too easily pleased."[1] Why? Because they are missing the one element that makes a genuine utopia possible at all: the presence of God himself.

GOD'S PROMISE OF A BETTER WORLD TO COME

The Bible also ends with a utopian vision. But this vision is different than any imagined one because it isn't a dream. It isn't something we have imagined. It is where the universe is actually heading. And everything we've explored in this book to this point leads to this reality. It is the endgame of God's redemptive story—a new creation, free from the curse of sin, where all who believe the gospel will enjoy life with one another and in the presence of God forevermore.

This is the vision for which *heaven* has become shorthand. But heaven is not the right word for this because it suggests a disembodied, ethereal existence. Our future is an embodied, physical one, where we will be able to touch, feel, and smell. Where we will have work to do, but it won't be characterized by toil and trial. Where we will have the freedom to be what we were always meant to be, as God's beloved children. And it all hinges on the return, or second coming, of Christ.

WHY WE MIGHT AVOID TALKING ABOUT THE SECOND COMING

Depending on your background, the concept of the second coming might be totally foreign to you. You might know of it only through weird internet memes, peculiar speculative fiction (and even worse, movies), and stories of frauds claiming to know the exact date of Jesus' return (and always being wrong). Or if you grew up as a Christian, you may have been part of a church where they talked about the end times a great deal, but often omitted Jesus from it. What they described probably sounded a lot more like a dystopian nightmare instead of good news. Also, it had charts.

So. Many. Charts.

When I first became a Christian, I noticed how much the people I knew were divided on this topic. Some made me wonder if they were building a bunker in their basement, ready for the world to end. Others, because of the perceived weirdness, simply didn't want to talk about it. They hadn't given the end times any serious thought at all. They had adopted a perspective of *pan-millennialism*: We don't know much, but we know that it all pans out in the end. While that might be satisfying in the short term, they do themselves—and the Scriptures themselves—a disservice because there is so much good news for us in Christ's return if we know what to look for.

WHAT CAN WE KNOW ABOUT JESUS' RETURN?

So what does the Bible actually say about Jesus' return and everything that happens after? Both a lot, and not very much. And even the *a lot* is fairly open-ended.

We know that Jesus' return will be unexpected (Matthew 24:44). While Jesus did say that there are signs to watch for—false teachers (Matthew 24:4-5), wars and rumors of wars (Matthew 24:6), earthquakes and famines (Matthew 24:7), and persecution (Matthew 24:9)—his return will happen suddenly, at a time we can't predict. Only the Father knows when Jesus will return (Matthew 24:36). But when it happens, everyone will know—it will be unmistakable (Matthew 24:30-33). But one of the key signs of his return is the rise of one the Bible calls the "man of lawlessness" (2 Thessalonians 2:3).

When Jesus returns, he will have a physical body, and his power and glory—his *God*ness—will be fully seen by all (Matthew 24:30). The dead will rise and Jesus will judge them all (Matthew 25:31-46). All of creation will be made new, including us (2 Peter 3:13). We will live in a holy world as entirely holy people in the presence of Jesus forever.

Those are the essentials of what Scripture says about Jesus' second coming, or at least the points on which Christians have generally agreed for the last 2,000 years. But there are some points on which not all have been able to agree, or at least not completely. The millennial reign is one of these (Revelation 20).

WHAT IS THE MILLENNIAL REIGN?

The millennial reign (Revelation 20:1-10) refers to what appears to be a 1,000-year period of Christ's rule on earth before the final judgment and the inauguration of the new creation. It is a picture of peace and human flourishing. In this era, people of all nations, languages, and people groups are united in joyful service to Christ as their King (Daniel 7:13-14). This kingdom will be free of weeping and sorrow, where all will have what they need, and reaching 100 years of age will be considered *young* (Isaiah 65:17-25). The vision of this future kingdom is beautiful. It is the world we long for. The world as it was meant to be, and will be, when sin is no more.

However, Revelation is an apocalyptic book full of symbolism and imagery drawn from the Old Testament (especially the Prophets), as well as writings that were influential but not considered Scripture. This means that there will inevitably be challenges in understanding aspects of its message, especially when it comes to the timing of events and how it affects our understanding of this millennial reign and its relationship to Christ's return. Over the centuries, interpretations have largely fallen into three broad categories: *premillennialism*, *postmillennialism*, and *amillennialism*.

Premillennialism teaches that Jesus will return before the millennium described in Revelation. This was the dominant position of the early church, held by Polycarp, Justin Martyr, Tertullian, Irenaeus, and other notable leaders.[2] This view declined in popularity in favor of amillennialism in the fourth through eighteenth centuries, but rose to prominence once more, especially in the form of premillennial dispensationalism, in the nineteenth and twentieth centuries. (And with it came all the charts.)

Postmillennialism teaches that Jesus' return will follow the millennium. It will be the result of good progressively overcoming evil as Christians share the gospel and positively influence society.[3] While still held by a minority of Christians, this view largely fell out of favor due to the unspeakable horrors that plagued humanity in the twentieth century.

Amillennialism takes a different approach than either of the preceding views. This position, which became the dominant perspective of the church in the Middle Ages and Reformation period, views the millennial reign as being symbolic of Christ's reign in this present age.[4] This was the favored view of Clement of Alexandria, Origen, Cyprian, and Augustine, among others.

Regardless of their differences, all three perspectives agree that when Jesus returns, all things will be made new. Death will die. Sin will end. And finally, we will be made fully new. Jesus' return is what every Christian longs for, the hope of every believer.

THE PROMISE THAT MOTIVATES OUR LIVES

The Bible shows us a vision of a world we can hardly imagine. A world that no human vision of the future can possibly imagine; one that offers more fulfillment than exploring strange new worlds with new civilizations that are, more or less, the same as ours. It will be the world as God intends it, and so also, we will be. Randy Alcorn says it this way, "When God is finished, we'll be ourselves without the sin—meaning that we'll be the best we can be."[5]

This promise has been the heart of the Christian witness in the world for 2,000 years. It has been a source of hope and comfort as we've faced genuine persecution, suffering, and strife.

But it's not just a promise to sustain us in persecution. It's a promise for right now. The hope of Jesus' return acts as an antibody to the false promises of the world; visions that are more in line with fantastical utopias than anything Scripture has to offer. The false promises of power, reputation, and wealth—the source of so much of the moral rot and fractionalization permeating the Western evangelical movement. Instead, the Bible's promise challenges us to see those things for what they are: to see them as worthless compared to the surpassing riches of Christ (Philippians 3:7-8). And that should shape how we live in the world (Titus 2:11-14).

The promise of the new creation reminds us that we are playing a different game (not merely by different rules). We can't live like everyone else because we are *not* everyone else. And that means, no matter what circles we walk in, whether we're in the private sector, the public sphere, or the political arena, we operate in a distinctively Christian way, full of honesty, integrity, and charity.

The promise encourages us to be more focused on *our* shortcomings than on faultfinding. While we should not excuse or endorse sin, we should not be surprised when non-Christians act like non-Christians. Instead, Christians who are pursuing holiness—people fueled by a vision of a new world—ought to be more tenderhearted toward nonbelievers because we know that we were once such as these (1 Corinthians 6:11). And if Jesus saved us, who can he not save?

The promise challenges us to live as people with good news to share. Christianity is both radically exclusive—salvation is found only through faith in Jesus Christ—and radically inclusive—everyone who believes, no matter their background or history, will be saved! The vision we have of the future—the promise of Jesus' second coming—is for everyone who believes. And the promise of the new creation, the fruit of the second coming of Jesus, is something that is more glorious than anything any human can imagine. That's something I want everyone to share in. So I want to tell all the people I can about it and invite them to join in. How about you?

REFLECT, EXPLORE, AND DISCUSS

1. What idea or concept stood out to you as you read this chapter? Why?

2. Read some of the Bible passages about the return of Jesus and the new creation referenced in this chapter. How do these passages encourage or challenge you?

3. What new questions do these passages raise?

4. Why is it important to embrace what we can know about Christ's return and the world to come?

5. Why is it just as important to admit what we can't know?

WHAT WILL YOU DO WITH WHAT YOU KNOW?

When I started teaching in my church, I struggled with oversharing. By that, I don't mean I got uncomfortably personal. There were no awkward moments that would have embarrassed Emily or my kids. My struggle with oversharing had to do with needing to learn that not everything I was learning in my own preparation at that time was ready to deliver to our church. Some of it was just for me. They were moments where the Holy Spirit was addressing a specific need or fear of mine or giving me needed encouragement or comfort.

As I wrote this book, I found myself wrestling with that same kind of push and pull, this tug of war between wanting to share everything I could say and what I felt compelled that you need to read. And that's probably a good thing for both of us because when it comes to the faith-defining truths of Christianity, there is always more to say. There is always more to learn. There is always more to inspire us to delight.

EMBRACE THE DELIGHT OF DOCTRINE

While not everyone would agree, *doctrine* and *delight* are two words I believe belong together. What we believe about God shapes our love for God. Theology, the application of God's Word to our lives, draws us closer to Jesus, the One in whom Christians delight. Doctrine is not stuffy, academic subject matter. It is something that cuts to the core of who we are and what we believe.

Augustine, the Bishop of Hippo, understood that doctrine and delight go together. In his youth, Augustine was a member of a hedonistic cult, turning away no pleasure that was set before him because he believed that the pursuit of pleasure was our purpose in life. Yet he found those pleasures to be empty. What he pursued failed to satisfy. The pursuits only made him long for more to try and satisfy a longing inside him—a longing that was, finally, only satisfied in the joy he discovered in Christ.

His delight in Christ made all that was once sweet to him sour. They were as nothing compared to "the surpassing value of knowing Christ Jesus" (Philippians 3:8 CSB). And so he set them aside. Is it any wonder Augustine could say, "Thou awakest us to delight in Thy praise; for Thou madest us for Thyself, and our heart is restless, until it [find rest] in Thee"?[1]

Like Augustine, it took me many years to grasp what the Scriptures so plainly revealed: Lasting delight cannot be found in anyone or anything but Jesus. The more I experience this, the truer it becomes, and the more I find myself desiring to learn more. To know Christ better. To delight in him. And to live from that delight.

THERE IS NO END TO OUR EXPLORATION

Christian teachers have spent centuries plumbing the depths of Scripture, exploring the truths found within its pages. Countless volumes have been and will continue to be written on every single truth that I've outlined in the pages of this book, and more besides. (And I've even read some of them.) There are times when I look at new books,

I find myself echoing the words of Ecclesiastes, for there is no end of the making of them (Ecclesiastes 12:12).

But honestly, I'm only upset about it because I don't have time to read them all.

Despite the negative tone of Ecclesiastes, I find it to be a counterintuitive encouragement: There is no end of the making of books because there is no end of learning. We are all always learning, always growing, and always changing.

That's why, even in seeking to pass on some of what I've learned over the last 20 years about what Christians believe, I haven't told you everything. And I haven't told everything, because this book is an invitation for you, no matter who you are and what you believe about God, to keep exploring. To keep learning for yourself.

I want you to question and wrestle with the Scriptures. I want what you learn to shape your convictions and to create and grow a lifelong love for the Lord. I even want you to figure out where I am wrong (because I'm probably wrong somewhere). And I want that for you because I want it for me too. While this book is the result of many years of study, I'm still learning. I'm still asking questions and still wrestling with Scripture because to wrestle with the things of God is a privilege—an opportunity to delight in the One who made us, saves us, and is with us until the end of the age, and forevermore (Matthew 28:20).

So what do you say? Let's get started.

NOTES

TRY THE UNTRIED

1. You can read about how I became a Christian in the opening chapter of *I'm a Christian—Now What? A Guide to Your New Life* (Bellingham, WA: Lexham Press, 2023).

2. "The Christian ideal has not been tried and found wanting. It has been found difficult; and left untried" (G.K. Chesterton, *What's Wrong with the World* [New York: Dodd, Mead and Company, 1910], 48).

3. Chesterton, *Orthodoxy* (New York: John Lane Company, 1909), 218.

4. This isn't to say that I agree with Chesterton on everything, then or now. As a Roman Catholic, he viewed Protestants as "Catholics gone wrong" (Chesterton, *The Catholic Church and Conversion* [San Francisco, CA: Ignatius Press, 2006], 99). As a Protestant, I disagree with him on purgatory, among other points of Catholic doctrine. We both, however, agree that cheese is delicious.

5. C.S. Lewis, "Introduction," in *St. Athanasius On the Incarnation*, trans. and ed. (Crestwood, NY: St. Vladimir's Seminary Press, 1944), 8.

6. Lewis, *Mere Christianity* (New York: HarperCollins, 2012), 78.

7. Lewis, *Mere Christianity*, 74.

8. J.I. Packer, *Knowing God* (Downers Grove, IL: InterVarsity Press, 2011), 42.

9. Packer, *Knowing God*, 42.

10. Packer, *Knowing God*, 44.

11. *Evangelical* in its adjectival form has historically referred to Christians who emphasize salvation by faith in the atoning death of Jesus Christ, the need for personal conversion, the authority of Scripture, and the importance of activism in two senses: evangelism (sharing the gospel with others) and acts of service and compassion (or "love and good works," as Hebrews 10:24 CSB says).

12. Ligonier Ministries and Lifeway Research, "The State of Theology (2022)," accessed January 25, 2024, https://thestateoftheology.com/data-explorer/2022/.

13. Ligonier Ministries, "The State of Theology (UK)," accessed January 25, 2024, https://thestateoftheology.com/uk/.

14. This is why one of my favorite definitions of theology is "the application of God's Word by persons to all areas of life" (John M. Frame, *The Doctrine of the Knowledge of God* [Phillipsburg, NJ: P&R Publishing, 1987], 76).

CHAPTER 1—ONE, AND ALSO THREE (WHO ARE ONE)

1. Jehovah's Witness missionaries use handbooks such as *Reasoning from the Scriptures* to answer objections and points of resistance to their message.

2. Genuine agreement is not possible due to Jehovah's Witnesses' belief that biblical truth can only be understood in light of the teaching of resources produced by the Watchtower Society, their official publishing organization.

3. *Essence* and *substance* are generally considered synonymous when describing God's nature.

4. Which many a prophet did, such as Elijah during his challenge to the prophets of Baal in 1 Kings 18 and Isaiah in Isaiah 44:9-20.

5. Some theologians advocate for the existence of an assembly of heavenly beings, who are subservient to the Lord, based on references to the "sons of God" (Genesis 6; Deuteronomy 32; Job 1–2) and reference to "gods" in God's great assembly (Psalm 82:1). However, these theologians do not advocate that any of these beings are God's equal, for, as the Lord said, "Before Me there was no God formed, nor shall there be after Me" (Isaiah 43:10 NKJV).

6. Theologian Michael S. Heiser (1963–2023) suggested that ancient Jews would not have been surprised or shocked by the idea that God is more than one. Based upon the narratives detailing the many appearances of the Lord to specific individuals, Heiser concludes, "Even in the Old Testament, God was more than one person, and one of those persons came as a man" (Michael S. Heiser, *Supernatural: What the Bible Teaches about the Unseen World—And Why It Matters* [Bellingham, WA: Lexham Press, 2015], 62).

7. While there is a functional subordination that is limited to the work of redemption—as a human being, Jesus submitted himself to the will of the Father, who sent him to rescue and redeem people from sin—it is not innate, or *inherent*, to the Father, Son, and Spirit's existence as three-in-one. While some teachers have attempted to popularize the belief in an innate subordination within the Trinity (usually referred to as the *eternal subordination of the Son*), such teaching is out of step with historic Christian beliefs.

8. To call a teaching heresy or a teacher a heretic is not something we should ever do lightly. It is a word that should be reserved for the most serious of errors, and used only after efforts at correction fail.

9. Modalism is found in the once-popular book *The Shack*, in which "Papa" (a woman representing God the Father) said to the lead character, Mack: "When we three spoke ourself into human existence as the Son of God, we became fully human. We also chose to embrace all the limitations that this entailed. Even though we have always been present in this created universe, we now became flesh and blood" (William P. Young, *The Shack* [Windblown Media, 2007], 99). The Father and the Holy Spirit did not take on human form; only Jesus, God the Son, became a human being in his incarnation.

10. Founded in the late 1800s, the Jehovah's Witnesses deviate from historic Christianity in their understanding of the Father, Son, and Spirit; their view of salvation (a highly complex works-oriented system); the rejection of eternal punishment; and in teaching that the New World Translation (their translation of the Bible) is the only faithful translation of the Word of God.

11. Such a reframing of heresy typically comes from a superficial understanding of complex subjects, of which the relationship between the Father, Son, and Spirit is undeniably one. Whether intentional or not, reframing heresy is the doctrinal equivalent of putting lipstick on a pig. Prettying it up doesn't change its nature.

12. The Church of Latter-day Saints (LDS) believes that Christianity became apostate after the death of the apostles and as new sects misinterpreted Jesus' teaching. LDS founder Joseph Smith taught that his movement was the restored church, with Smith as its prophet, apostle, and priest. According to their official doctrine, they view "the members of the Godhead in a manner that corresponds in a number of ways with the views of others in the Christian world, but with significant differences." Among those significant differences? They believe that each member of the Trinity (or Godhead as they prefer) is "a separate being…Although the members of the Godhead are distinct beings with distinct roles, they are one in purpose and doctrine" ("Godhead," *The Church of Jesus Christ of Latter-day Saints*, accessed January 25, 2024, https://www.churchofjesuschrist.org/study/manual/gospel-topics/godhead?lang=eng). In their view, the Father, Son, and Spirit's unity is not in their *being* or *essence*, but in their *purpose* and *teaching*.

13. Lutheran Satire, "St. Patrick's Bad Analogies," accessed January 25, 2024, https://www.youtube.com/watch?v=KQLfgaUoQCw/.

14. Fred Sanders, *The Deep Things of God* (Wheaton, IL: Crossway, 2010), 212.

CHAPTER 2—SIMILAR, BUT DIFFERENT

1. This sort of question is an attempt at a "gotcha" argument, one commonly offered by a smart-alecky skeptic trying to seem clever so they can avoid talking about Jesus. Such questions are not actually clever.

2. This is the error at the heart of a belief called *Deism*, which says that while there is a god that may have created the world, this god is not engaged with creation in any way. Essentially, he is like a clock designer or watchmaker who, after completing his work, wound it up and let it go to run on its own thereafter. Perhaps the most well-known Deist is Benjamin Franklin.

CHAPTER 3—PERFECTLY PERFECT IN EVERY WAY

1. Few people are either honest enough or self-aware enough to do so. I appreciated comedian and actor Dave Foley speaking this forthrightly when discussing the relationship between UFO experiences, the persistence of consciousness, and past-life experiences with journalist Leslie Kean: "I think I'll stick with not believing, or particularly even liking God, if there is one" (Dave Foley, "Episode 5: Leslie Kean," *Really?!. with Tom and Dave* [July 27, 2023], accessed January 25, 2024, https://podcasts.apple.com/us/podcast/really-with-tom-and-dave/id1694997896?i=1000622439788, 1:19:00–1:19:04).

2. R.C. Sproul, *The Holiness of God*, 2nd ed. (Carol Stream, IL: Tyndale House Publishers, Inc., 1998), 66-67.

3. This reality is, arguably, the most challenged in our current time, especially around issues related to what it means to be human, which we'll get to in chapter 7.

4. On the off chance you ever hear or read the word *immutable*, this is what it is referring to.

CHAPTER 5—IN THE WORDS HE GAVE US

1. This is what you're likely to see in the writings of scholars such as Marcus Borg and Peter Enns, as well as many popular-level philosophers such as Jordan Peterson.

2. Which is what you'd find expressed by leaders in many mainline denominations and self-identified progressive fellowships. Practically speaking, you'll hear it in a lot of teaching from otherwise faithful churches too.

3. You are also likely to find this approach among many progressive Christians and mainline denominations.

4. Revelation, the latter half of Daniel, parts of Isaiah, Zechariah, and Joel are also part of a subset of prophetic writing called apocalyptic literature. This genre is devoted to making explicit God's divine intervention in human affairs. Apocalyptic literature often uses highly figurative language that is sometimes difficult for modern readers to understand due to our distance from the culture in which they were written. Nevertheless, with careful study, we can understand them at least in part, if not in whole.

5. This concept, which is sometimes called the ecstatic or dictation theory of inspiration, has been rejected by the church from its earliest days.

6. First Corinthians 6:9-10 is one of those passages that doesn't sit well with this group. These verses unambiguously state that those who unrepentantly engage in all the sins the Western world celebrates—especially any kind of sexual immorality—will not inherit the kingdom of God. To not inherit the kingdom of God is to say that someone is not a genuine Christian.

7. Originally believed to be written in the eighth century BC, the oldest complete copy of *The Iliad* dates to the tenth century AD.

8. A fragment featuring John 18:31-33 on the front and John 18:37-38 on the back (P52), which has been dated c. AD 125–140 (John's Gospel is generally believed to have been written c. AD 90). The oldest complete copy of the New Testament, *Codex Sinaiticus*, dates to c. AD 350, and also includes the complete Old Testament in Greek. For the sake of comparison, only 10 copies of Caesar's *Gaellic Wars* exist, the earliest of which dates to one *thousand* years after the original was written, and few treat it with the same level of skepticism as they do the Bible.

9. Those seven are: Hebrews, James, 2 Peter, 2 and 3 John, Jude, and Revelation.

10. It should also be noted that I'm speaking here as a Christian within the Protestant tradition. The Roman Catholic Church canon includes seven additional books that Protestants do not recognize as inspired (although they can be helpful reading). These books were added to their canon during the Council of Trent in 1546 as a response to the Protestant Reformation. Churches within Orthodox traditions do not have an official number within their canons (yes, canons). Orthodox Bibles include between 73 and 81 books, depending on the specific tradition.

11. "The Chicago Statement on Biblical Inerrancy, Article XII," *Themelios*, Volume 4, Issue 3, accessed January 25, 2024, https://www.thegospelcoalition.org/themelios/article/the-chicago-statement-on-biblical-inerrancy/.

12. The importance of this cannot be overstated, as there can be a temptation to reinterpret both inerrancy and infallibility as referring less to Scripture and more toward one specific interpretation of it. This reinterpretation weaponizes both words to become instruments of control and coercion instead of tools to communicate a beautiful truth.

13. Clement of Rome, "The First Epistle of Clement to the Corinthians," in *The Apostolic Fathers*

with *Justin Martyr and Irenaeus*, ed. Alexander Roberts, James Donaldson, and A. Cleveland Coxe, vol. 1, *The Ante-Nicene Fathers* (Buffalo, NY: Christian Literature Company, 1885), 17.

14. For example, archaeological evidence confirming the existence of Kings David and Solomon was found in 1993. ("The Tel Dan Inscription: The First Historical Evidence of King David from the Bible," *Biblical Archeology Society* [September 23, 2023], accessed February 24, 2024, https://www.biblicalarchaeology.org/daily/biblical-artifacts/the-tel-dan-inscription-the-first-historical-evidence-of-the-king-david-bible-story/.)

15. The technical term for this is the *perspicuity*, or *clarity*, of Scripture.

16. See Exodus 20:12; Deuteronomy 5:16; Ephesians 6:1-4; Colossians 3:20; Romans 13:1-7; Titus 3:1-2; 1 Peter 2:13-17.

17. Where we see the Bible being manipulated to give human authorities more authority than fits their station, that is a misuse—an abuse—of Scripture.

CHAPTER 6 – A GOOD WORLD THAT HE RULES

1. Tolkien, for example, set about developing whole mythologies, histories, and languages for the different races within Middle Earth. While not every great author goes to that depth, the principle still applies.

2. The Latin phrase *creatio ex nihilo* (*creation out of nothing*) is the technical name for this belief.

3. It's not uncommon to see Genesis described as functioning as a counter-narrative to these. And there is a sense in which that is true. All contain similar imagery and describe some similar events. But Genesis is unique among the ancient creative narratives in that its starting point isn't violence.

4. To put all my cards on the table, my answers are:

    1. Yes, I understand this to be describing both historical and theological truths.

    2. I'm inclined to read the word *day* as *day*, largely because the Hebrew word used typically refers to a 24-hour period, but it's not a hill I'm willing to die on.

    3. I don't know. I do know Christians should approach our views on this question humbly. The point of the creation account is *not* to determine the age of the earth. Augustine, one of the early church's greatest teachers, cautioned against rash assertions, of "talking nonsense" on topics where there is room for disagreement, not to avoid embarrassment for ourselves but for the sake of those outside the faith for whose "salvation we toil" (*The Literal Meaning of Genesis*, Book 1, Chapter 19, Paragraph 39).

    4. That's a very personal question and I'm sure it's not any of our business.

5. *Apologetics* does not refer to the art of apologizing (although training on that might be helpful). It is a discipline focused on offering a reasoned defense of the Christian faith.

6. The ultimate goal of evolutionary theory seems to be to convince us that we are mere accidents, with no greater value or purpose than anything else in the universe. This unique obsession with convincing ourselves that we are not unique is telling.

7. The word for God in Genesis 1:1, '*elohim,* commonly refers to plural nouns, but it is also often used to make concrete abstract concepts. This is the best way to understand the word when it

references God. Just as the royal plural of English may be used to indicate the positional superiority of a ruling monarch (e.g., "We are not amused"), *'elohim* indicates God's deity and his absolute authority.

8. Theorists have suggested the odds of life, particularly intelligent life, emerging via evolutionary processes are less than 1 in 10^{24}, which means it borders on the impossible (Andrew E. Snyder-Beattie, Anders Sandberg, K. Eric Drexler, and Michael B. Bonsall, "The Timing of Evolutionary Transitions Suggests Intelligent Life is Rare," *Astrobiology* [March 2021], accessed January 28, 2024, https://www.ncbi.nlm.nih.gov/pmc/articles/PMC7997718/).

CHAPTER 7—A WORLD FOR BEINGS LIKE HIM

1. This is a key reason why many LGBTQIA+ advocates demand not mere toleration or acceptance, but celebration of their choices.

2. Outside of being the descendants of those of out-fought, out-hunted, out-bred, and/or out-smarted their opponents in a quest for genetic dominance.

3. Even denying their existence is self-defeating since it requires a rational argument that is also a moral one.

4. Some might wonder on this point about how to address those among us who might be intersex (a genetic or chromosomal condition describing developmental sex disorders). These individuals experience the brokenness of our world distinctly, and we want to walk alongside them with sensitivity and compassion. But intersex individuals are not a third gender, nor is their condition another form of transgenderism, as they most often affirm their maleness or femaleness based on their sexual anatomy. For a short but thoughtful treatment of this subject, see Katie J. McCoy, *To Be a Woman: The Confusion Over Female Identity and How Christians Can Respond* (Nashville, TN: B&H Publishing Group, 2023), 137-142.

5. Nor should we try, because one of the words frequently used in the Bible and translated as *soul* means *living being* or *person*. This is the word we find in Deuteronomy 4:29, for example.

6. Paula A. Johnson, MD, "Every Cell Has a Sex," *The Boston Globe* (January 1, 2014), accessed January 28, 2024, https://www.bostonglobe.com/opinion/2014/01/05/every-cell-has-sex/lgnbRyR1FvVqA9ccbKM5iI/story.html.

7. This phrasing is important: not every woman can or chooses to bear children, but part of what it means to be female is to have the potential to do so. Roman Catholic theologian Abigail Favale advocates for this as an essential defining characteristic. (Abigail Favale, *The Genesis of Gender* [San Francisco, CA: Ignatius Press, 2022], 120-121.)

8. Transgenderism as a *movement* seeks to codify these contextually driven performative behaviors as more essential to our identity than our biology; essentially, how we feel becomes more important than what we are.

9. I love how Dutch theologian Herman Bavinck described this: "While all creatures display vestiges of God, only a human being is the image of God. And he is such totally, in soul and body, in all his faculties and powers, in all conditions and relations. Man is the image of God because and insofar as he is truly human, and he is truly and essentially human because, and to the extent that, he is the image of God" (Herman Bavinck, John Bolt, and John Vriend, *Reformed Dogmatics: God and Creation, vol. 2* [Grand Rapids, MI: Baker Academic, 2004], 555).

CHAPTER 8—A WORLD WHERE WE ARE NOT ALONE

1. Occasionally you will find Christian teaching that tries to use Matthew 22:30 ("For in the resurrection they neither marry nor are given in marriage, but are like angels in heaven") as the biblical foundation for such a belief. But to do so is to entirely misunderstand what Jesus was describing in that passage. Rather than describing a transformed state, Jesus was speaking of the end of marriage in the new creation, since it will no longer be needed.

2. Some Christians do teach that guardian angels exist, with Matthew 18:10 and Acts 12 serving as their biblical basis for that belief.

3. Some Bible teachers suggest that it might have been possible, at one time, for them to procreate when they are in a human form (see Genesis 6:1-4).

4. *Messenger* is the meaning behind the word *angel* in both Hebrew and Greek. Interestingly, the Greek word for *evangelism* also shares a root word with *angel*: evangel, meaning *good news* or *good message*. When used in this sense, the meaning of angel may extend beyond supernatural beings to human representatives or messengers (see Revelation 2–3).

5. Genesis 16:7-11; 18:1-3; 22:11-18; Exodus 3:1-22; 23:20-21; Joshua 5:13-15; Judges 2:1-5; 6:11, 14; Isaiah 6:1-13; and Zechariah 12:8 are among the many passages showing this angel as different than the rest.

6. These appearances are referred to as *Christophanies* or *theophanies*, meaning visible manifestations of God to human beings. Origen was among the early church leaders who held to this view, as did Martin Luther, the sixteenth-century Protestant reformer.

7. Unidentified Anomalous Phenomena (UAP) has become the preferred term to describe what was previously described as Unidentified Flying Objects (UFO). This change was made primarily to avoid the negative stereotypes associated with the UFO designation. Non-human intelligence is a broader term to describe what might be behind these phenomena.

8. Helene Cooper, Ralph Blumenthal, and Leslie Kean, "Glowing Auras and 'Black Money': The Pentagon's Mysterious U.F.O. Program," *nytimes.com* (December 16, 2017), accessed February 8, 2024, https://www.nytimes.com/2017/12/16/us/politics/pentagon-program-ufo-harry-reid.html.

9. Michael S. Heiser, "Aliens and Demons: Evidence of an Unseen Realm - documentary film featuring Dr. Michael S. Heiser," Faithlife Films, (October 12, 2022), accessed February 8, 2024, https://youtu.be/ThmF7OErkxY?si=Ys42ElS6www5yicQ/. Heiser was among many who have noted that there are parallels between ritual sexual abuse and alien abduction experiences, as well as how the messages of these beings—even the seemingly benevolent ones—tend to minimize or reinvent Jesus.

CHAPTER 9—A WORLD WHERE GOD IS ALWAYS WORKING

1. This is typically offered with the arrogance and condescension that only the greatest of chronological snobs can muster. It should also be noted that these so-called less-enlightened people routinely spoke multiple languages, produced works of art and architecture that remain to this day, and developed indoor plumbing and complex irrigation systems among other accomplishments. Meanwhile, most of us in the West struggle to know the difference between *affect* and *effect*.

2. The most common challenge to any health-related miraculous event is to argue for the possibility

of misdiagnosis. While it is true that misdiagnoses do occur, we would be wise not to allow skepticism to lead us to our jump-to-conclusions mats too quickly.

3. Elijah's signs and wonders are recorded in 1 Kings 17–18 and 2 Kings 1–2; Elisha's are found in 2 Kings 2–5; 13. Isaiah's lone recorded miracle is found in 2 Kings 20:8-11.

4. Acts 2:4; 3:4-6; 5:12-16; 9:32-43; 13:6-11; 14:8-10; 16:16-18; 19:11-12; and 20:9-12 record some of the miracles done through them.

5. Matthew 8:1-17; 9:1-8; 14:22-33; Mark 5:1-43; 8:22-25; Luke 8:23-25; and John 6 include only a few of Jesus' miraculous deeds.

6. Jared C. Wilson, *The Wonder-Working God* (Wheaton, IL: Crossway, 2014), 29.

7. "Divine providence is…bound up with the interests of the individual Christian, with the interests of all Christians—the Christian church—and with the interests of the whole of the creation animate and inanimate." Paul Helm, *The Providence of God* (Downers Grove, IL: InterVarsity Press, 1993), 21.

8. While human activity—specifically our overconsumption of natural resources—has a negative effect on the world's climate, the general patterns remain the same. We'll also talk about humanity's actions and our effect on the world in a few chapters from now.

9. Incidentally, this is the worry that bad actors, including most politicians, prey upon. They set themselves up as the only hope for a better tomorrow or a return to a (real or imagined) sense of past greatness. They also always fail to deliver on their promises.

10. A line of thought that fuels the concept of deism.

11. King David's coercion of Bathsheba into a sexual relationship and subsequent murder of her husband (2 Samuel 11–12) is one of the most prominent examples of this: a good king chose to do something evil in the eyes of the Lord (2 Samuel 11:27). But it was through that evil act that Jesus is connected to David's family, as Bathsheba was the mother of both King Solomon (Matthew 1:6b) and David's son Nathan (Luke 3:31; 1 Chronicles 3:5).

CHAPTER 10—THE DIFFERENCE BETWEEN GOOD AND EVIL

1. Madison McQueen and Olivia Burnett, "How Porn and Trafficking Are Undeniably Connected," *Exodus Cry* (February 7, 2023), accessed February 23, 2024, https://exoduscry.com/articles/porn-and-trafficking/.

2. This is especially prevalent with so-called gender-affirming care, which takes a backward approach to treatment by starting from the viewpoint that the patient is correct in his or her self-diagnosis. Vanderbilt University Medical Center was forced to pause its gender-affirming surgeries for minors after footage of one doctor describing these surgeries as "huge money makers" surfaced online in 2022. (Kimberlee Krueski, "Vanderbilt to review gender-affirming surgeries for minors," *APNews.com* [October 7, 2022], accessed February 23, 2024, https://apnews.com/article/health-business-tennessee-nashville-vanderbilt-university-6deb93f7dea92f1b2082c39f72b59776.)

3. Statistically speaking, you're more likely to win the lottery than even recoup your investment as an affiliate for an MLM. See Abby Vesoulis and Eliana Dockterman, "Pandemic Schemes: How Multilevel Marketing Distributors Are Using the Internet—and the Coronavirus—to Grow Their Businesses," *Time.com* (July 20, 2020), accessed February 23, 2024, https://time.com/5864712/multilevel-marketing-schemes-coronavirus/.

4. Robert Downen, "20 years, 700 victims: Southern Baptist sexual abuse spreads as leaders resist reforms," *The Houston Chronicle*, February 10, 2019 (accessed February 23, 2024), https://www.houstonchronicle.com/news/investigations/article/Southern-Baptist-sexual-abuse-spreads-as-leaders-13588038.php.

5. Moral relativism, as a philosophy, is intellectually and ethically dishonest for the very reason that the only relative aspect of morality is people's application of it. So if someone advocates for this view, do as the late theologian R.C. Sproul once quipped, "Steal his wallet." Their relativism will disappear in an instant.

6. See Genesis 4:8; the book of Judges (all of it); Jeremiah 19:4-5; 2 Samuel 13:1-22; 1 Kings 12; 2 Kings 21; Acts 5:1-11; and Romans 1:29-32 for a few examples.

7. D.A. Carson makes this point in *From the Resurrection to His Return: Living Faithfully in the Last Days* (Fearn, UK: Christian Focus Publications, 2010), 36.

8. This is the argument as popularized by the eighteenth-century philosopher David Hume, which he attributed to the ancient Greek philosopher Epicurus. David Hume, Esq., *Dialogues Concerning Natural Religion*, 2nd edition (London, 1779), 186.

9. C.S. Lewis, *The Problem of Pain* (New York: HarperOne, 1996), 16.

10. Greg Welty, a professor of philosophy at Southeastern Baptist Theological Seminary, notes that these theodicies—justifications for the way God deals with humanity—entirely lack biblical support, so they should be disregarded. (Greg Welty, "The Problem of Evil," *The Gospel Coalition*, accessed February 23, 2024, https://www.thegospelcoalition.org/essay/the-problem-of-evil/.)

11. This seems to be the point of the question posed in Job 38:2: "Who is this who darkens counsel with words without knowledge?" God seems to be warning Job (and us) to be appropriately open-handed about matters we cannot fully comprehend.

CHAPTER 11—THE EVIL THAT WE DO

1. That would be 1994 for those who are curious. See Thomas Aichner, et al., "Twenty-Five Years of Social Media: A Review of Social Media Applications and Definitions from 1994 to 2019," *Cyberpsychology, Behavior and Social Networking*, v. 24, no. 4 (April 1, 2021): 215-22, https://doi.org/10.1089/cyber.2020.0134.

2. J.K. Rowling has experienced this since late-2019, as formerly adoring fans turned on her for affirming that biological sex is immutable, despite her long-standing support of LGBTQIA+ individuals ("J.K. Rowling Faces Backlash after Tweeting Support for 'transphobic' Researcher," *NBC News* [December 19, 2019], accessed April 21, 2024, https://www.nbcnews.com/feature/nbc-out/j-k-rowling-faces-backlash-after-tweeting-support-transphobic-researcher-n1104971).

3. Bible teacher and bestselling author Beth Moore has repeatedly been harassed online because she spoke out against Christians' support for Donald J. Trump's presidential candidacy. This ultimately led to her disfellowshipping with the Southern Baptist Convention, although she still lives rent-free in the heads of many of its clergy (Bob Smietana, "Bible Teacher Beth Moore, Splitting with Lifeway, Says, 'I Am No Longer a Southern Baptist,'" *Religion News Service* [blog], March 9, 2021 [accessed April 21, 2024], https://religionnews.com/2021/03/09/bible-teacher-beth-moore-ends-partnership-with-lifeway-i-am-no-longer-a-southern-baptist/).

4. J. Jordan Henderson, "Sin," in *The Lexham Bible Dictionary*, ed. John D. Barry et al. (Bellingham, WA: Lexham Press, 2016).

5. Victor P. Hamilton, *The Book of Genesis, Chapters 1–17*, The New International Commentary on the Old Testament (Grand Rapids, MI: Wm. B. Eerdmans Publishing Co., 1990), 165-166.

6. Darrell L. Bock, *Ephesians: An Introduction and Commentary*, ed. Eckhard J. Schnabel, vol. 10 (Downers Grove, IL: InterVarsity Press, 2019), 61.

7. *Monty Python and the Holy Grail*, directed by Terry Gilliam and Terry Jones, featuring Graham Chapman, John Cleese, Terry Gilliam, Eric Idle, Terry Jones, and Michael Palin (1975; Culver City, CA: Sony Pictures Home Entertainment, 2015), Blu-Ray.

CHAPTER 12—PEOPLE WHO LOVE WHAT THEY SHOULD HATE

1. C.H. Spurgeon, "Jacob and Esau," *The New Park Street Pulpit*, vol. 5 (London: Passmore & Alabaster, 1894), 120.

2. F.L. Cross and Elizabeth A. Livingstone, eds., *The Oxford Dictionary of the Christian Church* (Oxford, NY: Oxford University Press, 2005), 1257.

3. Augustine of Hippo, *Four Anti-Pelagian Writings*, ed. Thomas P. Halton, trans. John A. Mourant and William J. Collinge, vol. 86, *The Fathers of the Church* (Washington, DC: The Catholic University of America Press, 1992), 132.

4. D.A. Carson, *The Gospel According to John*, The Pillar New Testament Commentary (Grand Rapids, MI: W.B. Eerdmans, 1991), 207.

CHAPTER 13—ACCORDING TO A PLAN FOR THE WHOLE UNIVERSE

1. Christopher Hitchens, *God Is Not Great: How Religion Poisons Everything* (New York: Twelve, 2007), 102.

2. Unitarian Universalism is a movement born out of rejection of the doctrine of the Trinity, and is in no meaningful sense Christian, liberal, or otherwise.

3. Although there is such a thing as an unhealthy fundamentalism (an unnecessarily rigid dogmatism, especially related to secondary or tertiary beliefs), *fundamentalist* is most often used by those who reject essential Christian beliefs to dismiss anyone who continues to hold to those essentials, in the same way one might name check Hitler or use any word ending in *phobic* when making a weak argument.

4. "The Hitchens Transcript," *Portland Monthly* (December 2009), accessed May 5, 2024, https://www.pdxmonthly.com/articles/2009/12/17/christopher-hitchens.

5. James was the second son of Mary, the first of her children with Joseph. Jesus and James had three other brothers, Joseph, Jude, and Simon, as well as two or more sisters, although they go unnamed in any of the Gospels or the Epistles (Matthew 12:46-50; 13:55-56; Mark 3:31; 6:3; Luke 8:19; John 2:12; 7:3; Acts 1:14; 1 Corinthians 9:5; Galatians 1:19).

6. Some individuals and groups—including, sadly, some otherwise faithful Christians—have used the Bible to justify the barbaric form of slavery that was practiced in the United States up until the end of the Civil War (April 12, 1861–April 9, 1865). Many have attempted to justify segregation, racism, and the subjugation of women in their misuse of Scripture. Their justifications do not stand up to even the most basic scrutiny.

CHAPTER 14—BY BECOMING A HUMAN BEING

1. This argument emerged during the Enlightenment movement (c. 1685–1815) and had a brief moment of popularity in the nineteenth century as the Christ Myth Theory, which argues that the New Testament is historically unreliable as evidence of Jesus' existence, there are no non-Christian references to Jesus from the first century, and Christianity itself is a revision of ancient Persian and Babylonian mythology (Robert E. Van Voorst, *Jesus Outside the New Testament: An Introduction to the Ancient Evidence* [Grand Rapids, MI; William B. Eerdmans Publishing Company, 2000], 8-9). Archaeological evidence and careful study have seen this theory debunked, though not entirely eliminated. It still has proponents among the fringiest fringes of scholarship and internet chicanery.

2. The quest for the historical Jesus sees the New Testament as a reliable guide for reconstructing aspects of Jesus' life but assumes that any miraculous acts or claims of divinity are later additions as Christians' understanding of Jesus transformed from his being a wise teacher to a divine figure.

3. This is called *Docetism*, although its origins are obscure. Docetism is connected to another belief system called *Gnosticism* (meaning hidden or secret knowledge). One of the key tenets of Gnosticism is that the material world is itself evil, along with the Creator God of this world himself being a lower (and evil) deity. Salvation is found in the rejection of the material world. This teaching was also radically anti-women, with several Gnostic texts advocating for a view of non-gender or uni-gender as our intended state of being. Functionally, transgender ideology is a repackaging of this ancient heresy.

4. "Away in a Manger" has been criticized as promoting Docetism by some Christians, but if it does this, it was most likely not an intentional choice on the part of its author. It is much more likely an example of bad poetry leading to accidental heresy.

5. H. Bettenson and C. Maunder, *Documents of the Christian Church*, 4th ed. (Oxford, UK: Oxford University Press, 2011), 54. This statement comes from the Definition of Chalcedon, an ancient creedal statement written in response to controversies related to the two natures of Jesus.

6. John Murray, *Collected Writings of John Murray*, vol. 2 (Edinburgh: Banner of Truth, 1977), 132.

7. While many of these passages do not directly use the phrases connected to them, they are conceptually tied to these titles that are used in reference to Jesus.

8. "Christ" is a transliterated Greek word, "Christos," where "Messiah" is taken from the Hebrew word "מָשִׁיחַ," ("*mashiyach*"). Transliteration is the process of representing the characters of one alphabet into another, which essentially creates a new word in the target language in the process.

9. Names in the Old Testament often carried prophetic meaning, foreshadowing or clarifying specific events. In this case, "Immanuel" is a name that means "God with us."

10. Gabriel is one of two angels with a specific name in Scripture. He is referenced by name in Daniel 8:16; 9:21; and Luke 1:26-38. The only other angel to be named in the Bible is Michael in Daniel 10:13, 21; 12:1; Jude 9; and Revelation 12:7.

11. A virgin birth or conception does not play a role in the stories of Zoroaster, who had a human mother and father, or Mithras, who sprang forth from a rock, for example.

CHAPTER 15—AS A MEDIATOR WHO WILL NEVER FAIL

1. Or by being Canadian, since being equally unhappy about different situations is more or less the standard operating procedure of my former home but still native land.

2. Deborah, Samuel, Nathan, Elijah, Elisha, Isaiah, and Amos are just a few of the prophets who played a critical (if not always large) role in books like Judges, 1–2 Samuel, 1–2 Kings, and 1–2 Chronicles.

3. Derek Kidner notes that although "Phoenicians and Canaanites used this term for their supreme God," it is clear from the context of the chapter that whatever his predecessors and successors meant by it, the "God Most High" Melchizedek served was *Yahweh*, the true God worshiped by Abram (Derek Kidner, *Genesis: An Introduction and Commentary*, vol. 1, *Tyndale Old Testament Commentaries* [Downers Grove, IL: InterVarsity Press, 1967], 132).

4. Jewish philosopher Philo of Alexandria, for example, viewed him as the divine Logos who proceeds from God as the firstborn of God (Charles Duke Yonge with Philo of Alexandria, *The Works of Philo: Complete and Unabridged* [Peabody, MA: Hendrickson, 1995], 59).

5. Many English Bibles refer to David's sin against Bathsheba (2 Samuel 11) as "adultery" in the pericope (which is the fancy name for the summary statement that appears before a passage in the Bible). This potentially obfuscates the severity of his sin, since there is textual ambiguity about whether there was legitimate consent on Bathsheba's part. And given that David was the king of Israel, I'm not sure that consent—in the way we think of it today—can even apply.

CHAPTER 16—THROUGH THE STRANGE BEAUTY OF DEATH

1. The word *atonement* comes from Anglo Saxon words that mean "making at one." This is why you might sometimes hear or read the word described (somewhat cheekily) as "at-one-ment," which is basically the theologian equivalent of a dad joke.

2. See Genesis 5:5, 8, 11, 14, 17, 20, 27, and 31. Enoch (Genesis 5:21-24) is the only notable exception to this pattern, as is the description of him being one who "walked with God." Instead of being told "he died," we're informed that God "took him away," suggesting that God overruled humanity's death sentence in this case because it pleased God to do so for this man who trusted him (Hebrews 11:5).

3. Cain also brought an offering of the vegetables of his field, but his offering did not please God (Genesis 4:5). This isn't to suggest that vegetables were an unacceptable offering because offerings of fruit and vegetables are included in the Mosaic Law (see Leviticus 2). Cain's offering wasn't rejected because of its content, but because of Cain's heart in offering it—it was perfunctory, not offered out of sincere love and devotion.

4. Despite what we believe in the Western world, sacrifices of these kinds continue to be offered today, including *human* sacrifice. Some acts are overt and obvious. Others are more subtle, such as the way we sacrifice our health and well-being when we overwork ourselves.

5. What is the difference between these offerings? A sin offering symbolized the purging or cleansing the people of sin. A burnt offering was a gift or peace offering that was a "soothing aroma to the Lord" (Leviticus 1:9).

6. "Azazel" is a difficult word to understand, with four significant positions offered for what it might mean, with the fourth being favored by many modern scholars: (1) It could relate to its function—"the goat that departs," giving us the term *scapegoat*; (2) it may be an abstract

noun referring to the theological concept of *expiation*, the removal of sin; (3) it may refer to the wilderness where the goat departed; (4) it may be the name of a demonic being, possibly the Devil himself (Mark F. Rooker, *Leviticus*, vol. 3A, The New American Commentary [Nashville, TN: B&H Publishing Group, 2000], 216-217).

7. Scripture doesn't give his age, but some commentators have suggested he could have been as young as his mid-teens or as old as 37.

8. While some who describe Jesus' death this way genuinely struggle to see its goodness, to call it cosmic or divine child abuse is a straw man argument set forth by the uninformed, ignorant, or combative.

9. This is the heart of what's called the *ransom theory* of the atonement. Origen (185–253), an early church leader, understood that ransom as being paid to the devil, who is then obligated to release us from sin's bondage. However, while we are in bondage to sin, Satan is not our master, which is where this perspective falls short.

10. This perspective is what's called the *satisfaction theory* of the atonement. Developed by Anselm (1033–1109) as a reaction to the ransom theory, at least as it pertains to whom the debt of our sin is owed and the dishonor it causes toward God. However, when viewed in isolation, it is at an incomplete picture of what Christ accomplished in the atonement.

11. This theory is known as *Christus Victor*.

12. This is what Christians refer to as *penal substitution*, a perspective that, although it regained prominence in the Reformation era, existed in some nascent form in the early days of the church.

13. John R.W. Stott, *The Cross of Christ* (Downers Grove, IL: InterVarsity Press, 2006) 159.

CHAPTER 17—THROUGH AN EMPTY TOMB

1. Sleep is frequently used as a metaphor for death in the Bible, especially in Paul's writing (1 Corinthians 15:6, 18, 20; 1 Thessalonians 4:13-15; 5:10).

2. Jesus predicted his death and resurrection three times in Matthew (16:21-23; 17:22-23; 20:17-19), Mark (8:31-32; 9:30-32; 10:32-34), and Luke (9:21-22; 9:43-45; 18:31-34). His predictions of his death and resurrection are a little more enigmatic in John's Gospel, but they are present as well (John 12:7-8; 13:33; 14:25, 29).

3. "But let not the testimony of women be admitted, on account of the levity and boldness of their sex…" (Flavius Josephus, "Antiquities of the Jews 4.219," in *The Works of Josephus: Complete and Unabridged*, trans. William Whiston [Peabody: Hendrickson, 1987], 117).

4. The James referenced here is Jesus' younger brother, the eldest biological son of Jesus' adoptive father, Joseph. James went on to lead the church in Jerusalem and wrote the New Testament book that bears his name.

5. This is what makes Christianity the most potentially *falsifiable* religion in history, which is just a clever way of saying that it can easily be disproven. Importantly, no one has ever been able to unearth the dead body of Jesus.

6. Joseph of Arimathea donated his tomb to hold the body of Jesus (John 19:38-42). The location has traditionally been attributed to a tomb housed at the western end of the Church of the Holy Sepulchre in Jerusalem.

7. The Talpiot Tomb, about three miles south of the old city of Jerusalem, is one such example. Discovered in 1980, it became the focus of a 2007 Discovery Channel documentary produced by James Cameron (of *Terminator*, *Titanic*, and *Avatar* fame) and a companion book that claimed this tomb belonged to Jesus of Nazareth and some of his family and associates (Simcha Jacobovici and Charles Pellegrino, *The Jesus Family Tomb: The Evidence Behind the Discovery No One Wanted to Find* [San Francisco: HarperOne, 2008]). Archaeologists, linguistic experts, statisticians, and scholars largely rejected this conclusion due to the weakness of the evidence.

8. Jesus' name in Hebrew is *Yeshua*, which was a very common name among the Israelites and later Judeans. Its closest modern English equivalent today is Joshua, another very common name.

9. This doesn't mean people won't endure persecution or even die believing a lie, of course. After all, Joseph Smith, the founder of Mormonism, seemed to genuinely believe what a supernatural being claiming to be an angel told him; but believing does not make Mormonism true.

10. Adrian Warnock, *Raised with Christ: How the Resurrection Changes Everything* (Wheaton, IL: Crossway, 2009), 51.

11. *Austin Powers: International Man of Mystery*, directed by Jay Roach, featuring Mike Myers, Elizabeth Hurley, and Will Ferrell (1997; Burbank, CA: New Line Cinema, 2011), Blu-Ray.

12. John Dominic Crossan, a scholar who rejects historic Christian teaching, advocates for a view similar to this throughout his writing, including *The Birth of Christianity: Discovering What Happened in the Years Immediately After the Execution of Jesus* (San Francisco: HarperOne, 1999).

CHAPTER 18—BY MAKING THE DEAD LIVE

1. Whitefield's legacy, like many of his era, is complicated. God brought many to saving faith through his ministry. He was also a slaveholder, a practice out of step with Christian beliefs about the dignity and value of human beings (despite many Christians of his day also being slaveholders).

2. While this story has been shared in multiple forms, this retelling is adapted from *The God Who Is There*, by D.A. Carson (Grand Rapids: Baker Books, 2010), 131.

3. The Pharisees were not just fastidious about keeping the Law; they added layers of commands over the Law in their efforts to avoid violating its commands. Ironically, their efforts led them to consistently violate the Law by tying up "heavy loads, hard to carry, and put them on men's shoulders, but they themselves are not willing even to lift a finger to move them" (Matthew 23:4).

4. D.A. Carson, *The Gospel According to John*, *The Pillar New Testament Commentary* (Grand Rapids, MI: W.B. Eerdmans, 1991), 195.

5. D. Martyn Lloyd-Jones, *Revival* (Wheaton, IL: Crossway, 1987), 57.

6. Aaron Armstrong, *I'm a Christian—Now What?: A Guide to Your New Life with Christ* (Bellingham, WA: Lexham Press, 2023), 2.

7. While I am typically wary of using analogies to explain complex theological realities (remember, every analogy used to describe the Trinity ends in heresy), this is one of the few instances where one might be useful.

CHAPTER 19—WITH A GOAL IN MIND

1. Joe Carter, "Study: Majority of Self-Identified Christians Don't Believe the Holy Spirit Is Real," *The Gospel Coalition*, September 18, 2021, https://www.thegospelcoalition.org/article/christians-dont-believe-spirit/.

2. Sinclair B. Ferguson, *The Holy Spirit*, ed. Gerald Bray, Contours of Christian Theology (Downers Grove, IL: InterVarsity Press, 1996), 54.

3. Leon Morris, *The Epistle to the Romans*, The Pillar New Testament Commentary (Grand Rapids, MI: W.B. Eerdmans, 1988), 332.

4. Theologians call this *imputed* righteousness, which means Christ's righteousness is attributed or assigned to us.

CHAPTER 20—A UNITED PEOPLE

1. While Scripture does describe the tabernacle and later the temple as being central to the worship of the Jewish people (Exodus 26; 1 Kings 5–8), these physical locations are not analogous to the church. Jesus hints at this truth in John 4.

2. Sally Lloyd-Jones, *The Jesus Storybook Bible* (Grand Rapids, MI: Zonderkidz, 2007), 36.

CHAPTER 21—OUR RELATIONSHIPS WITH ONE ANOTHER

1. For thoughtful explorations of the effects of social media from a Christian perspective, I recommend *The Wolf in Their Pockets: 13 Ways the Social Internet Threatens the People You Lead* and *Terms of Service: The Real Cost of Social Media*, both written by Chris Martin; and also *Digital Liturgies: Rediscovering Christian Wisdom in an Online Age* by Samuel D. James.

2. Marjorie Weidenfeld Buckholtz, "The Key to Our Lasting Marriage Embracing Our Differences," *HuffPost* (October 9, 2023), https://www.huffpost.com/entry/opposites-attract-marriage-60-years_n_6511be0ce4b018d0253a440e.

3. Maureen Shaw, "The Sexist and Racist History of Marriage That No One Talks About," *Teen Vogue* (November 28, 2017), https://www.teenvogue.com/story/marriage-racist-sexist-history.

4. Jennifer Wilson, "How Did Polyamory Become So Popular?," *The New Yorker* (December 25, 2023), https://www.newyorker.com/magazine/2024/01/01/american-poly-christopher-gleason-book-review-more-a-memoir-of-open-marriage-molly-roden-winter.

5. Susan Dominus, "Is an Open Marriage a Happier Marriage?" *The New York Times Magazine* (May 11, 2017), https://www.nytimes.com/2017/05/11/magazine/is-an-open-marriage-a-happier-marriage.html.

6. These are also the sort of men who will declare that being married is the only consent required for sex, which is a dehumanizing approach to marital intimacy. To not put too fine a point on it, it is a sin.

7. Timothy Keller with Kathy Keller, *The Meaning of Marriage* (New York: Penguin, 2011), 42-43.

CHAPTER 22—OUR GREATER PURPOSE

1. David Foster Wallace, *This Is Water: Some Thoughts, Delivered on a Significant Occasion, about Living a Compassionate Life* (New York: Little, Brown and Company, 2009), 98-102.

2. In Roman Catholic teaching, a sacrament is a vehicle for imparting God's grace upon a believer, which is why some Protestants prefer the term *ordinance*.

3. See Acts 2:41; 8:12, 36-38; 9:18; 10:47-48; 16:15, 33; 18:8; 19:3-7.

4. Gregg Allison, *Historical Theology: An Introduction to Christian Doctrine* (Grand Rapids, MI: Zondervan Academic, 2011), 611-612.

5. I also believe this method is most in line with biblical teaching as it is what is depicted in Scripture. However, this is a matter upon which Christians can disagree.

6. The Roman Catholic doctrine of the Eucharist teaches that the elements become the body and blood of Christ while retaining the appearance of bread and wine (*transubstantiation*). The Lutheran doctrine of *consubstantiation* takes a step away from Catholic dogma, teaching that while the elements are unchanged from being bread and wine, the substance of Christ's body and blood is present with them.

7. John Calvin, one of the most prominent voices of the Reformation era, understood the Lord's Supper in this fashion, with John 6:35—Jesus' declaration of being the bread of life—undergirded his understanding of the Lord's Supper (Allison, *Historical Theology*, 652-654). Jonathan Edwards, the eighteenth century theologian, held to a similar view.

8. How to define *sacrificial* here is a matter of friendly debate among Christians.

9. Christopher Wordsworth, *A Church History to the Council of Nicaea, A.D. 325* (London: Rivingtons, 1881), 465.

10. Wordsworth, 465.

CHAPTER 23—OUR GREAT COMMISSION

1. "Living the Principle of Oneness—One Human Family—Essential Relationships—What Bahá'ís Believe," *bahai.org*, accessed July 27, 2024, https://www.bahai.org/beliefs/essential-relationships/one-human-family/living-principle-oneness.

2. The Bahá'í view of Jesus is similar to that of Islam, redefining him as a great prophet, a worker of wonders, and the Lord of Compassion, but not God himself.

3. There are also certain choices I don't make when it comes to entertainment that, if I'm asked, I'll explain. Usually, it's enough to say, "I'll pass."

4. Aaron Armstrong, *I'm a Christian—Now What?: A Guide to Your New Life with Christ* (Bellingham, WA: Lexham Press, 2023), 119.

5. Armstrong, *I'm a Christian—Now What?*, 86.

CHAPTER 24—OVER LIFE AFTER DEATH

1. *Star Trek III: The Search for Spock*, directed by Leonard Nimoy, featuring William Shatner, DeForest Kelley, and Christopher Lloyd (1984; Hollywood, CA: Paramount Pictures, 2013), Blu-Ray.

2. *Bill and Ted's Bogus Journey*, directed by Peter Hewitt, featuring Keanu Reeves, Alex Winter, and William Sadler (1991; Los Angeles, CA: Orion Pictures, 2018), Blu-Ray.

3. Seriously, I think they killed her three times throughout the run of the series.

4. Pew Research Center Report, "Few Americans Blame God or Say Faith Has Been Shaken Amid Pandemic, Other Tragedies – 2. Views on the Afterlife," *Pew Research Center* (November 23, 2021), https://www.pewresearch.org/religion/2021/11/23/views-on-the-afterlife/.

5. Reincarnation is a horribly depressing belief, functioning as a sort of metaphysical prison, as it offers no true escape from the cycle of death and rebirth.

6. Worship of the old Norse gods has seen a resurgence in recent decades, with between 500 and 1,000 adherents in Denmark today ("The Old Nordic Religion Today," *National Museum of Denmark*, accessed July 14, 2024, https://en.natmus.dk/historical-knowledge/denmark/prehistoric-period-until-1050-ad/the-viking-age/religion-magic-death-and-rituals/the-old-nordic-religion-today/).

7. The Hel of Norse mythology is similar to Sheol in the Old Testament, which, while having a distinctly negative sense in many references, functions as a general realm for all the dead (Genesis 42:38; Psalm 6:5; 16:10; 86:13; Isaiah 7:11).

8. "Life after Death" in "Basic Doctrines," accessed July 12, 2024, https://www.churchofjesuschrist.org/study/eng/manual/new-testament-seminary-teacher-manual/appendix/basic-doctrines.

9. Pew Research, "2. Views on the Afterlife."

10. Purgatory, as a doctrine, was codified in 1274 during the Second Council of Lyon. This doctrine has two features: First, that some who are saved still require purification from sin after death, and second, that they can benefit from the pious deeds and prayers of the living. Eventually, this fell into the hucksterism and functional witchcraft of the indulgence controversy, where time in purgatory was reduced through the purchase of relics alleged to have been connected to a significant figure from within the faith.

11. Clement of Rome, Polycarp, and Clement of Alexandria are among the many early church leaders whose teaching suggests they understood judgment as conscious eternal punishment. *The Epistle of Barnabas*, a widely read and respected document from the first century, also supports the prominence of this view.

12. Annihilationists point to Irenaeus, Justin Martyr, and Ignatius of Antioch as early proponents of this view. However, this may be a misreading as some of their work (Ignatius in *Letter to the Ephesians*, 16:1-2; Irenaeus in *Against Heresies* 4:28:2) calls that assertion into question. The subject is complex.

13. C.S. Lewis, *The Problem of Pain* (New York: HarperOne, 1996), 94.

14. Rob Bell, *Love Wins: A Book About Heaven, Hell, and the Fate of Every Person Who Ever Lived* (New York: HarperOne, 2011), 136-137.

15. Lewis, *The Problem of Pain*, 94.

16. J.C. Ryle, *Expository Thoughts on the Gospels*, vol. 2 (London: William Hunt and Company, 1856), 404.

CHAPTER 25—OVER A NEW CREATION

1. C.S. Lewis, *The Weight of Glory* (New York: HarperOne, 1980), 26.

2. David Nah, "The Millennium," in *Lexham Survey of Theology*, ed. Mark Ward et al. (Bellingham, WA: Lexham Press, 2018).

3. Nah, "The Millennium."

4. Nah, "The Millennium."

5. Randy Alcorn, *Heaven* (Carol Stream, IL: Tyndale, 2004), 280.

WHAT WILL YOU DO WITH WHAT YOU KNOW?

1. Saint Augustine Bishop of Hippo, *The Confessions of St. Augustine,* trans. E.B. Pusey (Bellingham, WA: Logos Research Systems, Inc., 1996).

To learn more about Harvest House books and
to read sample chapters, visit our website:

www.HarvestHousePublishers.com

HARVEST HOUSE PUBLISHERS
EUGENE, OREGON